A Garden Book for Houston
and the Gulf Coast

A garden at the Forum of Civics.

A Garden Book for Houston
and the Gulf Coast

River Oaks Garden Club

Pacesetter Press
A Division of Gulf Publishing Company
Houston, Texas

Printing History

ISBN 0-88415-350-9
Library of Congress
Catalog Card Number
75-5316

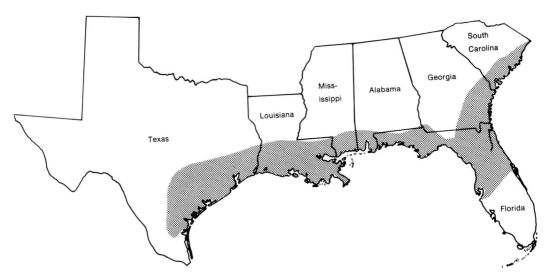

Map showing areas of approximately similar growing conditions for which this book is applicable.

Foreword

Almost fifty years ago Will C. Hogg recognized the need for a gardening book adapted expressly to the climatic conditions characteristic of Houston and surrounding areas of the Gulf Coast. With Mr. Hogg's support and the concerted efforts of several knowledgeable Houston gardeners, that concept came to fruition in 1929 with the publication of *A Garden Book for Houston*. In 1944 the Hogg family generously gave the book copyright to the River Oaks Garden Club, which has continued to revise and publish this popular gardening guide.

A member of the Garden Club of America, the River Oaks Garden Club is a non-profit organization. The monies obtained from its fund-raising projects, such as the Pink Elephant Sale and the Azalea Trail, are returned to the community in support of the purposes to which the Club is dedicated: encouraging interest in civic beautification, conservation, and horticulture. Exemplifying its own goals, this group of women maintains gardens open to the public at its historic building, The Forum of Civics, arranges fresh flowers in the rooms of The Bayou Bend Collection, and supervises, works in, and contributes financially to maintain the surrounding fourteen-acre Bayou Bend Gardens. By often assisting in urban landscaping, the Club improves the environment of the City of Houston, while lending its efforts to promote conservation throughout the United States—from the Big Thicket in Texas to the Redwood Groves in California. In celebration of Spring, the River Oaks Garden Club's annual Azalea Trail focuses the attention of thousands of visitors on the potential of garden beauty inherent in Houston's near-tropic clime.

With this third revision of *A Garden Book for Houston and the Gulf Coast* the River Oaks Garden Club remains steadfast in its aim "to stimulate the knowledge and love of gardening among amateurs," making available to them practical horticultural information known to bring success in this growing zone. By participating in the many enjoyable and beneficial facets of gardening, we can all improve that portion of the environment now in our care, leaving it healthier, more productive and more attractive than we found it.

All animals on our planet, including us, are guests of the plant kingdom.
No plants = no people and no animals. It's that simple.
                                                              —Malcolm C. Shurtleff

Acknowledgements

Assisting members of The River Oaks Garden Club

Advisors: Mrs. Royden B. Bowen, Mrs. Sam J. Lucas, Jr. and Mrs. Edward A. Blackburn, Jr.

Garden Book Chairmen: Mrs. W. Burres Head and Mrs. Will H. Thanheiser.

Special Consultants: Mrs. Stayton Nunn, whose help and advice were invaluable, Mr. and Mrs. John D. Marr, authors of "Azaleas" and "Camellias," Mrs. Louis A. Stevenson, Mrs. Hal Houseman, Mrs. Gail Borden Tennant and Mrs. Jay W. Colvin, Jr.

Assistants: Mrs. Thomas D. Anderson, Mrs. Conrad Bering, Jr., Mrs. Hans J. Bohlmann, Mrs. Spurgeon Britt, Mrs. James L. Britton III, Mrs. Ben A. Brollier, Mrs. Richard F. Burns, Mrs. Douglas S. Craig, Mrs. Robert P. Doherty, Jr., Mrs. Ray L. Dudley, Mrs. Jack D. Head, Miss Ima Hogg, Mrs. George F. Horton, Mrs. Harry H. Hudson, Mrs. William A. Langdon, Mrs. J. Griffith Lawhon, Mrs. Vernon L. Miller, Mrs. Charles B. Moore, Mrs. William H. McDugald, Mrs. F.O. McGehee, Mrs. James Noel, Mrs. James A. Reichert, Mrs. Raymond S. Risien, Mrs. E.K. Sanders, Mrs. Gardiner Symonds and Mrs. Herbert Wells.

Special appreciation to:

——Don Newman and Jack Crout with the Soil Conservation Service of the United States Department of Agriculture for their assistance with the chapters "Soil and Soil Improvement," "Drainage" and "Watering."

——Gary Outenreath with Tierra Wholesale Greenhouses and Busch Bird Park, co-author of "The Tropical Garden."

——Dr. Richard L. Duble and A.C. Novosad, Extension Turf specialists with Texas A&M University, College Station, Texas, for sharing their information on lawn grasses.

——The Houston Rose Society.

——William D. Adams and other staff members of the Harris County Extension Service, Horticulture Department.

——Lee Marsters, horticulturist and garden column editor for *The Houston Post.*

——Janet Wagner

Photographs and Sketches

Rob Muir: Cover photograph and those on pages ii, viii, 8, 19, 24, 29, 30, 35, 62, 71, 75, 79, 82, 99, 103.

Mrs. Louis A. Stevenson: Roses, page 52; Magnolia, page 75; and "Spring," page 119.

Mrs. George Horton: sketch of tree, page 14; and photographs "Summer," "Autumn," page 119.

William H. McDugald: assistance in design, page 119.

Mrs. John P. Bullington for allowing the photography of her vine, page 29.

The Texas Horticulturist, Winter 1975, for the sketches of "Weeds" pages 110-11.

Iowa State University Press, Raymond Fassell, for permission to use quotation by Malcolm C. Shurtleff in "Plants vs. Pollution," *Flower and Garden* Magazine, October 1970.

Contents

Garden Design

When any great design thou dost intend,
Think on the means, the manner, and the end.
                                        —Denham

Styles in garden design change as do styles in other artistic fields. Fortunately, current trends in landscaping approach garden design with the goal of creating a pleasing yet functional environment. This is accomplished by making the grounds an aesthetically satisfying complement to the living quarters, by fulfilling outdoor living comforts, by providing the necessary service areas and by assuring the sun and soil needs of the plant materials used, all the while considering time required for maintenance.

Importance of a Plan. Planning *before* planting is essential. Your most diligent efforts may be wasted by the lack of a definite, well-conceived plan, preferably drafted to scale on graph paper. To prevent costly mistakes it is wise to seek professional advice. This can be accomplished in one of several ways: a landscape architect can completely design and plant your home grounds; he can make a design plan only, which you can carry out; or he can have a verbal consultation with you on an hourly or per diem fee basis. In any case it is worthwhile to consult some of the many excellent books on garden design to gain a clearer understanding of unity, proportion, balance, perspective, focal points, and plant material with its varying colors, textures, and shapes. As you study these pages a

mental picture of your garden will come into focus.

There are basic decisions to make before a plan can be executed. Visualize the path of the sun's rays through the year to establish where shade is needed so that trees can be properly placed to provide cooling shade from the summer sun in this near tropic climate. Note the most convenient paths between house and garden, from garden to the storage area for garden supplies and equipment, and from street to house. From inside the house, create attractive perspectives; plan to screen unattractive views. Decide where your car and your guests' cars can be parked. Select the most convenient place for storage. Choose the coolest spot in summer and the warmest in winter for relaxation areas. If you want open space for lawn games, plan for them. Study plant materials—their form, mature size and growth requirements, and decide upon your favorites. Do you want a food garden? Who will maintain the home grounds and how much time can be given to this maintenance? All these points must be carefully considered before plans are made by whoever is drafting the garden design. Since it is *your* garden, be sure it will meet *your* desires. The goal of garden design is to enhance the lives of the inhabitants—plants and people.

Soil and Soil Improvement

To the solid ground of nature trusts
the mind that builds for aye.
—Wordsworth

Soil is the basic element for growing any plant. It must be friable enough to allow the penetration of the roots which support the plant, fertile enough to supply nutrients to the plant, and porous enough to retain air and moisture, so essential to plant growth. To supply these needs a soil must contain organic matter to increase its fertility and microorganisms to change the organic matter into a form which the plant can use. Organic matter and microorganisms also act as a bank, storing surplus nutrients and moisture for the plant's future needs.

Think of the soil as a living, ever-changing element and you will develop an understanding of this very complex material.

Soil Testing. Before you try to alter the soil in your garden it is important to find out all you can about the existing properties of the soil you are working with. One way to begin is to consult the nearest office of the Soil Conservation Service of the U.S. Department of Agriculture to see if a soil survey has been made in your area. These soil surveys furnish valuable information about your particular soil such as its texture, reaction and ability to transport or hold water and air.

Soil analysis is the only reliable method for determining the chemical condition of the soil. Always have a soil test before attempting to alter the pH; otherwise you will be working in the dark. The letters "pH" represent the barometer-like scale from 0 to 14 on which the hydrogen ion concentration is tabulated. The pH rating indicates the degree of acidity or alkalinity of the soil—a pH of 7 is neutral; higher pH numbers represent increasing alkalinity, lower numbers show increasing soil acidity. Soils which are either too acid (below 4) or too alkaline (above 8) seriously retard or kill plant growth. To be complete and really helpful a soil test should be made by an expert. Contact your nearest County Extension Agent to get forms and procedures for having your soil analyzed. There is a very nominal charge, but you will easily recover the price by avoiding mistakes. The results of the test will indicate the materials required to modify your soil pH and the appropriate fertilizer materials for the plants you are growing. There are home testing kits available, but the results are not so accurate. Home testing kits are useful for checking the results of your efforts *after* you have had an expert test made and have implemented the procedures suggested by it.

Basic Soil Composition. For home gardening purposes, soil can be divided into three simple classifications by texture: sand, clay and loam. Sand is composed of irregularly-shaped particles which do not cling together and can be seen with the naked eye. Nearly all sandy soils contain some fertile clay particles. Moist sand will form a ball under hand pressure, but promptly falls apart when the pressure is released. Sand is very loose and drains so rapidly that soil moisture is not retained and nutrients are readily leached through the soil, beyond the reach of plant roots. This property makes sand quick-drying and subject to rapid heating. Sand, by itself, is not a good soil for gardening, but it can be improved by adding large quantities of organic matter and some finely-ground clay. If you are not in a great hurry, green manuring, the planting of a cover crop later to be tilled into the soil, improves the texture of sandy soil. Sand is especially adapted to bulb culture and to other plants that are very hardy, drought resistant and deep-rooted.

Clay is composed of smooth, slightly flattened particles so minute that they can be seen only through powerful microscopes. Clay particles hold nearly all of the plant nutrients in any soil. These tiny particles cling together to form a hard, cement-like soil when dry, and a sticky, cloddy soil when wet. Clay soils hold large amounts of moisture for plant use, but in wet periods they often become waterlogged and soil air is expelled. Plant roots, water and air generally move very slowly in clay soils; yet when clay is loosened by modifiers such as organic matter, sand, gypsum, vermiculite or perlite it usually becomes friable and easy to manage. The additives alter the soil structure, which in turn improves the aeration and drainage of the clay soils. Black gumbo is a clay soil commonly found in Houston.

Loam is a mixture of sand and clay, giving it the good properties of each in a satisfactory proportion. Moist loam can be formed into a ball by hand pressure, and the shape will not crumble until some pressure is applied. A loam soil is usually well drained, well aerated and fertile. It retains nutrients, water and air for moderate periods. Loam is generally considered to be the best textured soil for most garden plants.

Organic matter and humus. These are sometimes referred to as "garden miracles" because they promote so many helpful accomplishments in soil. These two materials are so closely related that it is almost impossible to discuss one without discussing the other. Organic matter (plant or animal) is the material we add to the soil in any of several forms such as: manure, peat moss, pine bark mulch, rice hulls, compost, leafmold, lawn clippings, leaves, cottonseed meal, dried blood, bones, hair, etc. Through the process of decomposition organic matter becomes the dark spongy substance known as humus.

It is generally in this final stage, as humus, that organic matter has the greatest nutritive value and the most lasting effects on the soil. In all stages, however, organic matter helps soil in several ways: it pushes the tiny particles of clay apart, leaving spaces or pores which can be filled with water and air; it improves a sandy soil by addding material for the large sandy particles and water to cling to; it adds fertility to the soil, improves aeration and provides an excellent medium for the growth of soil organisms. If organic matter is not in a well-advanced stage of decay when incorporated into the soil, microorganisms will extract nitrogen from the soil, stealing it from the growing plant in order to carry out the process of decomposition. Therefore, extra nitrogen should be added when large amounts of organic matter are incorporated. This way the microorganisms can decompose the organic matter and the growing plant will still have an adequate supply of nitrogen.

Mulching, the covering of soil with loose material, usually organic matter, serves many purposes: it promotes healthy growth of plants, keeps the soil surface from cracking and hardening, deters weeds, keeps the roots at an even, beneficial temperature, adds organic matter to the topsoil, and it prevents loss of moisture from evaporation. Organic matter is often used for mulching, especially during hot weather. A mulch composed of a mixture of several different materials allows more aeration and better penetration of water because the variety of textures in the mixture retards compaction. A mulch keeps the soil crumbly and easy to work, providing good tilth. The practice of mulching differs to some extent according to soil and climate. There are times when newspaper, plastic or gravel may be desirable as a mulch, but these neither add desirable nutrients to the soil nor change its texture, nor do they provide a medium for organism growth. Leaves and other plant residues are Nature's own mulch.

Essential Soil Elements. Although many elements are necessary for plant growth in a good garden soil, the three most essential are nitrogen, phosphorus and potassium. The numbers on packages of fertilizers always refer to the percentages of those elements in that order—nitrogen, phosphorus and potassium. A fertilizer marked 5-10-5 means that it contains 5% nitrogen, 10% phosphorus and 5% potassium (potash). The other 80% of the mixture may contain a small percentage of trace elements, but most of it is filler to facilitate application. The abundance of these elements in the soil is best determined by a soil analysis, but a successful gardener is always alert for plant symptoms signaling deficiency or excess.

Nitrogen accelerates the growth of stem and foliage, gives a healthy green color to plants, stimulates rapid early growth, and improves the quality and crispness of leafy crops. Nitrogen is especially beneficial when plants are making buds. A yellow-green leaf color may be indicative of nitrogen deficiency, which sometimes causes premature development. An excess delays maturity, reducing the development of flowers and fruit, and is symptomized by flaccid, unhealthy growth. The principal inorganic sources of nitrogen are sodium nitrate, ureaform, ammonium sulfate, and calcium nitrate. (Ammonium phosphate is also an inorganic source but is seldom available.) Some organic sources of nitrogen are compost, organic material, dried blood or blood meal and cottonseed meal.

Phosphorus, called by some the master key to agriculture, stimulates root growth, gives plants a vigorous start, hastens maturity, promotes abundant seed and flower formation, increases the proportion of seed and fruit to stalk and hardens plants to winter injury. Virtually all plants need phosphorus to maintain flower and fruit production, and it is generally recognized that organic material in the soil increases the amount of phosphorus available to the plant. A phosphorus deficiency is usually indicated by low vigor in the plant, weak stems and few flowers. There is seldom a phosphorus surplus in soils. The principal inorganic source of phosphorus is normal or triple superphosphate, produced from raw rock phosphate. Raw and steamed bone meal are organic sources of phosphate.

Potassium, commonly called potash, strengthens plants and enables them to resist diseases, insects and winter damage; it promotes the production of starches, sugar and oil in the plants, and improves the quality of the crop yield. The main inorganic sources of potash are potassium chloride, sulfate of potash, and potassium nitrate. Wood ash is an organic source, and granite dust is a mineral source.

Other elements plants use, such as magnesium, calcium, sulphur, boron, etc., are not generally needed in the quantities of the principal three, so they are usually grouped under the term "trace elements." This term is printed on the package of some fertilizer mixtures as being present in the filler with which the elements are mixed for convenient use.

Commercial Fertilizers. To be highly productive most soils require a blend of all three essential elements. "Organic" gardeners try to obtain all the elements from organic or natural mineral sources. The inorganic sources of the elements are more rapidly available to the plant, but they do not improve the soil's tilth or texture. Elements from natural sources give slower results but they do improve the soil's texture, remain in the soil longer and, in the case of manure, compost, and other organic material, expedite the availability of the elements to the plant by promoting the growth of microorganisms, retaining moisture, and giving the soil body. Although the organic and inorganic fertilizers have different functions, they complement each other when wisely used. Each has its purpose, and it seems sensible to combine them as needed. The principal caution is to follow the manufacturer's directions, resisting the impulse to use quantities greater than specified. It is also important to follow the dictum: *Never fertilize a dry plant, and always water a fertilizer in thoroughly.* Fertilizers cannot become available to the plant until water is added.

Foliar feeding, the use of fertilizers in a water solution sprayed on the leaves of plants, is based on the ability of a plant to absorb nutrients through the leaves. Fertilizers are usually dug into the soil to allow a plant's roots to absorb them, but leaves also have the ability to absorb. Most liquid or soluble fertilizers have high concentrations of nutrient salts which may burn the foliage if used in concentrations stronger than recommended. Moreover, in the hot summers of Houston and the upper Gulf Coast it may be wiser to dilute 50% more than the proportions recommended by the manufacturer to avoid defoliating or even killing your plant. For example: when plants like azaleas, camellias, and any others that like acid soil begin to show an iron deficiency (indicated by the yellowing of the leaves between the veins) a foliar spray of iron chelate in solution is often recommended. In our hot weather use 50% more water than is recommended on the label. The leaf surface has maximum absorption when fresh, not wilted.

Manure. Barnyard manure is very useful as a fertilizer and especially as a soil conditioner because it promotes the growth of soil organisms, adds nutrients to the soil and helps change minerals into forms more available to plants. Fresh, or "hot," manure is apt to burn plants when touching them, but well-composted manure is an excellent mulch, particularly when mixed with other organic materials such as pine needles, peat moss, pine bark mulch or old hay. An old but still accepted way of using manure is to make manure "tea." Steeping a burlap bag of manure in a barrel of water for at least two weeks results in a liquid manure. When diluted to the color of weak tea it can be applied to plants as a quick stimulant. The soil around the plants should be loosened and moistened before application, and watered again after application. Chrysanthemums are encouraged into good bloom by this treatment, as are many other plants in bud.

Other Fertilizers. Bone meal is one of the safest and most efficient fertilizers. It is slow-acting and tends to make the soil alkaline.

Cottonseed meal has a somewhat acid effect, is rich in nitrogen, contains small amounts of phosphorus and potassium, and is especially fine for lawns and bulbs.

Activated sewage sludge and tankage are good soil conditioners with slowly-available nutrients. They improve the physical condition of mixed fertilizers, but are better used on inedible plants.

Organic matter is indispensable to soil conditioning.

In all gardening activities the safety of the gardener must always be foremost. Protection from overexposure to sprays and chemicals is advisable. Wash your hands after handling chemicals. If you use manure check with your physician as to the advisability of tetanus shots.

Soil pH. Most garden plants, vegetables and ornamentals prefer a slightly acid soil, while most herbs prefer a slightly alkaline soil. Soil acidity may be increased by the addition of organic matter, iron sulfate (copperas), agricultural sulphur, gypsum (calcium sulphate) or magnesium sulphate, used according to directions. The latter is the quicker-acting, but the other materials are longer-lasting. Gypsum adjusts the pH and thus aids bacterial growth. Organic matter serves the many purposes discussed earlier. Three or four inches of organic material worked into the soil help make it more acid; the same material used as a two- to three-inch mulch tends to maintain an acid soil condition. If soil is too acid, lime, wood ashes, limestone sand or bone meal will help neutralize it or, in greater quantities, bring it to the alkaline side. Again, information from your soil test will point this out.

Compost. Composting is the process used to speed decomposition of organic matter in humus. Because carbon is the principal element of all plants, it is the principal constituent of compost. The goal in composting is to encourage the growth of more bacteria so they will decompose the carbonaceous materials. Since the bacteria or microorganisms must have nitrogen to carry out the decomposition process, you should add some form of nitrogen to your compost piles. Raw rock phosphate is another desirable additive. The weak acids in the organic material help break the phosphate down into forms readily available to the plant. Soil should be added to the compost to increase the nutrients, serve as a base to which the nutrients can cling, and be a host for microorganisms. The compost must be aerated because air is necessary for the bacteria to carry out their work of decomposition. Therefore, the pile must be turned regularly or built around a wire chimney or flue. Moisture in the compost keeps the bacteria activated and prevents the compost heap from becoming a fire hazard. The compost pile should be at least three feet high to build up heat, but may be of any design you choose as long as you assure the presence of the necessary elements. Composting, as well as other recommended gardening practices, is aimed at making the environment more favorable to the all-important soil microorganisms.

Drainage

We learn wisdom from failure much more than from success. We often discover what will do by finding out what will not do; and probably he who never made a mistake never made a discovery.
—Smiles

This chapter should be in boldface type because no other facet of gardening is more important than drainage. It is an absolute necessity, for without the proper removal of excess water from planting areas, all is for naught, particularly in low coastal country.

If the soil is well drained, water should disappear from a planting hole in ten minutes. If the water stands as long as one hour, the soil is slow-draining and corrective measures are indicated. The water itself does not injure the plants; but standing water excludes oxygen from the soil, and plants, like people, suffocate without oxygen. Yet drainage can be too rapid; this too is harmful because the quickly-draining water takes with it valuable minerals and prevents the retention of reserve moisture.

Shaded planting areas require more rapid drainage than those in the sun, since evaporation is slower and the soil is cooler in the shade. With excess water standing, the soil may become waterlogged and unproductive. As long as water is moving down into the soil slowly it is seldom harmful because it draws air and nutrients deep down into the root area.

New property should be graded, preferably by an expert, before construction begins. Excess surface water should be directed to flow to the street or to an appropriate drain, away from the house and the planting areas.

When faced with improper drainage, ascertain if the problem is due to the quality of the soil. Tight clay can fail to absorb any water at all or, in the presence of standing water, can become water-soaked; sand can allow excessively rapid drainage. However, both can be turned into productive soil (see "Soil Improvement").

If the quality and texture of the soil are not causing the drainage problem, try checking at various locations by digging holes to see if there is a hardpan layer of soil under the top level. This condition may arise after heavy equipment has been driven over wet ground during construction, compacting the soil into a hard layer, virtually impervious to water or roots. Plants growing improperly should be dug up. If their roots show downward and abruptly horizontal growth they have probably encountered an impenetrable layer. This condition may have been hidden and worsened by the spreading and leveling of the layer of sand usually used to level after construction, and by failing to incorporate it into the existing soil. There are alternative solutions to this problem. Either dig down deep enough to break up the hardpan and mix into it great quantities of gypsum, organic matter and some sand to form a homogenous soil which should then become productive, or lay drain pipes leading downward to a drain outlet. Though the latter may seem too difficult or too expensive an operation, drainage is so vital to all future gardening activities that every effort should be made to correct drainage problems before planting is attempted. The nearest Soil Conservation Service can give helpful advice.

Another means of providing good drainage is to build beds whose surfaces are several inches above ground level. Raised beds offer the opportunity to have the soil well aerated and especially prepared to meet the plants'

needs. When attractively attuned to other landscaping, raised beds provide a refreshing change from flat terrain.

There is a chain reaction—poor drainage leads to insufficient aeration, and both conditions encourage the spore development of disease organisms and the infection of the plant. The plant sickens and dies. The object is to reverse the order—well drained soil promotes good aeration and maintains reserve moisture and nutrients. The plant is nourished and thrives.

Watering

The thirsty earth soaks up the rain, and drinks, and gapes for drink again.
The plants suck in the earth and are with constant drinking fresh and fair.

—Abraham Cowley

Plants depend more on water than on any other element we add to the soil. Water is the chief agent for transporting nutrients in the soil to plants, and plant roots grow only in the presence of water, air, and soil nutrients. Three common questions are how, how much, and how often to water. In general, the answer is water thoroughly and infrequently.

The observant gardener gradually learns which plants need a great deal of water and which need less. Resist the temptation to take hose in hand on a pleasant evening, sprinkle a while and go away under the impression that the garden is watered. Sprinkling moistens only the top inch or so of the soil, forcing the roots to come up to obtain the moisture they require. When close to the surface of the ground the roots are prey to insects, fungus disease, and drying heat. However, there is a proper occasion for light sprinkling. Most plants benefit from having their foliage rinsed off occasionally, and shallow-rooted plants like azaleas enjoy an overhead sprinkling, but this should not replace thoroughly watering their root systems, shallow though they may be.

Water travels through soil particle-by-particle and through soil pores. It moves downward through soil, not spreading out fanwise. Obviously then, water must be allowed to flow long enough for it to seep down at least eight to ten inches for small plants and to greater depths for shrubs and trees. The proper use of water is intrinsic with all other essentials to plant growth.

The texture of the soil affects watering. Sandy soil becomes soaked quickly, but it also dries out quickly. Loam is not soaked so quickly as sand, but neither does it dry out so quickly. Clay soil takes more time to saturate and retains water longer, but it may also present a runoff problem. If this happens leave the sprinkler on until puddles form; turn it off until the water soaks in and then turn it back on.

The amount of water put out by a sprinkler may be tested by setting several coffee cans in the area reached by the "rain." After 30 minutes, check the amount of water in each can. You will get a good estimate of the amount actually going into the soil and can judge future sprinkling time from this test.

If there is some doubt as to whether the soil is dry enough to need watering insert a trowel or stick. If it does not go easily into the soil at least four or five inches, water is needed.

Weather conditions affect the frequency and amount of watering. Hot, dry winds certainly dry the soil out by transpiration quicker than cool humid air. Look at your plants. They will usually show you when they need water. Wilting at noon on a hot day does not indicate lack of water, but the same appearance in early morning or late afternoon does. Freshly transplanted stock and plants about to bloom need more water than usual.

There are root-watering wands that are very effective for getting water down to the root areas of large shrubs and trees. Broad shallow furrows made at the time of planting seeds or alongside small plants in rows are effective for irrigating these plants with a gentle flow. If the hose head is put in a can or a box, or if a soaker head is used, the soil will not wash away.

Wherever water goes, air follows, unless the water stands too long and forces the air out. Plants depend on the oxygen in the air. After the ground is saturated with water the roots begin to take it up, gradually leaving space between the soil particles. Air then fills these spaces. When the water has been completely depleted by roots and transpiration, only air remains between the particles, and the plant wilts. This is the time to water again, but not by sprinkling lightly.

Become acquainted with your plants' needs by observation. Soon there will be no reason to ask when to water—your plants will show you.

Lawns

Give me a clear blue sky over my head
And the green turf beneath my feet.
                                        —William Hazlett

A lush, green lawn can be as pleasing to the eye as an ocean vista or an open expanse of terrain. A well-kept turf is one of the most important parts of a garden and is a rewarding horticultural endeavor as well. A lawn serves other useful purposes, as it provides an inexpensive surface for recreation and inhibits soil erosion.

A lawn properly begun is much easier to maintain, healthier, and therefore, more resistant to diseases and insects. Grass has the same needs as other plants: food, water with good drainage, and proper soil with organic matter. The chapters on "Drainage" and "Soil and Soil Improvement" will be of great help before you plant your grass. The turf is the floor of your garden, so prepare the foundation carefully if you want a healthy green lawn, resistant to diseases and insects. Grass needs sandy, well-draining soil with an adequate amount of organic matter, fertilization, and proper watering.

Once the ground has been graded, proper drainage established and the soil cultivated thoroughly, rake the surface carefully to remove all stones, rubble, weeds and tree roots to provide a fine tilth before planting. A dressing of good fertilizer and organic matter applied prior to planting is beneficial and should be worked into the soil to a depth of several inches.

St. Augustine Grass. St. Augustine grass *(Stenotaphrum secundatum)* is the most widely used grass for lawns in the Gulf Coast area, and it is the best for planting under trees. This broad-leaved grass grows equally well in sun or shade, makes an excellent year-round green turf that is springy and soft underfoot, chokes out all other grasses and endures heat and drought. It remains green longer, but is not so cold-hardy as Bermuda. Besides its value as a lawn grass, St. Augustine is widely used for holding steep banks that are subject to erosion. As St. Augustine does not make satisfactory seed, it is planted by sod or stolons. The best time to plant it is from March to October. When using sod, cut it into three-inch blocks and plant 12 to 15 inches apart, pressing the soil firmly around blocks but not covering the grass blades. Plant stolons, or runners, about ten inches apart, covering the roots firmly with soil, leaving the grass blades above ground. It is estimated that one bushel of stolons is sufficient to plant 600 square feet. The grass is sometimes planted in blocks covering the entire area for an "instant lawn."

A process for rapid establishment of new lawns, called "hydraulic mulching," has been successful throughout the South. State highway departments find it fast and economical. Either seeds or sprigs of the grass variety selected are mixed with water and a fibrous mulch material to form a slurry which is sprayed under pressure onto the prepared area. The surface must be kept moist until the grass is established, but some lawns have required mowing in about a month.

A Bermuda grass lawn may be converted to St. Augustine simply by digging out small chunks of sod and inserting stolons of St. Augustine. St. Augustine should be well-watered after planting, and rewatered as needed until healthy growth is established, then water only when the grass shows the need, and soak it to a depth of eight inches or more, as sprinkling is usually more harmful than helpful (see "Watering"). Your lawn will benefit each spring and fall from the application of a complete fertilizer in a proportion equivalent to one pound of nitrogen per 1,000 square feet. Remember, the numbers on a bag of complete fertilizer represent, respectively, the percentages by weight of nitrogen, phosphorus, and potassium in the total. Apply evenly to dry grass and water in. At other times a light dressing of weed-free manure is helpful. Organic sources of nitrogen, such as cottonseed meal or sewage sludge, are very desirable. Sufficient fertilization produces more verdant growth. Mow as soon as the grass is about two inches high. Clip your lawn often enough to prevent removing more than half the growth at any one time. St. Augustine grass should be kept between 1½ to 2 inches tall; too dense a turf leads to a build-up of stems and leaves that harbors disease and keeps new roots from penetrating the soil; too close a cutting leads to dry soil and heat damage.

Opinions differ concerning the removal of lawn clippings. They may be raked in to add the nutrients in them and to act as a mulch, or they may be removed and added to your compost pile. To avoid the build-up of too thick a thatch, a light dressing of a topsoil mixed with some organic matter and fertilizer may be applied to abet the decomposition of the thatch (see "Compost"). If the thatch builds up too thickly the grass becomes more susceptible to diseases and insects. A thatching machine may be used to remove the accumulated material. Aeration of the soil—the removal of small plugs of earth to allow water and air to penetrate the soil—produces a healthy turf and restores compacted areas. Whatever tool you use for this purpose should remove, not displace, the soil.

Brown patch and chinch bugs, two major problems affecting St. Augustine grass, appear somewhat similar but require different treatments. Brown patch is a fungus infection (*Pellicularia filamentosa*) which develops in early autumn in enlarging brown rings. Apply a fungicide, preferably in granular form, and water in. The brown area may revive, and further infection may be avoided by proper fertilization. Chinch bugs, which appear in late spring, are black with white wings and are only ⅙ inch when full grown. Their presence may be ascertained by sinking a cylinder (such as a coffee can with both ends removed) in the lawn and filling it with water so that the insects will be forced to climb the sides. They can be destroyed by a stomach poison spray, used carefully and according to directions. St. Augustine grass is susceptible to a virus disease known as St. Augustine Decline (SAD) for which there is no known cure. Agricultural Experiment Stations have been trying to develop a grass that is resistant to SAD. Several are being tried, but the most promising at this writing seems to be Floratam. It is said to be resistant to both SAD and chinch bugs. Floratam can be planted as stolons in an infected St. Augustine grass lawn and will spread over the entire lawn.

Despite its problems, St. Augustine is still the grass most often recommended for Houston and the upper Gulf Coast. St. Augustine grass will thrive if it is planted in properly prepared, well-draining soil, watered by soaking and only when necessary, cut at regular intervals with a sharp mower blade and fertilized about twice a year. Few other varieties of grass have as much tolerance for shade and traffic as St. Augustine. *All* lawn grasses, however, require careful maintenance.

Bermuda and Zoysia Grasses. In colder areas, where St. Augustine cannot stand the winters, Bermuda grass *(Cynodon dactylon)* planted from seed is generally used. Bermuda grass is the most practical because it is planted from inexpensive seed and is disease resistant; but it does not grow in shade, it is brown from the first fall frost till after the last spring frost, and it is more difficult to remove from flower beds because of its rhizomes. There are some hybrid Bermudas, such as Tifway, Tiflawn and Texturf-10. All are high-maintenance grasses requiring frequent clipping with reel-type mowers adjusted to less than one inch mowing height, but Bermuda grass and its hybrids make a fine-textured, soft, green lawn.

Zoysia grass is recommended for its dark green color, resistance to insects and disease, and fine texture, but it requires more care and time for developing a good lawn and thins out in shade. Rye grass *(Lolium multiflorum),* an annual winter grass, fills a particular garden need. It covers bare spots and is a green fertilizer, adding both humus and nitrates to the soil.

As desirable as it is to maintain an attractive green turf, it is extremely more important to take precautions to avoid accidents. The number of injuries from carelessness in the operation of mowing machines is rising, unnecessarily. Keep in mind these admonitions for your safety:

- Always wear sturdy shoes.
- Rake the lawn for debris before mowing.
- Keep other people out of area while mowing.
- Never allow anyone's hands or feet to come near a moving mower blade.
- Never handle electrical equipment with wet hands or when the lawn is very wet. Keep cords in good condition; repair breaks and tape exposed wire immediately.

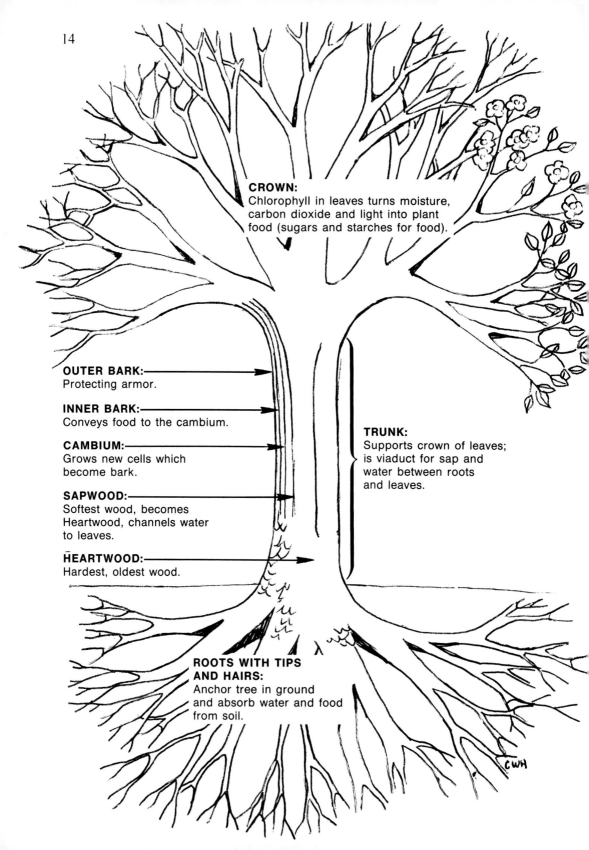

14

CROWN:
Chlorophyll in leaves turns moisture, carbon dioxide and light into plant food (sugars and starches for food).

OUTER BARK:
Protecting armor.

INNER BARK:
Conveys food to the cambium.

CAMBIUM:
Grows new cells which become bark.

SAPWOOD:
Softest wood, becomes Heartwood, channels water to leaves.

HEARTWOOD:
Hardest, oldest wood.

TRUNK:
Supports crown of leaves; is viaduct for sap and water between roots and leaves.

ROOTS WITH TIPS AND HAIRS:
Anchor tree in ground and absorb water and food from soil.

Trees

This learned I from the shadow of a tree / Which to and fro did sway upon a wall,
Our shadow selves, our influence may fall / Where we can never be.
—Anonymous

As the largest and most permanent of plant forms, trees should receive first consideration in planting home grounds. Spacing trees in the garden is extremely important because their position determines open lawn spaces, the location of flower beds and protection of the house from the sun's heat. Choose carefully and discriminatingly from among the numerous varieties of trees, evergreen and deciduous, which flourish in this area. Shade, foliage, bark texture, flower, fruit, picturesque form—there is a tree to meet every purpose. Visualize the tree in your garden at its ultimate height and breadth. To attain its natural beauty the tree must have space enough to accommodate it. Consider the proportions of the tree to its surroundings. Although intensely cold winters along the Gulf Coast are rare, there are several trees which celebrate fall with colorful foliage. These are so noted in the lists of trees in this chapter and in the "Flowering Shrubs and Trees" planting chart.

Shade Trees. The presence of one or two fine shade trees is often the deciding factor in selecting a homesite, yet trees which would add value and beauty to the completed home are often carelessly damaged or killed during home building. During this time it is essential to give them adequate protection by sur-

rounding them with barricades to prevent injury to the bark and forestall indiscriminate piling of soil around the root systems. Soil piled too deeply around the base of a tree trunk may suffocate the tree. Terraces built around trees should insure good drainage for the trees. Trees may also be damaged from chemicals such as those used for termite-proofing and weed-killing, even when 50 feet away from a tree.

The distribution of shade trees is important in planning the home grounds, for in this near tropical climate shade is almost as necessary as sunlight in a garden, particularly during the summer months when trees cast their long, cool shadows. Although many recommended shade trees are relatively slow-growing, they are long-lived and their beauty and dignity give lasting value to the garden. Many rapid-growing trees are shorter-lived, but they may be enjoyed until the permanent trees reach their desired size. When locating trees near flower beds or in lawns plant varieties that tolerate pruning to allow filtered sunlight to encourage the healthy growth of plants and grass beneath. When planting primarily for shade situate trees properly by plotting the path of the sun's rays at different seasons. Allow enough space between tree and house for air circulation and natural growth. When a shade tree is placed on the west side of the house remember that the shade lengthens as the sun goes down. If the tree is placed too close the slanting rays will come under the tree and onto the house. Planted on the east side the tree may be placed closer to the house, perhaps 20 feet away, if its mature size permits.

In addition to the trees appearing in the "Flowering Shrubs and Trees" Planting Chart the following can add their own charm to a landscape, providing shade, form, flowers, fruit or fall color:

d = deciduous   e = evergreen

ACACIA WRIGHTII: e—to 30', shrub or tree, irregular-shaped crown, ornamental, bee food.

AILANTHUS GLANDULOSUS (Tree of Heaven): d—to 100', native, symmetrical open head, light moist soil, rapid growth.

ANAQUA (Ehretia anaqua) e—native, to 50', rounded, disease-resistant, red and yellow berries, bird food.

ASH
Green *(Fraxinus pennsylvanica lanceolata):* d—to 70', spreading, rounded, bird food.
White *(Fraxinus americana):* d—to 100', narrow, rounded, bird food, needs good drainage.

BIRCH, River *(Betula nigra):* d—native, to 90', fast growth, attractive trunk and bark.

BUCKTHORN, Carolina *(Rhamnus caroliniana):* d—native, to 35', handsome leaves, red to black fruit, bird food.

CAMPHOR TREE *(Cinnamomum camphora):* e—to 40', tough, aromatic.

CHINABERRY or TEXAS UMBRELLA *(Melia azedarach umbraculiformis):* d—to 45', native, rounded crown, stylistic form, insect-resistant, bird food.

CHINESE PARASOL *(Firmiana simplex):* d—to 35', round crown, smooth green bark, hardy, fine shade tree in lawn.

ELM*
Cedar *(Ulmus crassifolia):* d—native, to 90', drooping branches, rounded crown, dependable, fall color (American Elm subject to disease).
Chinese *(Ulmus parvifolia):* d—Small, hardy, tough, somewhat weeping.
Siberian *(Ulmus pumila):* d—small, graceful, disease-resistant. (*U. pumila pendula* is weeping form.)
Winged *(Ulmus alata):* d—to 60', fast growth, corky wings on branches, disease- and insect-resistant.

GINKGO or MAIDENHAIR TREE *(Ginkgo biloba):* d—to 50', irregular form, smooth bark, slow, plant male only, fall color.

GUM, Black *(Nyssa sylvatica):* d—to 100', rich moist soil, bird food, fall color.

HACKBERRY, Sugar *(Celtis laevigata):* d—to 100', spreading crown, berries for birds. (*C.l. smallii* is smaller variety; *C. occidentalis* is common hackberry.)

HICKORY, Black *(Carya texana):* d—to 80', narrow crown, crooked branches, ridged trunk.

HOLLY
American *(Ilex opaca xanthocarpa):* e—yellow-fruited; variety "Savannah"—heavy bearing upright columnar form.
Dahoon *(Ilex Cassine):* e—shrub or small tree to 30', bee food, flowers Apr.-May, bright red berries remain until Feb.-Mar. (rare yellow-fruited variety also).

HORNBEAM, American *(Carpinus caroliniana):* d—to 35', fluted trunk, pendulous branches, bird food.

LINDEN, American *(Tilia americana):* d—to 130', spreading roots, broad, round head, bird food.

LOBLOLLY BAY GORDONIA *(Gordonia lasianthus):* e—to 60', good ornamental, moist peaty soil, large single white fall flowers.

LOCUST, Honey *(Gleditsia tricanthos):* d—to 100', native, open crown, thorny, hardy, trouble free, bee food.

SWEET BAY *(Magnolia virginiana):* e—to 30', large white fragrant flowers, leaves white beneath, likes to be wet.

MAPLE,
Drummond's Red *(Acer rubrum drummondii):* d—to 40', small rounded form, good foliage, fall color, ornamental.
Japanese *(Acer palmatum):* d—to 25', graceful, fall red color, round habit, moist soil.
Red* *(Acer rubrum):* d—native, to 50', oval form, quick growth, short-lived, prey to root rot, fall color.
Silver* *(Acer saccharinum):* d—to 100', ornamental, leaves silvery white beneath, rapid but short-lived, not resistant, brittle, bird food.

MULBERRY, Russian White *(Morus alba tatarica):* d—to 30', hardy, fruit messy but good bird food. ('Teas Weeping'-*M.a. pendula*-d.)

OAK
Burr *(Quercus macrocarpa):* d—to 80', broad spreading crown, Chinquapin *(Quercus muhlenbergii):* d—to 60', insect- and disease-resistant, lustrous leaves, needs drainage.
Laurel *(Quercus laurifolius):* d—to 70', dense, round-topped.

---

* The roots of the red and silver maples, willow, elm and poplar will clog water lines or sewers, unless planted well away from them.

Live *(Quercus virginiana):* e—to 70', large, spreading limbs close to ground, resistant, 50' spread, dependable.

Overcup, *(Quercus lyrata):* d—native, open, irregular head, slow but long-lived, insect- and disease-resistant.

Post *(Quercus stellata):* d—to 75', large, dense, rounded head, leaves whitish beneath, native.

Shumard *(Quercus shumardii):* d—to 130', native, open, spreading branches, large, fall color.

Southern Red *(Quercus falcata):* d—open rounded form, to 80' with 30' spread.

Swamp Red *(Quercus falcata pagodaefolia):* d—to 80', large.

Swamp Chestnut, *(Quercus prinus):* d—to 100', narrow, long-lived, compact narrow head, bird food.

Texas *(Quercus texana):* d—to 35', small, good form, medium growth rate, fall color.

Water *(Quercus nigra):* d—to 85' with 45' spread, fast growth.

White *(Quercus alba):* d—native, to 150', desirable, large broad open head, white bark, resistant, needs careful transplanting, quail food, grows rapidly.

Willow *(Quercus Phellos):* d—native, to 90' with 45' spread, rounded form.

OSAGE, Orange (Bois D'Arc) *(Maclura pomifera):* d—native, balls said to be insect retardants in house.

PAPAW, East Texas *(Asimina triloba):* d—to 30', dramatic, purple flowers, yellow edible fruit, needs rich soil.

PECAN *(Carya illinoensis):* d—to 100' with 35' spread, rounded form, medium rate growth, Texas State tree.

PISTACHE

Chinese *(Pistachia chinensis):* d—spreading, sturdy, beautiful foliage, medium growth rate, female trees have berries, fall color.

Texas *(Pistachia texana):* e—native, excellent.

POPLAR,* White *(Populus alba nivea):* d—to 70', few pests but short-lived, bark greenish-white, leaves white beneath, root suckers invasive, ornamental.

QUINCE, Chinese *(Chaenomeles sinensis):* d—to 20' tree or shrub, pink flowers, yellow fruit, fall color, smooth attractive bark.

SASSAFRAS *(albidum):* d—native, very interesting, fall dark red color.

SOAPBERRY *(Sapindus drummondii):* d—to 50', small, ornamental, erect rounded crown, moist soils, Golden yellow fall color; desirable.

SWEETGUM *(Liquidamber styraciflua):* d—to 100' with 40' spread. (*L. formosana* good for Houston.) Fall color, symmetrical, cone-shaped, fast-growing, long-lived, trouble-free.

SYCAMORE *(Platanus occidentalis):* d—to 170', largest deciduous tree in U.S., smooth white bark with age.

TALLOW, Chinese *(Sapium sebiferum):* d—to 40', fast but brittle growth, rounded crown, fall color and seeds; milky sap is poisonous.

WITCH HAZEL *(Hamamelis virginiana):* d—to 30', attractive ornamental with yellow flowers in fall.

Transplanting Trees. Modern methods permit transplanting large, mature trees at any season of the year, but this is a job to be undertaken only by experienced people with adequate equipment. While mature trees can be placed where they are most needed, smaller, younger trees are more economical. Small trees which are dug, balled and burlapped, and properly cured are comparatively easy to move, and their growth continues uninterrupted after replanting.

Before planting any tree check the drainage and the soil (see "Drainage" and "Soil and Soil Improvement"). Any tree too large to be handled easily should be planted by experts with the proper equipment. Large or small as the tree may be, in our low coastal areas of high rainfall the method of planting remains the same. Contrary to instructions for other parts of the country, do not make the planting hole larger than to allow a clearance of about ten inches all around the ball of the tree, deep enough to let the top of the root-ball be two or three inches above soil level after settling. Most of our soil is slow-draining, and the slightly raised position assures better drainage.

When the tree is properly placed in the hole fill in the bottom third of the hole with the original soil that has been broken up. Water. While the water is draining mix equal amounts of peat moss, pine bark mulch or other soil conditioner with the original soil and fill the remainder of the hole, covering the top of the ball and an area about three feet around the trunk of the tree. Water again. Mulch with organic matter to a depth of about two inches to conserve moisture and prevent weeds. Once the tree is watered thoroughly, wait until the soil is almost dry before watering again. Many trees in Houston die from root rot caused by overwatering. When the soil seems slightly moist, almost dry, water well. Sprinkling does not get the water down deep enough into the soil and the roots are forced to come to the surface in search of moisture, weakening the tree.

When transplanting bare-root trees, take great care not to injure or bruise the roots. Dip the roots in a thin watery mud to protect them and prevent drying out during moving. The hole should be sufficiently large to spread the roots out in their natural position and deep enough for the old soil line on the trunk to lie about two inches above the soil. The earth should be well firmed between and about the roots so that no air pockets are left, and watered thoroughly.

Care of Trees. Adequate fertilization and care keep trees in a healthy condition and do much to eliminate repair problems and insect or disease damage. Trees may be fed in February or March. Fertilizer is most efficiently applied by means of a series of holes, made by a crowbar, about two inches in diameter and 18 inches deep, dug about three feet apart just inside the drip line of the branches. Two or more rows of holes are necessary for large trees. Follow directions on the label of fertilizer used. The holes should be half filled with fertilizer, then filled up with earth and watered thoroughly.

Spanish moss should not be allowed to proliferate beyond control. It may be pulled off by hand or removed with a rake. Dead wood should be cut from trees as soon as it is noticed. Whenever a limb is removed or the trunk of a tree becomes damaged, the wound should be painted with a special tree paint to prevent entry of insects or disease. If you are not familiar with the practice of corrective pruning, spraying and staking, consult a local nurseryman or tree surgeon who will recommend the proper methods.

Flowering Trees. There are a number of beautiful trees which, when well placed, add interest and variety to the garden and the entire neighborhood. Varieties may be selected to provide a succession of bloom from early spring, through summer, and into early fall. Some of the smaller varieties are especially

valuable as accents or specimen trees near the corner of the house, against a bare wall, at the edge of the property, overhanging a pool, or wherever height and interest are desired.

The espalier method of training trees is adaptable to a wide range of small ornamental trees or shrubs. The technique of training trees and shrubs differs widely from that used for fruit trees. More pleasing effects are obtained if the tree or shrub is allowed to follow its natural characteristic growth. Branches may be held in place by wall nails or long staples. Yaupon, pyracantha, hawthorns, flowering plums, loquat, and pillar or climbing roses are especially effective when displayed against a wall. Professional skill is advised, as the planting and pruning must be done with extreme care, and all twigs and branches must be cut off except those growing in a single plane.

Native species of flowering trees are vigorous and require little care. Many of the less hardy varieties require special care, but their beauty is well worth the extra work. (See the "Flowering Shrubs and Trees" planting chart.)

Native Trees. The South is rich in native plants, and there is a growing appreciation of their charm and suitability in landscape design. Native trees should be more widely used for shade and decorative purposes, as adaptation has acclimated them to our weather, soil, moisture, and drainage conditions. There are native trees to fit most situations.

Nursery-grown native trees are better for transplanting than those dug in the woods, and they stand a much better chance of survival. Those grown in the nursery fields have been regularly fed and watered and root-pruned to develop a compact root system, enabling successful transplanting. Trees taken from the woods have long taproots and usually die after the first season. By observing conservation laws and using only nursery-grown stock in our gardens, our valuable native dogwood, redbud, haw, holly, yaupon, magnolia, and others will be preserved and perpetuated.

Trees and People. The amount of carbon dioxide gas that Man and his machines and factories release into the air is increasing year by year. It therefore becomes even more important to plant trees since they absorb the noxious gas. It takes 78 trees per person per day in modern civilization just to maintain carbon dioxide in atmospheric balance. One man's breathing, for example, equals the carbon dioxide absorbed by one tree, while an automobile using five gallons of gas per day requires two trees to maintain a carbon dioxide balance, and oil and gas for home heating require five trees.

Fruit Trees and Fruits

And the fruits will outdo what the flowers have promised.
—Francoise de Malherbe

Clouds of blossoms embellish the early spring garden that has fruit trees, whether fruit is produced or not. Fruit is a bonus to the beauty of these trees, and many are grown successfully in Houston and the upper Gulf Coast area. No other ornamental quite compares in decorative effect with these small trees.

Fruit trees react differently to differing soils in different climates. The selection of the particular varieties of fruit adapted to local soil and climatic conditions is of utmost importance. Most varieties that bloom and fruit in this area of long summers and mild winters are dwarf or semi-dwarf. Some fruit trees require exposure to a certain number of hours of temperature below 45° as a stimulus to break dormancy and initiate spring growth. Almost all peaches, for example, need about 700 chilling hours to fruit, though fruit trees may blossom even when they don't produce fruit without sufficient cold. "Self fruitful" species bear fruit as a result of pollination from their own blossoms, but many other species require the pollen from another variety to set fruit; these are termed "self-unfruitful."

It is advisable to spray fruit trees with an oil emulsion during dormancy to protect against scale. When 75% of their flower petals have fallen the trees benefit from a spraying with a solution of six tablespoons wettable sulphur per one gallon of water to avoid Brown Rot in the fruit. Repeat every two to three weeks until harvest time. Your County Extension Agent can supply you with a list of the kinds of fruit which grow especially well in your area, and will, upon request, send you bulletins with detailed instructions as to species and varieties, soil preferences, approved sprays for diseases and insects, and pruning advice.

Fruit trees are attractive when espaliered against a wall, but skillful pruning is necessary to develop and maintain the precise pattern of branches and stems. Even though the trees are already trained when purchased, they must be pruned often to keep the desired pattern, and many gardeners feel the beauty is worth the effort.

Mulberry trees are sometimes grown for shade and as an invitation to birds, and persimmon trees are grown for the striking effect of their showy orange-red, oblongish fruit. There is also a native persimmon with small fruit particularly enticing to birds. To a limited extent, tropical fruit trees such as bananas, avocados, and papayas are grown in protected locations, but these seldom bear fruit except following very mild winters (see "The Tropical Garden"). Pecan trees are grown throughout the Gulf Coast, and there are many varieties. Grapes may be trained attractively and usefully on arbors and fences. Blackberries and dewberries are a worthy addition for their fruit and as a food for birds, though the plants are of little ornamental value. Strawberries produce when in beds to themselves, as decorative borders, in strawberry pots or as an interesting ground cover. You and the birds will enjoy them.

Plant fruit trees in January and February while they are dormant. If, however, they are in containers, baskets, or B & B they may be planted in March or April. To avoid disturbing the roots some gardeners do not remove basket or burlap. Be sure to plant fruit trees slightly above regular level of surrounding ground for they must have good drainage (see "Drainage;" for planting procedure, see "Trees"). Use a root stimulator solution at planting time, and repeat at two-week intervals for two months, unless the soil is wet from heavy rainfall. In this event suspend application of stimulator until ground dries out.

Give yourself a spring bouquet by planting fruit trees. They may not be the longest-living trees, but their beauty is breathtaking.

FRUITS FOR THE GARDEN

Fruit	Variety	Ripens	Description
Peach	Junegold	May	Yellow clingstone, hardy. 650 hours cold required
	Rio Grande	May-June	Yellow, good quality. 500 chilling hours.
	Luttichau	June	White freestone, very sweet, medium size, prolific.
Plum	Bruce	May	Large, red color, acid, self-unfruitful, good jams and jellies.
	Methley	June	Medium, purple color, very sweet. Best pollinator for Bruce.
	Excelsior	June	Medium size, tart, red color.
Pear	Pineapple	July-Aug.	Medium. Beautiful for flowers and foliage.
	All Red	August	Mainly ornamental.
	Garber	August	Semi-oval shape, medium size, prolific.
	Keiffer	August	Bears at young age, fair quality, very productive.
	Orient	August	Good quality. Spreading-type decorative tree, shade and fire-blight resistant.
Orange	Marrs Early	Sept.-Oct.	Medium size, sweet, tender, on trifoliata root stock.
Satsuma	Owari	October	Medium to large size, prolific, tree cold resistant.
	Silverhill	October	Small, both on trifoliata root stock.
Lemon	Meyer	Sept.-Oct.	Smooth skin, good quality, hardy, self-fruitful.
Fig	Celeste	June	Small blue fruit, sweet, good fresh or preserves, self-fruitful.
	Texas Ever-bearing	July	Medium to large size, brown color, good quality, needs water.
Loquat	(*Eriobotrya japonica*)	March	Yellow, firm flesh, prolific.
Persimmon	Eureka	October	Roundish, oblong red fruit, excellent quality, self-fruitful.
	Tane Nashi	October	Large cone-shaped orange-turning-red fruit, self-fruitful, seedless, ornamental tree.
Pomegranate	(*Punica Granatum*)	September	Showy, orange-red fruit.

(Continued on next page)

FRUITS FOR THE GARDEN

Fruit	Variety	Ripens	Description
Pecan	Caddo	August	Medium, very prolific, good kernel quality, resistant
	Desirable	October	Large, well filled, resistant
Blackberry	Brazos	May	Very large fruit, prolific, upright canes, self-fruitful, jams, jellies, freezing.
Dewberry	Boysen	May	Large wine-red fruit, good quality, vining, self-fruitful.
	Young	May	Large size, good quality.
Strawberry	Sequoia	April-May	Exceptional size, quality and color. Plant crown just above soil level, self-fruitful.
Grape	Herbemont	July	Small, brownish-red, vigorous, resistant, good juice.
	Scuppernong	July	Vigorous vine, small bunches, sweet. Good for jelly and juice.

Coniferous Evergreens

I remember, I remember/The fir trees dark and high:
I used to think their slender tops/Were close against the sky.

—Thomas Hood

Conifers are evergreen trees and shrubs which have narrow, needle-like foliage and bear cones or berries. In landscape design they provide year-round foliage mass, ranging from picturesque low-spreading types to distinctive cone-shaped varieties for vertical accents.

All conifers should be moved with balled roots and may be transplanted throughout the year, although August and early spring are considered the most favorable times. Most conifers are slow-growing and require less pruning than other trees and shrubs. The lower limbs should be allowed to remain, for removing them destroys a conifer's natural beauty. Conifers are usually resistant to blight, but when infested with red spiders and basket worms they should be treated promptly (see "Diseases and Pests").

Pines may be grown successfully on the home grounds if secured from nurseries, but they are difficult to transplant from the woods because their long taproots and heavy root systems are easily damaged by digging and prolonged exposure. Pines prefer a well-drained, deep loamy soil, and it is important to maintain their natural needle mulch which keeps the ground moist, cool and slighty acid. Mature pines are susceptible to any shock or damage, such as cutting away or destroying part of their roots, which can kill the trees. Soil carelessly thrown over root area may well cause a tree to die. Some conifers for this area are:

CEDAR—*Cedrus deodara*
    Japanese—*Cryptomeria japonica*

CHINA FIR—*Cunninghamia*

CYPRESS
    Arizona—*Cupressus arizonica*
    Bald—*Taxodium distichum* (Dwarf var.—*Taxodium distichum nanum*)
    Hinoki—*Retinospora (Chamaecyparis) obtusa*
    Italian—*C. sempervirens*
    Montezuma—*Taxodium mucronatum*
    Mourning—*C. funebris*
    Portuguese—*C. lusitanica*

JAPANESE YEW—*Podocarpus macrophyllus*
    P.m. var. Maki

JUNIPER
    Blue or Silver Cedar—*Juniperus virginiana glauca*
    Chinese—*J. chinensis*
    Common—*communis*
    Creeping—*J. horizontalis*
    Dwarf Blue—*J. chinensis viridifolia*
    Greek—*J. excelsa*
    Pfitzer—*J. chinensis pfitzeriana*
    Redcedar—*J. virginiana* (native)
    Savin—*J. sabina*
    Sylvester—*J. chinensis femina*

PINE
    Japanese Black—*Pinus thunbergi*
    Loblolly—*P. taeda* (native yellow)
    Longleaf—*P. palustris*
    Shortleaf—*P. echinata* (native)
    Slash—*P. caribaea*

REDWOOD, Dawn—*Metasequoia glyptostroboides*

Shrubs

Shrubs are so versatile that an exquisite garden can be planted with choices from the extensive variety of flowering and berried shrubs, evergreen and deciduous. Shrubs once considered too tender are now grown successfully in our gardens. Hybrids and other unusual newcomers are frequently introduced, and many dwarf forms of old favorites offer plants more appropriately sized for small gardens or for potting. Visit gardens and nurseries to become familiar with the diverse assortment of shrubs. There are those of graceful habit, varying leaf textures, and flowers or berries for different seasons. You will derive more satisfaction in your final selections if you first acquaint yourself with the characteristics of a number of different shrubs.

Hedges. Shrubs are often used to emphasize salient parts of the home grounds. As hedges, they provide seclusion and privacy, outline boundary lines, absorb street noises, screen service areas and provide an effective background for colorful blossoms of lower-growing plants.

When plantings are to serve as a background they may be composed of various species of shrubs. In this case the bushes are often allowed to grow naturally, with only occasional pruning for shaping. Such a combination of shrubs offers interesting material for arrangements in the home. Hedging plants may be of one species, perhaps kept pruned in a formal manner. To achieve the density necessary in a clipped hedge begin pinching off the terminal buds of each branch soon after planting. A trapezoidal shape is recommended for hedges, with the lower portion of the hedge forming the base of the trapezoid. By keeping the top narrower than the bottom, the sides of the hedge receive equal sunlight from top to bottom, stimulating even growth. If the top of the hedge becomes broader than the bottom, unattractive legginess at the bottom of the hedge results from lack of sun.

If hedges are to be composed of only one variety, equally spaced and kept trimmed, plant them in a trench. The procedures for assuring drainage, preparing the soil, planting, and care are the same as for planting shrubs individually. Information in the "Drainage," "Soil and Soil Improvement," and "Propagation" chapters will be useful for both situations. A word of caution in planning hedges: when they are to border driveways or walks, allow ample space for the inevitable growth and spread of the plants. Little plants become large shrubs. If the hedge outgrows its assigned environs, hard, frequent pruning will be required. Pruning is time-consuming and in crowded locations the plants' natural beauty may easily be ruined by it.

Planting. Always group plants of similar sun, soil and moisture preferences together, assuring each plant sufficient space for its natural mature size. With so many choices of plant material available, there is a shrub for every purpose and it is not difficult to follow this principle. Every garden has both sun and shade, and some locations are drier than others. Just as you should become familiar with your plants, also study your garden to become familiar with its subtleties and particulars.

Shrubs are a long-term investment which pays increasing dividends in beauty as the years go by. Consider year-round appearance of foilage as well as floral or berry display. Locate aromatic plants where you can enjoy their fragrance.

When you have decided where the shrubs will be planted, prepare the soil, preferably several weeks before the bushes will actually go into the ground. Hopefully, any drainage problem will have been corrected. If necessary, mend the texture of the soil by incorporating about 40% organic matter (including manure), gypsum and sand, vermiculite or other similar substance. The organic matter encourages the growth of vital soil bacteria. Tilling the soil will blend the additives. If the bushes to be planted like a slightly acid pH, and if the test on your soil shows the need for it, mix in a sprinkling of sulphur. Detailed instructions are provided in the "Soil and Soil Improvement" chapter.

Make the planting holes or trench just deep enough to allow the top of the root ball or the top surface of the soil in the container to be at ground level or even a bit above, because plants often sink lower after planting. Replace the soil around the plant, and water. Watering settles the soil, forcing out the air pockets, giving the plant the moisture it especially needs to survive the shock of transplanting. A solution of root stimulator poured around the plants aids quick root recovery and growth. Mulch about two inches

with a loose organic material such as pine bark mulch (see "Mulching").

Water the shrubs thoroughly every week during dry weather but only after determining if the soil is really dry. Do not water lightly, this brings the roots to the surface and weakens the plant.

Trimming. Training shrubs to tree form with one or several bare trunks can provide trees more suitable in size for the smaller garden. Shrubs pruned to raise a tree-shaped head are especially pleasing, adding height without adding lower foliage bulk. Crape myrtles, viburnums and yaupons are among the many shrubs which can be easily pruned into small, sculpted trees which are quite elegant when situated beside a terrace or in a courtyard. Tree-trimmed shrubs are delightful when planted to form pleached allees or trained and interlaced to form an arbor. So trimmed, the color and texture of the trunks become pronounced.

Selection. For discussions of particular shrubs which grow well in Houston and the upper Gulf Coast region see "Flowering Shrubs and Trees" (Planting Chart), "The Tropical Garden," "Azaleas," "Camellias," and "Roses." The followiing plants, among many others, make attractive hedges.

d = deciduous   e = evergreen

Abelia, flowering—e
Azaleas, flowering—e
Bamboo (if spreading is controlled)—e
Camellia, flowering—e
Cape Jasmine, flowering—e
Cherry Laurel (Wild Peach)—e
Elaeagnus—e
Euonymus, flowering—e
Holly (in variety), berried—e
Ligustrum (in variety)—e
Oleander, flowering, tender—e
Pineapple Guava, fruited—e
Pittosporum, flowering—e
Podocarpus—e
Pomegranate, flowering, fruited—e
Pyracantha, berried (very thorny)—e
Roses, flowering—e
Tamarix, flowering—e
True Myrtle (m. communis), flowering, fruited—e
Viburnum (in variety), flowering—e

Some plants for very low hedges are:

Asiatic Jasmine (12 inches)—e
Box (Japanese and Korean)—e
Confederate Jasmine, flowering (12 inches)—e
Dwarf Holly—e
Dwarf Pittosporum Tobira, flowering—e
Dwarf Pyracantha—e
Dwarf Viburnum—e
Dwarf Yaupon—e
Gardenia radicans, flowering—e

Native Shrubs. With increasing enthusiasm for plant conservation, gardeners use more of the native shrubs found to be dependable, hardy, resistant to disease and insects, and beautiful in the garden (see"Flowering Shrubs and Trees" in the Planting Chart). The native species have another advantage—they attract birds to our gardens. Selected for wildlife, native shrubs and trees provide nesting sites and necessary shelter while providing natural food as well. A variety of plants, combinations of trees, shrubs and vines, attracts native birds. The birds return the favor by helping keep insects under control.

Appropriate bird houses or nesting places, water to drink and bathe in, shallow containers of fine soil for dust baths, and feeders placed in locations that allow the birds to eat in safety all help foster your garden's "bird-appeal." Birds more often suffer from a lack of water than a lack of food. Some birds are more difficult to attract than others; woodpeckers, for example, like to have a stock of pruned limbs somewhere around, and purple martins prefer apartments high above the ground. Birds find some gardens more attractive than others, seeming to possess an uncanny discretion in choosing gardens which offer safe home sites and sufficient food. Hollies, crabapples, blackhaw, dewberry, dogwood, elderberry, grape, hackberry, mulberry, peppervine, pokeberry, sumac, Virginia creeper, yaupon, and wax-myrtle are among birds' favorites in this area. None of the above plants are poisonous to humans or carry diseases that affect crops or orchards in the Gulf Coast region. There are more than 40 species of birds which may frequent your garden if they find it attractive enough.

In addition to those listed in the "Flowering Shrubs and Trees" Planting Chart, the following are attractive garden shrubs:

ACACIA BERLANDIERI (Guajilio): large, tender fine ferny foliage.

ANISE, FLORIDA (*Illicium floridanum*): e—to 10', long aromatic leaves, purple flowers.

GORDONIA AXILLARIS: large with 5" shiny dark leaves, white fall flowers. Plant in moist sand-peat soil.

HOLLY (*Ilex*): in variety, evergreen usually red berries; neutral to slightly acid, porous loam in sun or semi-shade; mulch with pine needles and peat moss. One spring feeding before new growth starts with fertilizer containing organic source of nitrogen, like many azalea-camellia fertilizers. Prune when dormant before new growth starts for holiday greens, cutting at leaf or bud, not at trunk; tip-prune to shape. Use dormant oil spray early spring.

English (*Ilex cornuta aquifolium*, 'Albo-Marginata'): black-green waxy leaves with silvery-white margins and undersides.

Hume (*I. cornuta* 'Hume'): glossy leaves, large red berries.

Hybrid (*I. aquiperni* 'Brilliant'): ornamental shape, red fruit.

Japanese (*I. crenata*): black berries. Fine for hedge.

Little-Leaf (*I. crenata microphylla*): dwarf form.

Possumhaw (*I. decidua*): d—red or orange berries attractive on bare branches.

Tarajo (*I. latifolia*): e—elegant tree or large shrub, lustrous toothed leaves.

Winterberry (*I. verticillata*): e—red berries remain on bare branches *I. latifolia:* 'Variegata' has variegated foliage.

SAGERETIA THEEZANS: d—large shrub with long pendulous branches, small whitish flower spikes, purple fruit; bright yellow fall color.

VIBURNUMS: e—comprise a diverse group of plants with clustered, frequently fragrant flowers often followed by fruit birds like. They are of easy culture, tolerating various soils in semi-shade or sun and may be pruned into tree form. The following are some of the evergreen forms:

V. acerifolium: Texas native, foliage like maple, fall color.

V. japonicum: large medium green foliage.

V. Laurestinus: leaves rough to touch; also dwarf form.

V. nudum: shiny leaves, red fall color, found in wet places.

V. odoratissimum: bright green glossy leaves, good for screening; *nanum* is dwarf form; *variegatum* has variegated foliage.

V. rhytidophyllum (Leatherleaf): waxy, glossy leaves, trouble-free.

V. rufidulum (Black Haw): to 35'.

V. suspensum (Sandankwa): foliage glossy green above, paler beneath.

Vines

Where, twisted round the barren oak,
The summer vine in beauty clung.
—Longfellow

A morning glory to greet the day, a coral vine to add scintillating color, a confederate jasmine to fill the night with fragrance—vines offer all this and more. Grape vines covering pergolas in hot summers were a very early garden application of climbing plants providing welcome shade and edible fruits as well. Vines add charm and beauty to our gardens, needing only the gardener's imagination to use them interestingly and effectively. Select vines with consideration for habit of growth, ultimate density and desired effect of foliage, flowers or fruit, whichever is more important. Discriminately chosen for the appropriate purpose and space, vines are a joy.

Plants grow as they are destined to grow and vines are a prime example. They are going to form long shoots or branches needing support. Vines must have something to climb on, cling to or lean against, even on the ground itself. Those which cling by aerial rootlets with tiny suction cups at their tips are useful for wall coverage. Ivy, in partial shade, and fig vine are strong growers and have no difficulty covering large areas of masonry. These vines grow so profusely in this temperature climate that they need to be properly trained and trimmed to prevent their obscuring the house and invading flower beds. Unless you want complete coverage quickly,

consider using fewer plants. It will take longer to cover, but will reduce maintenance later. By keeping the vine pinch-pruned or clipped you can create a pleasant tracery effect.

Vines that climb by their tendrils or twining stems are excellent for covering pergolas, wire fences and trellises. Trellises may be hinged to allow painting a wood surface behind them. Special nails may be obtained to fasten wires for vines on mortared surfaces. Some of the annual vines, such as the morning glory and the moonflower, are delightful for summer color and make excellent temporary summer screening. They can be trained on strings or wires across sunny windows.

Some plants, such as climbing roses, must be tied to supports. These plants prefer to have their long canes trained horizontally to force breaks which produce more flowers. Pillar roses like to climb vertically. Either variety makes a stunning picture when properly placed.

Vines can be used creatively to fill in before permanent plantings get a start. When the space available in planting is too narrow for trees or shrubs, as against a house, a vine is a good choice.

Prepare the soil deeply when planting vines, and consider soil requirements (see

"Soil and Soil Improvement"). Some vines flower better in poor, others in rich soil. The chart of "Vines Easily Grown" offers helpful cultural information on good vine selections for this climate.

Once established, perennial vines will thrive for years with only occasional cultivation—an annual top dressing with manure or other fertilization, watering and pruning as needed (see "Pruning").

Vines do not harm adult trees when confined to the trunk and main branches, but do not allow them to cover the foliage, since food is manufactured in the leaves. The graceful, casual way vines grow embellishes any garden. You may find other ways to use vines to add character to your garden.

Ground Covers

All sorts are here that all the earth yields, variety without end.
                                                                —Milton

Various plants make excellent ground covers to take the place of or complement a lawn. Very few ground covers other than turf grasses can survive much foot traffic, but stepping stones may be laid if a path is necessary. Correct any soil and drainage problems before preparing the soil. Because ground covers are long-lived plants which eventually become very thick and dense, the only opportunity to prepare the soil properly is before planting (see "Soil . . ." and "Drainage").

Select ground cover plants for their form, shade of green, leaf shape and ultimate height to meet the purpose. Depending on the particular plant, ground covers range in height from three inches to several feet. A mass of "gold dust" aucuba, planted in the shade it loves, becomes a stunning ground cover. It may be pruned to any height between two and four feet. When planting under trees spread fertile soil in which to set the ground cover plants, taking care not to smother the tree (see "Trees"). Low-growing plants are often interplanted among bulbs to hide the withered ripening leaves and keep the blooms of taller plants protected from splattered mud after rains. Ground covers discourage weeds and provide a growing mulch which prevents water from evaporating too rapidly from the surface soil and keeps the soil at an even temperature.

Creeping plants are excellent for binding and holding the soil on steep banks, thereby preventing erosion. Small plants such as creeping thyme are charming growing between stepping stones set in sand, and trodding on thyme releases its fragrance.

More and more dwarf varieties of shrubs and perennials are being developed. Some of these provide a ground cover that flaunts a mass of blooms. Dwarf forms of pyracantha, lantana (tender to freeze) and nandina are among this interesting group of dwarf shrubs. Ground covers recommended for Houston and the upper Gulf Coast are:

AJUGA REPTANS
One of the best covers for dense shade. Blue or white flowers—low rosettes of leaves. Also bronze, variegated and giant types.

CONFEDERATE JASMINE (*Trachelospermum jasminoides*)
Vine used as ground cover will bloom. Dwarf sport *T. asiaticum* can be clipped and used for low edging but does not bloom.

CORAL BERRY (*Symphoricarpus orbiculatus*)
Low-running shrub for high ground cover. Pink, red or white berries through winter. Deciduous. Also white-berried form.

EUONYMUS FORTUNEI
Beautiful trailing evergreen, desirable for carpeting. Partial shade.

FORGET-ME-NOT (*Myosotis*)
Particularly desirable for interplanting in lily beds. Blue flowers. Sun or partial shade.

GILL-OVER-THE-GROUND (*Nepeta hederacea*)
Often called "ground-ivy." Desirable for carpeting, Sun or partial shade.

HONEYSUCKLE (*Lonicera japonica*)
Excellent cover for steep slopes where soil is not too good. Full sun or half shade. Very fragrant.

IVY (*Hedera*)
In a host of forms. Excellent trailer for foilage effect. Shade or semishade. Good under trees. Slow grower.

JAPANESE SPURGE (*Pachysandra*)
Low-growing plant. Glossy leaves, creamy white flowers. Sun or shade. Will tolerate acid soil.

LANTANA, Trailing
Lavender flowered. Full sun. Excellent soil binder. Also dwarf yellow variety.

LIRIOPE (*Muscari*)
Purple or white flowers, grass-like foliage. Any soil. Sun or shade. Makes dense carpet or edging.

MAIDENHAIR FERN
Semi-shade. Will grow in acid soil. Excellent for under-planting.

MONKEY GRASS (*Ophiopogon*)
Narrow-leaved evergreen. Sun or shade. Easy culture.

OXALIS
Pink, white and yellow flowered varieties. Sun or shade. Naturalizes. Grown from bulbs.

PARTRIDGE-BERRY (*Mitchella*)
Native, dainty trailing plant with glossy leaves. Red berries in winter.

PERIWINKLE (*Vinca Minor*)
Blue or white flowers. Forms dense carpet. Best in part shade.

PHLOX, Moss (*P. subulata*)
Pink flowers. Moss-like evergreen foliage. Sun. Good drainage. Pavement planting.

PLUMBAGO, Creeping (*Ceratostigma plumbaginoides*)
Evergreen. Deep blue flowers. Sun or semi-shade.

ROSES, trailing types
Useful for embankments. Sun or partial shade. Max Graf and Wichuraiana best varieties.

SEDUM
Many varieties having varied flower display. Dense evergreen mat. Any soil. Sun to partial shade. Pavement planting.

STRAWBERRY BEGONIA
Trailing perennial, round variegated leaf. Delicate white flowers on slender stem. Shade.

VIOLETS
Will grow in partial shade. Good soil.

WANDERING JEW (*Tradescantia*)
Used under shrubs, rank-growing. Sun or part shade. Green, purple or variegated.

See also: Vines, Bulbs, Flowering Plants, Ferns, Shrubs.

Gray-Leaved Plants

Soon as the evening shades prevail,
The moon takes up the wondrous tale.
—Joseph Addison

Gray foliage gives a garden a luminous quality, adding cool tones on a hot day, assuming a silvery-white appearance in the moonlight. Yet the charm of these plants belies their strength. Almost all gray-leaved plants withstand long periods of drought and intense heat and are rarely troubled by insects. Used skillfully, gray-leaved plants provide contrast and background for garden color, accentuating vivid colors and complementing soft pastels. The gray effect is usually due to hairs on the surface of stems and leaves which protect the plants' surfaces and keep them cool and moist in the same manner that a mulch protects the soil.

Some gray-leaved plants suggested for gardens in this area are:

TREES

Arizona Cypress (*Cupressus arizonica*)—Pyramidal specimen tree.
Veitch's Silver Cypress *(Chamaecyparis pisifera squarrosa)*—soft textured conifer, may be sheared.
White Poplar (*P. alba, nivea* and *pyramidilis*)—leaves flutter gracefully in breeze, showing white under side of leaves, tolerates poor soil.

SHRUBS

Elaeagnus pungens—Silver-lined leaves, small white, fragrant flowers in fall.

Lavender Cotton (*Santolina incarna*)—gray foliage, ideal for bordering—will stand shearing.
Pineapple Guava *(Feijoa sellowiana)*—red tassel-like blossoms.
Pittosporum, Variegated—gives gray-green effect, blooms in spring.
Salt Cedar (*Tamarix*)—feathery foliage, pink flowers.
Senesa or Desert Sage (*Leucophyllum texanum*)—Lavender flowers following rain.

PLANTS

Butterflyweed or Pleurisy Root (*Asclepia tuberosa*)—native plant—bears orange flowers.
Catnip (*Nepeta*)—useful as a border plant.
Garden Pinks (*Dianthus allwoodi*)—perennial, tufted plant form, gray-blue-green foliage, flowers.
Lead Plant (*Amorpha canescans*)—short stemmed native plant, small pink flowers.
Mealy Sage (*Salvia farinacea*)—blue flowers.
Penstemon grandiflorus—tall-growing annual plant, silver-green succulent foliage—blue or purple flowers.
Silverleaf Nightshade (*Solanum elaeagnifolium*)—native, silver-gray foliage, purple flowers, good border plant, does well in summer.
Silver Queen (*Artemesia albula*)—perennial, white felt-like leaves.
Silvery Wormwood (*Artemisia filifolia*)—native, soft green margined with white.
White Leaf Mint (*Pycnanthemum albescens*)—native perennial.
Dusty Miller (*Centaurea gymnocarpa*).
Spanish Dagger (*Yucca*)—Needs hot sun, little water.
Succulents and Cacti—Ideal for rock gardens.

Azaleas

Perfume, colors and sounds echo one another.
—Charles Baudelaire

Azaleas, native to the Orient, were originally brought to Europe and England by the East India Companies, and reached America about 1784. Meanwhile, native deciduous azaleas had been found in Virginia in 1690 and in Florida and the Carolinas in 1730, but it was not then recognized that the imported azaleas and the native azaleas were related. Today, almost every garden azalea is the product of hybridization.

Species, Hybrids, Varieties, Clones. Azaleas belong to the genus Rhododendron. Latinized names of the azalea species should be preceded by Rhododendron or R. Collectively, azaleas constitute one series of Rhododendron—the series *Azalea*. Azaleas may be species, hybrids, or clones selected from either species or hybrid groups. These categories become important when discussing a particular azalea or appreciating a recent azalea introduction.

It is impractical to list the vast number of azalea varieties, but many clones of the following hybrids have been successfully grown in the Gulf Coast area, including Houston: Southern Indian, Kurume, Pericat, Glenn Dale, Rutherford, and the late-blooming hybrids. Some clones of Belgian

Hybrids and new clones from current hybridizers have also flourished.

Azaleas may be divided into related groups according to their specific characteristics. Most azaleas are evergreen. Some are deciduous, but other than some native American species, they do not grow in a warm climate, so this eliminates for the South the beautiful Ghent and Mollis Hybrids which prefer a cool climate.

Landscape Utilization. The versatility of azaleas is unlimited, with some type available for any garden or landscape use. Mature plants range in size from one to ten feet high, with a spread up to 15 feet. Azaleas also vary in their preferred growing conditions of sun and shade. Most thrive under a high canopy of pines, gums, and deciduous oaks. Some require full sun to grow and set buds; others flourish in shade. Very few bloom in dense shade.

Azaleas may be utilized in a variety of ways: as pot plants, in mass plantings, as hedges, as specimen plants, espaliered, and as tree types. Though all start small none remain that way. Consider all facets of your landscape plan before selecting the varieties of azaleas for your garden.

(Text continued on page 36)

Many varieties of azaleas may be seen at Bayou Bend Gardens, #1 Westcott St., Houston.

Blooming azaleas are most effective when planted in groups. You have the choice of rich and varied coloring, from white through pale to deep hues, with many shaded and variegated sorts as well. Azaleas in full bloom present a stunning display of color with flowers in such profusion that they hide the foliage. Groups or masses of azaleas of a single variety are dramatic, but beautiful and interesting effects can also be attained by planned shading of colors or by using accent plants here and there with flowers of contrasting size, form or color. If you desire a particular color effect, select and plant your azaleas while in full bloom.

You can confine your plantings to azaleas which bloom at the same time; or, by careful selection, you can enjoy a prolonged season of bloom from September to May, with the greatest flowering in February and March. For maximum bloom effect, it is best to group together plants which bloom about the same time. In Houston the very late-blooming varieties tend to put out new growth before they bloom, obscuring the blooms somewhat. The only serious disadvantage to an extended blooming season is the fungus disease, azalea petal blight, which may be controlled only by spraying all the blossoms two or three times a week during the blooming season to keep them beautiful.

The basis of any new planting should consist of varieties which have been tested and found adaptable to this climate. Plants should be secured only from reliable sources and should be in a strong and healthy condition at time of planting. Azaleas are permanent investments, increasing in beauty and value from year to year and, properly planted, they are likely to outlive their growers.

Southern Indian Hybrids. The Southern Indian Hybrids, known in the South as "Indicas," are the most widely known azaleas, largely because of the fine specimens of great age in famous old southern azalea gardens. Indicas grow rapidly and form large, wide-spreading bushes. The flowers are single and, like the leaves, are larger than those of the other hybrids and species. As to habit, there are two general classes: tall plants (to about eight feet) usually of faster and more open growth and earlier blooming; and low plants (to about four feet) compact, dense and spreading, of slow growth and usually late-blooming.

There are numerous varieties, but the following early, midseason, and late-blooming clones thrive and are usually available in the Gulf Coast area:

*Good bloom in moderate to considerable shade.
**Good bloom only in moderate to full sun.
   T = tall, M = medium, L = low mature height

WHITE
*Fielder's White—early midseason. M
 Indica Alba (*mucronatum*)—early midseason. T
**King's White—late midseason. T-M
*Mrs. G.G. Gerbing—early midseason, large flowers, sport of George Lindley Taber. T
*Lady Helen—midseason, green throat, sport of Pride of Mobile. M-T

PINK TO RED
 Brillantina (Brillant)—late, red. M
**Elegans—early, light pink. T
 Fisher Pink—midseason, light pink. M
**Judge Solomon—midseason, pink with violet red blotch, sport of Formosa. T
*Mardi Gras—midseason, pale pink with rose pink blotch, sport of Pride of Mobile. M-T
 Pride of Dorking—late, carmine red. M
*Pride of Mobile (Elegans Superba)—midseason, deep rose pink. M-T
**Southern Charm—midseason, pink, sport of Formosa. T

SALMON TO ORANGE-RED
**Daphne Salmon (Lawsal)—late midseason, salmon pink. M-T
**Duc de Rohan—early midseason, orange-red. M
**Moss Point Red (Triomphe de Ledeberg)—late, light orange-red. M
*President Claeys—midseason, orange-red. T
**Prince of Orange—late, dark orange-red. M

LAVENDER TO VIOLET
**Formosa—midseason, magenta, very hardy. T
*George Lindley Taber—early midseason, pale lavender pink, large flowers, sport of Omurasaki. T
*Omurasaki (Form of *phoeniceum*)—early midseason, violet red, large flowers; not generally available, but valuable for shady location. T
*Vittata (*Fortunei*) (*Vittata punctata*), variety of Simsi—very early (September to February), flowers very variable from almost pure white with faint lavender stripes to well-colored pale lavender. Valuable for its long blooming season. T

Kurume Hybrids. The Kurume Hybrids are probably the hardiest and most shapely azaleas. They vary in height to four feet, forming dense, compact bushes with small, glossy, evergreen foliage. Their small flowers are borne in profusion, some of single type, others hose-in-hose (two perfect corollas, one set within the other). In Houston Kurumes seem to do best in high filtered shade with protection from the hot afternoon sun. They respond well to pruning and become even more beautiful. These hybrids originated in Kurume, Japan, 150 years ago and were brought into the United States between 1915 and 1928. In many cases the difficult Japanese names have been replaced by English names.

Many Kurume varieties grow well in Houston. Those generally available are:

Snow—early, white, hose-in-hose, large flowers, blooms best in moderate sun.
Apple Blossom—pale pink with white, hose-in-hose.
Coral Bells—early, salmon pink, hose-in-hose, blooms in sun or shade.
Bridesmaid—salmon pink, early, large flowers.
Pink Pearl—early, pink shaded to light pink, hose-in-hose, blooms in sun or shade.
Salmon Beauty—early, salmon pink, hose-in-hose, blooms in sun to moderate shade.
Christmas Cheer—early, brilliant bright red, hose-in-hose.
Hexe—midseason, crimson, hose-in-hose.
Hinodegiri—early, scarlet, single, slow compact grower.

Pericat Hybrids. Pericat Hybrids are relatively new azaleas probably resulting from crosses of Belgian, Indian, and Kurume Hybrids. They resemble the Kurumes but bloom later, grow a little faster and have medium-sized foliage similar to the Kurume Hybrid, "Pink Pearl". The Pericats are very hardy and bloom well in sun or shade. Varieties generally available are:

Gardenia Supreme—early, white with faint pink blotch, hose-in-hose.
Hampton Beauty—late-midseason, pink, hose-in-hose, frilled.
Madam Alphonse Pericat—late-midseason, pale pink, hose-in-hose with rufffled petals.
Pericat Pink—late-midseason, deeper pink, hose-in-hose.
Sweetheart Supreme—late-midseason, light pink, hose-in-hose with ruffled petals. When opening they give a rosebud effect.
Twenty Grand—midseason, semi-double, tyrian rose.

Belgian Hybrids. The Belgian Hybrids were developed primarily for greenhouse culture in Belgium and England. There are many in America but they have not been tested extensively in southern gardens because they had been considered too tender for outdoor culture. The flowers are large, double, with twisted frilled petals. As a group they offer some of the most spectacular and beautiful blooms of all azaleas. Some clones have been grown outdoors successfully in Houston since 1960. Experience has proven their need for overhead filtered shade and a hedge or wall to break the strong north winds. Plants increased in hardiness with maturity. Other clones are probably cold hardy and probably can be grown under the same conditions as the Southern Indian Azaleas. Grown successfully were:

Albert-Elizabeth—semi-double, large frilled, white with orange-red edging.
Emil de Konnick—semi-double, white edged purple.
Hexe de Saffelaere—single, hose-in-hose, frilled, violet red.
Red Wing—recently introduced, large ruffled, hose-in-hose, brilliant red,
Triomphe—double, frilled, violet-red with dark blotch.

Glenn Dale Hybrids. The Glenn Dale Hybrids were developed by B.Y. Morrison, former chief of the Plant Introduction Section, United States Department of Agriculture. They are unusual in the great number of different crosses made, the wide range of species from which the parents were derived, and the tremendous number of seedlings from which the numerous named varieties were selected. Among the many varieties are plants of diverse habit, color and flower form for each blooming period of the entire blooming season for evergreen azaleas. Flowers are small to large, often up to 4½ inches. Plant habits are either upright or spreading and low, medium or tall. The Glenn Dale Hybrids were developed to be cold hardy for the Middle Atlantic States. They were formally introduced in 1953, but were not generally available until 1965 and still are not well known. There are over 400 clones to choose from. Many do well in Houston, including:

Eros—low spreading, dark glossy foliage, lovely Eosine
pink color.
Fashion—medium height, dark foliage, flowers 2 to 4 in
head, hose-in-hose, begonia rose with heavy blotch of
Tyrian rose.
Glacier—white with green throat, handsome foliage.
Polar Sea—frilled white, chartreuse blotch.
Refrain—lovely light Rosolane pink, hose-in-hose,
flowers 1 to 3 in head.
Sebastian—beautiful rose pink.
Treasure—heavy foliage, vigorous growth, white with
faint pink cast to buds.
Mary Margaret—dark foliage, spreading, outstanding
bloom of deep Rose Doree with heavy blotch of
purple-whole flower carries as a glowing orange.

Rutherford Hybrids. Rutherford Hybrids,
developed for greenhouse or florists' pot
plants, are medium height azaleas with
various types of blossoms in colors ranging
from white through pink to red, orange-red to
purple. Developed by Bobbink and Atkins of
East Rutherford, New Jersey, the plants are
evergreen and may be regarded as a United
States contribution to the Belgian-Indian
Hybrid azaleas. Many should do well outdoors in Houston. Most of the flowers are
double, frilled, hose-in-hose, two to three inches in size. Now growing in Houston are:

Constance—pink, midseason.
L.J. Bobbink—purple, frilled, midseason.
Pink Ruffles—semi-double, hose-in-hose, midseason,
pink.
Rose Queen—rose, white throat, midseason.

**The Late-Blooming Azaleas, Satsuki
Azaleas.** The late-blooming evergreen azaleas
are mainly derivatives of the dense, low-
growing native Japanese species Indica (indicum), and the Dwarf Indica (indicum Var.
eriocarpum) of lower growth, denser, slower
growing, less hardy than Indica, with larger,
frilled flowers, found wild farther south (to
Formosa) than the Indica. These azaleas are
not to be confused with the hybrids of the
South called "Southern Indicas."

They are known in Japan as the Satsuki
Azaleas because they bloom in late May or
early June. Under the old Chinese calendar
Satusuki is the fifth month, the equivalent of
our June. The Indica azalea is said to have
been in cultivation in Japan for 300 years.
There its varieties and hybrids are the favorite
azaleas for gardens and for Bonsai. They are

all the work of Japanese hybridizers. The
Dwarf Indica Azaleas were not introduced
into this country, so far as is known, until
1938. Once stems are pencil thick the plants
are about as hardy as the Indica azalea. The
Satsuki group sport readily. The Japanese
prefer singles and plants that sport. Their
development has continued in Japan and
these new varieties should be introduced in
this country.

The best-known Satsukis in this country
are the Gumpo clones of the Dwarf Indica
Azaleas, which have done well in Houston:

White Gumpo—upright, very low, dense, very late,
flowers singled frilled, occasionally flecked pink.
Pink Gumpo—rose pink with deeper flecks.

Another group of the Indica Azaleas has
come to us through England and Holland.
They were found wild in Japan in 1680 by the
Dutch East India Company. They were introduced to England in the 1830's under the
names danielsiana, macrantha, and lateritia
by ship's officers of the British East India
Company. These were the sources of the Indica Azalea commonly sold today under the
name "Macrantha," and also the source of
the very low-growing clone, "Balsaminaeflo-
ra." These plants are low (up to 24 inches),
spreading, with fine dense foliage, beautiful
even when not in bloom. The flowers are
larger than Kurumes and tend to dribble into
bloom, reaching peaks in June and early
autumn. Two varieties thrive in Houston:

Macrantha—single, clear pink.
Macrantha—double, hose-in-hose, clear pink.

Other American Hybrids. Fine new
American hybrids are being developed continuously. The following have been grown
successfully in Houston:

COOLIDGE HYBRIDS
Shimmer-Kurume type; rose pink.
KERRIGAN HYBRIDS
Ballerina—salmon pink, hose-in-hose.
Bride's Bouquet—white, medium size, full formal
double, gardenia styled bloom.
MOSSHOLDER-BRISTOW HYBRIDS
Desert Rose—large single to semi-double, salmon
pink with red throat.

Princess Caroline—Belgian type, ruffled, salmon pink with red throat.

White Orchids—large, single to semi-double, ruffled white with showy red throat.

NUCCIO HYBRIDS

The Nuccio firm currently has a extensive hybridizing program and has introduced a number of beautiful hybrids of several types which grow well in Houston.

Native American Azaleas. Native American azaleas are botanical species. They are deciduous and have a long blooming season which varies according to the species and latitude, from Florida north into Canada and west into Texas. The flowers are fragrant and the color range includes cream, yellow, and orange, as well as the white to pink to red shades. Two species are native to Texas:

R. canescens (Florida Pinxter A.)—near white to medium or deep pink. Grows from Florida west to Texas.

R. oblongifolium (Texas A.)—usually white, sometimes pale pink. Grows on open wooded hillsides and streams in east Texas. Clove scent. Discovered 1850. Blooms in July.

There are at least 17 native American species. Those most adaptable to Houston in addition to the two named above, are:

R. austrinum (Florida A.)—cream yellow to orange to red.

R. alabamense (Alabama A.)—white, usually with yellow blotch.

They are most successfully grown when their native habitat is simulated as nearly as possible as to drainage, soil, and shade.

Plant Selection. Having decided on the landscape plan and the type and varieties of azaleas you desire, you are ready to select plants. Buy only from reliable nurseries so you can depend on the labeling and previous care of the plants. Most nurseries now grow azaleas in containers, and most of those imported into the Houston area come in plastic containers rather than cans. Most are growing in a peatmoss mixture, usually 2/3 peat and 1/3 sandy soil. If they are in cans they may be in almost any acid mixture, from soil to sand, to sand and sawdust, or even a clay field ball stuck in a can. This applies to plants in containers from one to five gallon size, the latter being fairly large plants. Large plants are seldom available unless they are growing in soil in gardens. Large azaleas growing in soil must be transplanted, like trees, with heavy equipment. Select only plants with dark green, vigorous, dense foliage. If the foliage is light-colored, yellow or droopy, the culture has been bad or the plant has been damaged—do not buy it.

Planting. All container-grown plants should be bare-rooted. The method of planting and the particular soil mixture are governed by the plants' expected mature size and their usage. If they are to be used as container plants, the plants can be grown permanently in a container type mixture such as:

Pine bark (2 parts)
Oak leaf mold (1 part)
Top sandy soil (1 part)

To 10 gallons of mix add:

½ cup dolomite lime
½ cup superphosphate
¼ cup sulfate of potash
¼ cup chelated multitrace elements.

The pH should be about 5.5. The key to successful container culture is good drainage, which means a porous soil.

For all other types of growing media and all other uses, it is advisable to bare root the azalea and plant it in a bed of prepared soil mixture. Select a well-drained location. *Do not dig a hole,* unless you live in the rare sandy soil area of Houston. Work up the top four inches of native soil, add some agricultural gypsum to condition it and then add a foot or more of the prepared soil mixture in which to plant the azalea. It should be an acid, loose, friable, sandy mixture with at least 1/3 humus and a pH of 5.0 to 6.0. A mixture of 1/3 sandy loam, 1/3 humus from compost, manure, pine bark, etc., 1/6 torpedo sand, and 1/6 agricultural Perlite, plus one pound of 16-mesh agricultural sulphur per large wheelbarrowful to give a pH of about 5.5, is usually satisfactory. For determining soil pH and other testing procedures, see "Soil and Improvements."

To bare-root an azalea having a dirt ball, simply take a hose with a nozzle and wash off most of the ball. Azalea roots are unlike other plant roots; they are dense and fibrous and are usually right at the surface, so you can generally expose most of the roots and still have a small core of soil in the middle of the root system. When you have to bare-root an azalea grown in a peat-soil mixture or pure peatmoss, you have a job on your hands. Sometimes you can soak it thoroughly in water and then bare-root it adequately with the water pressure from a nozzled hose. Other times, in addition to this, you must use a 3-pronged tilling fork to tear the ball apart so as to free at least two inches of the roots to plant in the new growing mixture. You will think you are tearing your plant to pieces, but it is essential to remove most of the peatmoss ball mixture. A peatballed plant will not survive in a mixed soil bed. The peat moss either soaks up water and drowns the plant, or it dries out and kills the plant. Soak the root system in a hormone solution (Transplantone, OD-4, or equivalent) for a half hour.

To plant, dig a hole in the prepared bed to accommodate the plant's roots. Set the plant on a cone of dirt in the middle of the hole, with the roots spread out naturally over the cone. The top of the root system should be just barely below the surface of the bed. Cover the roots with the soil mixture and wash it in well into the root system. Mulch the bed with about four inches of pine needles or other coarse plant fiber. Do not use peatmoss as mulch; it will dry out, shed water and kill the plant.

Watering. Azaleas need good drainage. They should be moist at all times, but not waterlogged. An azalea's leaves wilt when it needs water. Of course it is not good culture to let the plant get that dry. Water thoroughly and deeply, then leave the plant alone until it needs water again. During the hot dry summers it is necessary to soak the beds deeply every four or five days. Plants also dry out during the winter, so be sure to check the azalea beds and keep them sufficiently damp. If a hard freeze is predicted, water deeply. Most plant damage from our hard northers is due to dehydration that can be prevented if the root system is moist. When they bloom in the spring, azaleas need plenty of water.

Fertilizing. Azaleas are light feeders. Fertilize them once in the spring, just after the blooming season, with an organic-base acid type fertilizer, such as an azalea-camellia mix. It should be a 5-10-10 with a cottonseed meal, or equivalent, base, with trace minerals and sulphur added. To fertilize azaleas, first be sure there is a mulch of about four inches of pine needles or other coarse plant fiber; next, scatter the fertilizer lightly on top of the mulch, spreading evenly over the bed and out beyond the drip line of the plants; work it in with your hands, then water in. Do not allow dry fertilizer to touch the stem of the plant. Do not use too much fertilizer. For a plant one foot high and one foot in diameter, one level tablespoonful is sufficient. If the plant is in a container, use half that amount. A cupful is plenty for a very large plant, say eight feet in diameter.

Never fertilize an azalea having light yellowish foliage. The plant is sick from poor drainage, or from an acid problem or iron deficiency which must be corrected before fertilizing. Check for adequate drainage and test the pH of the soil. If the pH is below 4.0 (too acid), sprinkle a little agricultural lime over the mulch and water it in. *Never cultivate around an azalea, you will injure the shallow roots.* If the pH is 6.8 or higher, the plant needs acid. Sprinkle a little 16-mesh agricultural sulphur over the top of the mulch in same amount and method as fertilizer, and water it in. In addition, use a chelated iron-mineral compound; add twice as much water as recommended by the manufacturer, and sprinkle with a watering can over the entire bed. Keep these chemicals away from the center of the plants. You want to treat the roots, not the stems. Changing the soil pH or treating a sick plant is a slow process. Retest the pH after three or four weeks, and repeat the treatment if necessary until the pH is in the 5.0 to 6.0 range and the plant has a dark green healthy look. Only then should you add a little fertilizer.

Where there are numerous trees their roots will take up some fertilizer, and it will be necessary to make a second azalea fertilization late in the spring, about May 15. Never apply fertilizer after June 1. For outdoor culture in an area where there can be freezing temperatures in the winter, it is essential for azaleas to stop growing, become dormant and harden off before the freezes. If they have been over-fertilized and have not gone into their normal dormant period, the hard freezes will split the stems and kill the plants.

Pruning. Though azaleas in informal plantings require little pruning except to cut back unsightly branches, the proper time for it is immediately following the blooming season before new growth starts. In late June cut tall canes down into the bush and pinch new growth shoots to thicken the plant and maintain a desired shape. Azaleas put out new growth all along the canes. Formally planted azaleas may be sheared rather severely, within the limits of their mature size, to maintain a shape or pattern. Hedges of large or dwarf types may similarly be clipped to a height appropriate for the variety used. Do some of your pruning when plants are in bloom and enjoy the blossoms.

Diseases and Pests. Azaleas in good growing condition are seldom troubled by insects or diseases, but it is probably advisable to spray once with an oil spray plus an insecticide, such as Malathion, as a precaution in the spring thirty days after the main blooming period. This delay is necessary because oil spray should not be used for thirty days after a fungicide spray such as is used to control azalea petal blight.

Azalea Petal Blight. There is one serious fungus disease, azalea petal blight, which attacks flowers but does not damage plants. The initial symptoms are small, wet-looking translucent spots on the flower petals. The spots rapidly enlarge and spread from flower to flower, bush to bush. The flowers become a wet slimy mass and the blooms in an entire garden can be destroyed almost overnight. The severity of this disease depends on the temperature and humidity. The spores of this fungus disease are widely spread by wind and bees, so you can protect your plants only by spraying the flowers with a fungicide two or three times a week during the blooming season, starting as soon as the flowers begin to open. Dithane Z-78, formulated by Rohm-Haas as a wettable powder, is currently used: 1½ lbs per 100 gal. of water plus 3 oz. sticker spreader. Spray the bed under the plants, all parts of the plants and inside the flowers. The fungus spore dies on contact with the fungicide. Use a fine, misty spray. By spraying the beds, you also disinfect your own yard. The only disadvantage is that the spray leaves white specks on the flowers.

WARNING: most insecticides and fungicides are poisonous to various individuals in varying degrees. Wear rubber gloves when mixing and spraying. Do not place yourself in a position where spray blows back on you or is inhaled. Wash face and hands with warm water and rinse eyes with water immediately after spraying.

Lichen Fungus. There is a "lichen fungus" disease which attacks azalea stems and stunts or kills them. It is not known to develop in Houston, but it is present on almost all mature azaleas imported from south Louisiana. It is an odd-looking greenish-gray growth on the stems. It can be eradicated by applying a strong fungicide, such as Captan, with a paint brush.

Leaf Gall. Azaleas may occasionally be attacked by the parasitic fungus, *exobasidium leaf gall,* which severely distorts young leaves as they develop. The leaves appear to be excessively thick and become pale or yellowish-green with a glossy surface. It is controlled by removing and burning all affected leaves.

Root Rot. Root rot is infrequent in azaleas, but it sometimes attacks them and may be caused by parasitic fungi. One, *phytophthora,* causes the leaves to turn a pale dull green and droop as if in need of water, but the leaves do not revive when watered. This disease may cause sudden death of the azalea as a result of infection in the fine feeder roots, evidenced by moist, brown decay at the tips. Sometimes the main root system is infected, the bark is killed, and the cambium is blackened at the soil line. Defective drainage and a heavy compact soil are contributing factors.

Another type of root rot is caused by the root-destroying fungus, *Clytocybe tabecens,* which forms a white, web-like growth resembling absorbent cotton. The growth covers and girdles the larger roots preventing their functioning. Sometimes light yellow mushroom growths are produced just at the ground. The plants suddenly turn yellow and wilt. Death is sometimes so rapid that the leaves die without being shed. Since there is no warning of the attack, there is little chance to save the plant. If these root rot fungi are detected early some of the plants can be saved by repeated applications of the fungicide Dexon, a wettable powder formulated by the Chemagro Corp. If the plant dies you will find that the fungus is mostly in the old silt or clay ball from the nursery of origin. Be sure to remove all of the old ball and thoroughly disinfect the good bed material with Dexon before planting another azalea in the bed.

Chlorosis. Chlorosis (yellowish and dropping foliage) is not a disease but a symptom of cultural deficiencies, most of which inhibit the availability of iron to the plant. The most common cause in Houston is an alkaline soil condition due to the alkalinity of the city's water (pH 8.4). The best pH for azaleas is 5.0 to 6.0, so chlorosis is common when much irrigation is necessary with Houston city water. This condition is so common in Houston that it needs special emphasis. The treatment is described in "Soils and Soil Improvement."

Iron Chlorosis may be due to:
1. Alkaline soil; pH 7 or higher.
2. Too acid soil; pH below 4.
3. Over watering and poor drainage.
4. Over fertilization.

5. Nitrogen deficiency.
6. Magnesium, calcium, potassium, manganese, boron, phosphorus deficiencies

Nitrogen deficiency is usually the result o using raw plant fiber such as sawdust o shavings or even stems and leaves as a mulcl instead of humus in the planting mixture. A the raw plant fiber breaks down it uses up nitrogen from the soil.

To correct chlorosis determine the prob able cause:

1. Test the acidity of the bed. If above pH 6.0, correct according to instruction under "Soil and Soil Improvement." I too acid, below pH 4.0, add bone mea in flour form. Move mulch back sprinkle bone meal on until the ground is fairly white, replace mulch and wate well.
2. Check drainage.
3. If you have a good reason to suspect a nitrogen deficiency because of the plan material added as humus to the planting soil, this condition can be corrected by adding nitrogen as ammonium sulphate like "peppering an egg" and watering it in. *Do not over-do it.*
4. If no other cause can be found, it may be due to a deficiency mentioned under number 6 above. Nitrogen, phosphorus and potassium are provided in all acid-forming azalea fertilizers. The others are trace elements that are manufactured and marketed as a chelated mineral mixture. This should be applied strictly according to the manufacturer's instructions.

Propagation. The only way to reproduce azaleas true to the variety or clone is by vegetative propagation. This is seldom done by the amateur home gardener who usually purchases the small plants from professional growers. For detailed information see the chapter "Propagation."

Camellias

And the spring arose on the garden fair like the spirit of Love felt everywhere.
—Shelley

Camellias were imported into Europe from Southeast Asia over 400 years ago and were brought to the United States nearly 200 years ago. They were reported at Middleton Place near Charleston, South Carolina, in 1787. They were soon reported north along the Atlantic coast states as far as Boston, where they were widely cultivated as greenhouse plants from 1800 to 1850. As outdoor plants, they spread across the South and reached California in 1852. They flourished as outdoor plants in the warmer parts of the United States, but the early greenhouse culture was largely abandoned. Interest in camellias declined around 1900 and revived again about 1930, becoming more widespread in 1945 with the founding of the American Camellia Society and in 1946 with the founding of the Southern Camellia Society and their dissemination of research, nomenclature, and cultural data. This stimulated plant development and introduction. New species of camellias were soon imported into the United States, and by the early 1950s a major hybridizing program was under way which has been of vast importance to all facets of the camellia industry, including the home gardener.

There are 89 known species of camellias of which 21 are now in the United States and eight have garden varieties. *Camellia japonica,* with over 3,000 named varieties, dominates all facets of camellia usage, including home gardening and hobby flower growing. *Camellia sasanqua* is the second most important species because of its early blooming, good landscape characteristics, and its excellent root stock value in the nursery trade for grafting. Since the Yunnan Reticulatas were imported in 1948, *Camellia reticulata* and many other species, particularly *Camellia saluenensis,* have been used extensively in hybridizing to produce many fine hybrid cultivars which may be important to the home gardener in the near future.

Many thousands of seedlings of many species and hybrids are grown each year, but only a few are worth introducing as new named varieties. Most of them are cut off and used as grafting stock. Selected new seedlings are grown and evaluated for several years before introduction. For two to ten years after introduction they are evaluated by growers and accredited ACS horticulture judges. A very few of the new varieties may ultimately receive outstanding awards of merit from the American Camellia Society or the Southern California Camellia Society.

Camellia Nomenclature, published biannually by the Southern California Camellia Society, is the official nomenclature book of the American Camellia Society. All the

Betty Sheffield Supreme

Crimson Robe

Guilio Nuccio

Tomorrow Park Hill

Lila Naff

Clark Hubbs

Camellias of numerous species may be seen in Houston at the Garden Center, the McAshan Arboretum and the Bayou Bend Gardens. Camellias and slides courtesy of Ferol and Sam Zerkowsky, Tammia Nursery, Slidell, Louisiana.

gistered named varieties in the United
tates are described in this volume and all the
ward-winning cultivars are listed. The
ybrids are divided into two classifications:
Species Reticulata and Hybrids with
eticulata Parentage," and "Hybrids With
ther Than Reticulata Parentage." This is
e result of the present belief that most of the
nported Yunnan Reticulatas were probably
ybrids.

Camellias bloom from early fall to late
pring in Houston and the Gulf Coast area,
epending on the horticultural temperature
one, the species and the variety. C. sasanqua
looms early, from mid-October to mid-
ecember; C. japonica blooms early to late,
om mid-October to mid-March; C.
ticulata blooms late, mostly in March; and
ost Hybrids bloom mid-season, probably
ecause one parent is usually a mid-season
aponica.

Camellias furnish beautiful and exotic
looms of all sizes and types for outdoor
ome garden display on the plants, for cut
owers in the home as specimens or
rrangements, for cut flowers and corsage use
the floral trade, for specimen flowers in
amellia flower shows, and as material for ar-
stic arrangements in flower shows. C.
asanqua blooms are small, varying from 1½
3 inches in diameter, and of all flower
orms from single to formal double. Many
ansanqua blooms are small, fragile singles
nd not good cut flowers. C. japonica blooms
ary in size from miniatures (less than 2½ in-
hes) to very large (up to 8 inches), include all
ower forms but very few singles, and usually
ave good texture and substance, so they
ake good cut flowers for the home, the
oral trade, and specimens for flower shows.
here is a size, flower type, and color for
very conceivable use. C. reticulata and
eticulata hybrids have mostly large to very
rge blooms, from four to seven inches, with
eep, rather complex, mostly semi-double
lower forms, good heavy texture, and a
pecial sheen to the deep rich colors. The
ther class of hybrids has smaller blooms,
rom small to large, mostly up to five inches,

all flower forms but few singles, more subtle
colors, even some pastel and many with a
lavender tinge due to the Saluenensis parent.
All Camellia species vary in cold hardiness.
C. sasanqua is the most cold hardy, C.
reticulata is the least cold hardy and, except
for 'Crimson Robe' and 'Captain Rawes,' will
not bloom after freezing weather. C. japonica
and the Hybrids vary from one extreme to the
other. Most Japonicas and many Hybrids are
cold hardy for outdoor culture in Houston.

Camellias furnish extremely valuable
landscape material with luxuriant dark green
foliage of rather heavy leaf structure. C.
sasanqua has small leaves and frequently
willowy growth habits; C. japonica has
medium to large leaves that are rounder in
shape and heavier in texture on plants which
vary from rather dense to quite open in
growth habits. C. reticulata has mostly large,
thick, reticulated, serrated leaves on open,
rangy-growing plants. All camellias are trees
with varying growth characteristics. Some remain relatively small after many years, but
there are also many old camellias in the Gulf
Coast areas 10 to 20 feet high, and there are
known Japonica trees over 400 years old and
over 30 feet high, and known Reticulata trees
300 to 500 years old and up to 50 feet high.

The home gardener has a vast array of
camellia plant material to choose from. There
are fine old varieties which have stood the test
of time for 50 to 150 years and belong in any
garden. However, most of the best camellia
plant material has been developed and introduced during the past 25 years, and the
camellias of tomorrow are just now being
developed and introduced. A few cultivars
considered best in each category are sub-
mitted, followed by some suggestions on how
to grow them.

Camellia Sasanqua. The following list includes the American Camellia Society Peer
Sasanqua Award winners from 1958 to 1974,
plus a few older reliables. Some are closely
related, later blooming species *Hiemalis* and
Vernalis. The plants have rapid, hardy growth
and free flowering characteristics which make

them particularly valuable in landscape planting as hedges, mass or foundation planting and as espaliered specimens.

*ACS Peer Sasanqua Award Winners.

*Bonanza—deep red, large, semi-peony form.
*Chansonette (species *Hiemalis*)—first Peer award winner—brilliant pink, large, formal double with ruffled petals.
Jean May—shell pink, large, double.
*Harriette Ruster—white tipped pink, large, anemone form with undulating outer petals.
*Leslie Anne—white tipped reddish lavender, large, semi-double with irregular petals to peony form.
Mine-No-Yuki or Snow—white, large, peony form.
*Miss Ed—light pink with lavender and deeper pink tints, medium, peony form with wavy and notched petals.
Shishi-Gashira (species *Hiemalis*)—red medium, semi-double to double.
Showa-No-Sakae (species *Hiemalis*)—soft pink, occasionally marbled white; medium, semi-double to rose form double.
Sparkling Burgundy—ruby rose with sheen of lavender, small to medium, peony form with intermingled stamens and petaloids.
*Star Above Star (species *Vernalis*)—white shading to lavender pink at edge, medium, semi-double.
*Yuletide—orange red, small, single, compact upright growth.

Camellia Japonica. The different varieties of *Camellia japonica* produce flowers which vary in color from white to pink to red, either solid color or variegated with white. The variegation is usually due to a fungus infection of the root stock which does not seriously injure the plant but does result in a new flower variety. Listed are a few old favorites plus some newer ones, including all the ACS Illeges Seedling Japonica Award winners since 1955 and all of the ACS Sewell Mutant Award Winners.

In all nomenclature lists: E = early blooming;
M = mid-season blooming;
L = late blooming;
1800 = date of introduction.

OLD VARIETIES

Daikagura—bright rose pink splotched white, E-1891; large, loose peony form; Daikagura Pink, mutant 1936; High Hat, blush pink mutant 1945; Conrad Hilton, white mutant 1955.
Early Woodville Red—full peony, light red mutant of Woodville Red, E-1822.

Alba Plena—white medium to large, formal double, E-M-1792; Fimbriata, formal double mutant with fringed petals, 1816; Mrs. Hooper Connell, peony form mutant, 1950.
Adolphe Audusson—dark red, large, semi-double, M-1877; Variegated, dark red spotted white, 1920s; Special, predominantly white with some red, 1942.
Elegans (Chandler)—rose pink with center petaloids often spotted white, large, anemone form. Produces outstanding mutants, M-1831.
Imperator-France—dark red, full peony form, M-1908.
Magnoliaeflora—blush pink, medium, semi-double hose-in-hose type bloom, M-1886.
Mathotiana (Purple Dawn)—crimson sometimes with purple cast; large to very large, rose form to formal double, M-1840s; there are many mutants of this variety, such as Flowerwood, Sultana, Red Wonder, Rosea Superba, etc.
Pink Perfection—shell pink, small, formal double, M-1875.
Ville De Nantes—dark red blotched white; medium to large, semi-double with upright fimbriated petals, M-1910. Mutant of Donckelarii, 1834.

NEWER VARIETIES

*Illeges Seedling Award
**Sewell Mutant Award

Betty Sheffield—white faintly striped red and pink; medium to large, semi-double to loose peony. This is a beautiful bloom, but its claim to fame is that it has produced 12 outstanding mutants which have been named and registered but have not received awards to date, M-1949.
**Betty Sheffield Supreme—mutant, white with deep pink to red border on each petal, M-1960.
*Carter's Sunburst—pale pink, striped deeper pink; large to very large; semi-double to peony form, M-1958.
**Carter's Sunburst Pink—mutant, deep pink. The variegated form is often considered the finest bloom, M-1964.
*Charlie Bettes—white with deep yellow stamens, large to very large, semi-double, E-M-1960.
Clark Hubbs—brilliant dark red, full to loose peony form with fimbriated petals, M-1960.
Don Mac—deep red semi-double to loose peony form with curled and creped petals around a large mass of white stamens. An excellent garden variety, M-1956.
Drama Girl—deep salmon rose pink; very large, semi-double; large foliage, vigorous, M-1950.
**Elegans Splendor—mutant, light pink edged white with deep petal serrations, M-1969.
**Elegans Supreme—mutant of Elegans, anemone form, rose pink with very deep petal serrations, M-1960.
*Grand Slam—brilliant dark red, large to very large, semi-double to anemone form, M-1962.
*Guilio Nuccio—coral rose pink, large to very large, semi-double with some upright petals. The variegated bloom is frequently the most beautiful, M-1956.

Gus Menard—white with canary yellow petaloids; large anemone form with center petals divided by petaloids. M-1962.

**Helen Bower (Chimera of Dr. Knapp grafted on Mathotiana Var.)—bloom very similar to Mathotiana, M-1964.

*Julia France—very light pink, large, semi-double with fluted petals, M-1958.

Kramer's Supreme—turkey red, large to very large, full peony form. An excellent garden variety, M-1957.

*Marie Bracey—coral rose, large semi-double to peony form. The variegated form is frequently the best bloom, E-M-1953.

**Mathotiana Supreme—mutant, crimson sometimes with purple cast; very large semi-double with loose irregular petals sometimes interspersed with stamens. An outstanding garden variety, M-1951.

*Mrs. D.W. Davis—blush pink, very large semi-double with large petals; also a peony form, M-1954.

Margaret Davis—mutant, white to cream white with a few rose red lines and dashed and edged bright vermillion; medium, full peony form, M-1961.

Snowman—white, large, deep semi-double with curled and notched petals, M-1964.

*Tomorrow—strawberry red, large to very large, semi-double with irregular petals and large petaloids, to full peony form. A tremendous parent plant with 8 outstanding mutants, M-1953.

**Tomorrow's Dawn—mutant, deep soft pink to light pink, shading to white at edge, with some white petaloids, M-1960.

**Tomorrow Park Hill—mutant of Tomorrow Var.; light soft pink generally deepening toward edge and variegated white. Another mutant without the white variegation has now developed, M-1964.

MINIATURES

Beautiful new Japonica miniatures (2½ inches or less) are being developed and introduced because many of the other new varieties are so large there is a need for some smaller blooms.

Fircone—blood red, similar in shape to a fir cone, semi-double, M-1950.

Little Red Riding Hood—crimson, formal double to peony form, M-L-1965.

Little Slam—rich red, full peony form, E-M-1969.

Pearl's Pet—rose red, anemone form, E-M-1959.

Pink Smoke—light lavender pink, anemone form, M-1965.

Tammia—white with pink center and border, formal double with incurved petals in a geometric design, M-L-1971.

Camellia Hybrids:

SPECIES RETICULATA AND HYBRIDS WITH RETICULATA PARENTAGE:

Reticulata 'Captain Rawes' and Reticulata 'Crimson Robe,' whether true Reticulatas or hybrids, produce magnificent carmine and crimson flowers on strong-growing rangy plants outdoors in Houston. The following Reticulata hybrids may be cold hardy and are worth a try outdoors, as well as protected, because of their parentage.

Aztec—deep rose red, very large semi-double to loose peony form. M-1971, Reticulata 'Crimson Robe' x Japonica 'Lotus.'

Dr. Clifford Parks—red with orange cast, very large anemone form. M-1971, Reticulata 'Crimson Robe' x Japonica 'Kramer's Supreme.'

Dream Castle—silver pink, very large semi-double with fluted upright petals. M-1972, Reticulata 'Crimson Robe' x Japonica 'Coronation.'

Francie L—rose pink, very large, semi-double with irregular, upright, wavy petals. M-1964, Reticulata 'Buddha' x Saluenensis 'Apple Blossom.'

Lila Naff—a proven cold hardy variety. Silver pink, semi-double, with wide petals, often upright. M-1969, Reticulata 'Butterfly Wings' x Japonica (?).

Milo Rowell—deep rich pink, very large, semi-double with irregular petals to loose peony form. M-1968, Reticulata 'Crimson Robe' x Japonica 'Tiffany.'

HYBRIDS WITH OTHER THAN RETICULATA PARENTAGE

The following group, except El Dorado, are Saluenensis x Japonica hybrids and bloom outdoors unprotected in Houston.

Angel Wings—white washed and shaded orchid pink, semi-double with narrow upright petals, medium size, M-1970.

Anticipation—deep rose, large peony form, M-1962.

Charlean—medium pink with faint orchid overtone, large, semi-double, M-1963.

El Dorado—light pink with lavender overtone, large full peony form, M-1967, Petardii x Japonica 'Tiffany."

Elsie Jury—clear medium pink; large, full peony form, M-L-1964.

Julia Hamiter—delicate blush pink to white; medium, semi-double to rose form double, M-1964.

Location. The climate, soil, and water of the Houston area are far from ideal for camellias, but if proper cultural practices are maintained they will flourish and bloom luxuriantly. Most of the Houston area is flat and poorly drained, and the soil is a heavy, dark gumbo or light-colored clay. This necessitates using prepared soils for camellias and selecting well-drained locations where they will have high tree shade in summer and some protection from hard north winds in winter. Other Gulf Coast areas to the east have ideal growing conditions.

Plant Selection. Camellias may be planted any time during their long flowering period from October to April. However, early planting before February gives them time to produce new root growth and become established before hot weather starts. Good medium-sized plants, which are two or three year old grafts, on strong root stock will bloom the first year. Select healthy, fresh looking plants with clean, dark green foliage and no evidence of dead twigs or scale.

Examine the balls of canned or burlapped plants. Many canned plants are dug from the field and stuck in containers and may have defective root systems and poor planting mediums. The soil or planting medium should be loose, friable, sandy loam, or a mixture containing that, plus sharp sand and humus similar to the medium in which you intend to place the plant. If there is heavy soil, a clay ball, a sand ball, or over one inch of soil above the first roots, bare-root the plant before planting.

Planting. *Do not dig a hole* to plant a camellia; rather, loosen the top soil down a few inches, work in some agricultural gypsum to condition the native soil, and add about four inches of prepared soil mixture over the bed area. Then set the ball of the plant on top of the mixed soil and add prepared soil around it to build the bed up to the level of the top of the ball. Do not put dirt on the top of the ball. Prepare the planting soil by mixing either: ½ good sandy loam, ¼ leaf mold, ¼ well-rotted manure, a little sharp sand, and one cup of 16-mesh agricultural sulphur per large wheelbarrow load of mixture; or ⅓ sandy loam, ⅓ humus (ground pine bark, compost, rotted sawdust, well-rotted barnyard manure), ⅙ torpedo sand, ⅙ agricultural perlite, 1 cup sulphur per wheelbarrow load of mixture. The sulphur is an important ingredient in Houston, for camellias require an acid soil (pH 5.5-6.5). Settle the bedding mixture around the ball and wash in well so there are no air pockets. Cut burlap from the top of the ball, and be sure there is no excess dirt over top feeder roots. Use the same procedure for canned plants.

If, however, the dirt of the balled or canned plant is not similar in texture and content to the soil in which it must now grow, plant it bare-rooted. Wash all the soil from the roots and treat the roots with a plant hormone (Transplantone, OD4, or equivalent) according to the manufacturer's instructions. Keep roots wet. Container-grown plants which have complete root systems may now be planted in the bed. Field-grown plants which have lost some roots being dug and burlapped should be heeled-in in sawdust for several months so new root growth will be put out prior to bare-rooting.

To plant a bare-rooted camellia prepare a complete planting bed about one foot high above ground surface, with soil mixed as previously directed, allowing at least 2¼ feet diameter of bed area for each inch of the plant's trunk diameter. In this artificially well-drained bed you may now dig a hole and arrange a cone of soil on which to set the bare roots of your camellia. Complete the planting procedure with soil around the roots, water down, and later add just enough soil to cover the top feeder roots. Do not fertilize for one year. Support the plant with a strong stake one foot taller than the plant. Bare-rooted camellias must be protected from damage by sun, wind, and dehydration. The best way is to envelope the entire plant in a plastic bag, sealed at the top, and supported on the plant stake to hold the bag off the plant. Pile dirt around bottom edge of bag to seal and hold securely. Protect the plant with a sun shade, such as burlap on a chicken wire frame. Water as needed to keep plant moist. After one month, loosen the bag and gradually remove it. If plant begins to wilt, replace the bag.

The final step is to add a thick mulch of at least four inches of pine needles, cane litter (bagasse), rice hulls or other coarse organic material. This keeps the bed from drying out and weeds from growing. Peat moss should not be used as mulch because it packs, dries, and sheds water. Beds elevated for perfect drainage may be protected against washing away by planting heavy edgings such as liriope or monkey grass (ophiopogan), or by simply bordering with rocks.

Camellias must have a slightly acid soil, but too acid (low pH) is just as bad as too alkaline (high pH). See "Soil and Soil Improvement." A small, simple soil test kit takes the guesswork out of maintaining the proper pH. Test the soil twice each year when much alkaline city water is being used. It is usually necessary to add acid to counteract Houston's water. A light sprinkling of 16-mesh agricultural sulphur over the bed will usually be adequate when the soil tests pH 5.5 to 6.5. If the soil tests pH 6.8 or higher, use a quick-acting chemical such as iron sulphate (technical copperas) or iron chelate. In large doses these strong chemicals can easily burn the feeder roots, so *use cautiously.* One tablespoonful in one gallon of water sprinkled over the foliage and bed of a five foot plant is adequate. If the soil is very alkaline this treatment may be repeated after two weeks. If the beds test pH 4.5 to 5.0 do not add acid. If the beds test very acid, pH 4.0 or lower, bone meal or a little agricultural lime may be used to raise the pH. Sickly, yellow, chlorotic plants may be the result of soil that is too acid, too alkaline, or poorly drained.

Insects and Diseases. Healthy, robust plants which have been properly planted in a suitable bed mixture, adequately watered, and kept slightly acid will not be particularly subject to disease.

Tea scale infestation is the most common problem in this area. In the dormant stage it appears as small brown specks, considerably longer than wide. In the active stage tea scale appears as cotton-like matter on the bottom of the leaves; when the infestation is severe the tops of the leaves become yellow and mottled. The scale is actually a sucking insect which attaches itself to the leaf of the plant and sucks out plant food and fluids.

Aphids are also troublesome to new growth. Chewing insects and bugs which inhabit the mulch around the beds may come up at night to feed on the new foliage. These do not injure the plant, but they chew holes in the foliage, making it unsightly.

To treat all these problems use a combination spray of an insecticide such as Malathion or equivalent and an oil spray such as Oil-i-cide. The insecticide will control the aphids, the oil spray will control the scale infestation, and spraying the bed in the vicinity of the plant helps control other bugs and chewing insects. It is usually necessary to spray twice in the spring after all danger of frost is past, and again in the early fall. Do not use an oil spray when temperatures get above 90° or later than October 15, as an oil-sprayed plant is particularly vulnerable to an early freeze. In addition to spraying, sprinkle an ant-killing material on the camellia beds.

Research on the commercial application of systemic insecticides has been extensive during the past few years. These chemicals, applied to the surface of a plant, either to the root system or above ground, are absorbed into the plant's circulation system and transmitted to all parts of the plant, rendering it repellent to certain insects for a period of time. CYGON 2E has proven effective for camellias. Cygon can be used as a soil drench over the area of the root system, in accordance with the manufacturer's instructions. It can also be applied full strength with a 2-inch paint brush, painting a narrow stripe around the trunk of the plant just above the soil line. It is effective against tea scale.

Dieback, a disease caused by the fungus *Glomerella cingulata,* frequently infects camellias grown in the Gulf Coast area. The first symptom usually noticed is wilting and death of small new growth, with the leaves falling off and the dead twigs remaining for a few days. Older twigs may be involved and killed, but the leaves turn brown and do not fall off. The fungus spores also enter and infect the plant through breaks in the bark caused by wounds, insect punctures, and normal leaf fall. At the base of an infected twig, leaf or in a wound, fungus invades and kills the wood cells and spreads up and down the stem. The surrounding healthy wood continues to grow, thus enlarging the stem diameter. The infected area of dead cells appears sunken and is called a canker. The canker provides the food base for the fungus and produces millions of spores each year. The spores are distributed by rain splashing to nearby plants and to other parts of the same plant. Crawling and flying insects may also distribute the spores. Severe infection may kill large branches or even the entire plant. There is no known cure for an infected area or canker except to cut it out down to healthy green wood and immediately disinfect the wound with a mixture of the fungicides Benlate and 50W Captan in water. Both chemicals are effective protectants but will not cure after infection has occurred. They should be used to disinfect pruning and grafting tools, to disinfect scions and stocks during grafting, and can be used as a plant disinfectant by spraying after pruning or at normal leaf fall. All the usual garden species and hybrids of camellias are susceptible to the fungus, but *C. sasanqua* is much more sensitive. Certain cultivars in each species are also much more sensitive than others. Excess high nitrogen fertilizer and too much acid contribute to the disease and overhead sprinkling spreads it.

Camellia flower blight, a disease caused by the fungus *Selerotinia camellia* Hara, infects camellia flowers grown in many parts of the Gulf Coast area. It attacks only petals of camellia flowers during the spring flowering season. Therefore, any fall flowers resulting from early-blooming varieties of any specie or hybrid, or those stimulated to flower early by gibberellic acid applications will escape infection. The fungus does not cause disease on leaf, stem, or root tissue, and in no way impairs the health of the plant. The fungus invades camellia flower tissue and its symptoms are brown specks or blotches which spread to invade most of the flower tissue. The brown diseased flower finally falls to the ground where it eventually forms sclerotia, small hard fibrous bodies which are the dormant form of the fungus. The fungus remains dormant until the next winter, when it becomes active and spores are ejected from January to April and are disseminated by air currents to infect the new crop of camellia flowers and thus start a new life cycle. There is no positive chemical cure for the disease. The spores can be carried at least one mile by air currents, so if infection is in the area it is difficult to avoid. There are contact fungicides which will kill the spores but discolor the flowers. The

fungicide PCNB (trade name Terrachlor) used as a ground spray in December prevents the activation of the fungus but gives no off-premises control. The best control procedures are to exclude it if possible by planting only bare-rooted plants, spray the bed areas early in December with PCNB at 2 lbs/1,000 sq. ft, and pick up from the ground all infected or spent camellia blooms.

Systemic fungicides are available for some non-woody plants, but so far none are systematic in camellias in the United States. It is possible that research may develop them for camellias in the future.

Pruning. Camellias are frequently pruned to control the shape and size. Sometimes the pruning is severe, but it is usually done the way trees are pruned. The weak interior twigs and branches should be removed along with all dead wood to provide air circulation and reduce insect and disease susceptibility. When pruning to shape a plant, care should be taken to prune down to a growth bud which is pointing in the direction you want a branch to take. Some pruning can be done when you cut flowers.

Fertilization. Fertilization is probably the least important aspect of camellia culture. A little fertilizer goes a long way, so be sure not to over-fertilize. Avoid high nitrogen fertilizers. A 5-10-10 acid fertilizer, balanced especially for camellias and azaleas, is available under several brand names. Use according to directions. The amount and frequency of fertilization depends on conditions in your garden and what you are trying to accomplish. It is best to start with two light applications in the spring—the first shortly after the plants have finished blooming, and the second about a month or six weeks later. Ordinarily, this is sufficient; but if the plants are competing with large tree roots or are growing in sandy, porous soil which has a tendency to leach out, give them a little foliar feeding as a small additional boost in the early summer. At this time, as soon as flower buds can be distinguished from growth buds, twist off all of the twin buds except one pointing outward, not upward, on each stem to produce a larger, more perfect flower. If a mass effect or longer flowering period with smaller blossoms is desired, do not disbud. If you want specimen flowers for a special occasion a light fertilization about one month prior to the expected date will help the plant mature ripening buds to blossoms of maximum size and vitality. Be extremely cautious with any of these experimental procedures; be moderate with your fertilizer.

Chemical Bloom Stimulation. Chemical treatment of camellias with a natural plant hormone, gibberellin (GIB), to accelerate the normal blooming cycle and increase the size of the blooms has been widely adopted by the camellia flower show group. The same hormone is used more commonly in commercial agriculture to accelerate the normal maturation cycle and increase the crop yield. For camellias, GIB can be used in the acid or potassium salt form in a 10,000 ppm solution. It is usually applied by removing, a growth bud adjacent to a mature flower bud and placing one drop of the solution in the vegetative cup at the base of the growth bud, as illustrated by Figure 1. This supplies the flower bud with an excessive amount of the same growth hormone that produces the normal flower. The effect of the treatment varies with species, variety, and bud. It speeds up blooming time in varying degrees, increases the bloom size, improves the quality of many blooms, damages others, does not damage mature plants if used in moderation, damages smaller plants if used to excess, and may kill very small plants.

GIB is useful to the camellia show hobbyists because it gives larger flowers early in the year so shows can be held before the flowers can be damaged by freezing weather and fungus diseases. Home gardeners are eligible to participate in all American Camellia Society shows, and some may desire to practice the GIB treatment for their own home enjoyment.

Propagation. Camellias can be reproduced by the conventional propagation methods: cuttings, layerings, or grafts. Seeds will not reproduce true to the parent plant. Rare varieties are propagated by grafting scions, using the cleft graft method, on large *C. sasanqua* or *C. japonica* root stock (see "Propagation").

It is possible to have a good specimen blooming plant after about three years; but it is usually cheaper and more satisfactory to buy well established two- or three-year old grafted plants from a reputable nursery.

The summer and winter care of camellias, as well as watering, is similar to that for azaleas.

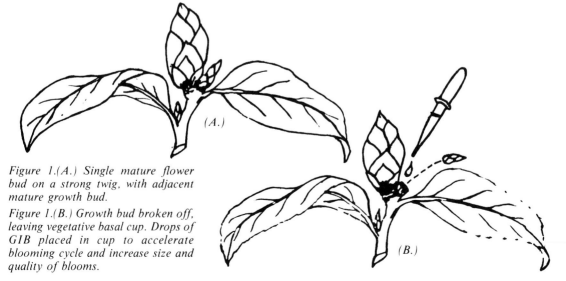

Figure 1.(A.) Single mature flower bud on a strong twig, with adjacent mature growth bud.

Figure 1.(B.) Growth bud broken off, leaving vegetative basal cup. Drops of GIB placed in cup to accelerate blooming cycle and increase size and quality of blooms.

Roses at Houston Garden Center.
The American Rose Society and Gardens are located at Shreveport, Louisiana.

Roses

And I will thee beds of roses
And a thousand fragrant posies.
—Christopher Marlowe

Symbolizing many ideals throughout the history of civilization, often called "The Queen of Flowers," the rose has a distinctive quality that has earned it a place not just in the gardens, but in the hearts of millions of rose enthusiasts. Surely no garden is complete without at least one of the several types of roses.

The would-be rose grower should not be discouraged when confronted with the list of procedures considered essential to rose care. Relax, take heart. Roses flourished forty million years before there were human hands to tend them. Roses have been found blooming in gardens abandoned for half a century.

Think of roses as you would other flowering shrubs. Don't be afraid to plant the flower whose form, colors and fragrance are enjoyed around the world simply because extra care and pampering are involved. Keep in mind that we often treasure most that for which we must expend effort.

Beautiful roses may be grown in Houston — if certain fundamental essentials are provided. Buy only #1 grade bushes, plant them properly in a sunny, well-prepared bed, maintain a regular dust or spray schedule, water and feed with discretion, and keep spent blooms removed.

Location of Beds. Since the rose is a shrub, it may be used in various ways in garden design; however, stronger, more floriferous plants usually result if the rose bed is set apart from other shrubbery. Like most blooming plants, roses must have sun—a minimum of four hours a day. Locate the bed away from shrubs and trees which not only cast shade, but whose roots rob the rose bushes of moisture and food. In this temperate climate roses bloom nine or ten months of the year; so, adequate service walks around and through the rose garden facilitate the cutting of blooms and the care of the plants. These walks also prevent stepping into the bed and compacting the soil.

In selecting an area for your rose bed, first look for ample sunshine, preferably morning sun to dry the foliage early.

Preparation of Beds. Provide your rose bed with good drainage. If water takes longer than twenty minutes to drain out of a foot-deep hole, read the chapter on "Drainage" for suggested improvements. Many growers prefer to assure drainage by raising the beds eight or ten inches with a bordering material such as boards or bricks.

Roses like good dirt which is slightly acid (pH 6.5). If you are in doubt about your soil, simply call your County Extension Agent for directions about getting a soil analysis. Reading the chapter on "Soil and Soil Improvement" will also be helpful. Try to prepare the soil for the rose bed at least a month ahead of planting time to allow settling and blending. Order your bushes early from a reputable source, specifying top quality #1 grade, with delivery at the proper time. The planting time usually recommended in the coastal country is January and February for bareroot roses. Rose bushes purchased in containers may be planted at any time with proper care. Most gardens in the Houston area have black gumbo, a type of clay soil, which is productive when amended for drainage and friability. For 100 square feet of bed area, mix the following into the top fourteen inches of the soil you have: 1 bale peat moss, ½ yard sand or sandy soil, ½ yard compost, 10 pounds superphosphate, 25 pounds agricultural gypsum, ½ yard barnyard manure and 5 pounds complete rose food. This mixture will be slightly acid. The phosphate is an especially important addition at this time because it must be down in the root area to be effective.

Well-grown roses often attain greater size in our almost tropical climate and this fact should be taken into consideration when spacing bushes in the bed. Ample spacing allows for better air circulation which discourages disease and insects. Suggested spacings are: Climbers 6-10 feet, Grandifloras 4-6 feet, Hybrid Teas 3-3½ feet, Floribundas 2-3 feet, Polyanthas 1-1½ feet, and Miniatures 12 inches. A single row of roses needs a bed at least three feet wide, and a double row at least four feet. Wide walkways around the bed make the bushes more accessible.

Care on Arrival. If plants are ordered from a distant nursery, be sure to inspect them on arrival. It is best to plant that day. If packing material is dried out from heat in transit, a small amount of moisture may be added by means of damp sphagnum moss or other material. This will keep plants in a cool place for a day or two. If still unable to plant, heeling-in is recommended. Bury all roots and most of the top in a horizontal position in moist soil. They will keep in this condition for about ten days. If the plants are potted, keep watered well until planted.

Planting. Proper planting and early care are essential steps for success with a rose garden. Regardless of whether the plants are plump and turgid or dried out on arrival, soak the roots or most of the plant in a tub of water just before planting, the time varying with the need. A plump plant should soak from thirty minutes to one hour, a dried out plant overnight—no longer. Never let the roots dry out, even for a few minutes. Have the hole ready before removing the plant from the tub of water. In the previously prepared bed, dig a hole about twenty-four inches in diameter and about ten inches deep. Shape some dirt into a cone-shaped mound in the center of the hole. Now remove a plant from the water, immediately check for broken or damaged roots and remove them with a pair of sharp shears; clip the ends from all large roots only. The roots of a rose bush usually have a natural spread that will fit down over the prepared mound; in any case the mound should be modified to the shape of the root system on each plant. Some forcing is permissible, but it is better if roots can be fitted comfortably.

It is important that the rose be replanted at approximately the same depth in the soil in which it grew in the field, with the bud union *above* the level of the ground. Adjust the height of the plant when resting on the mound to pregrown elevation. Next start filling in around roots with either a little fine-textured prepared soil or the best material removed from hole. Work this dirt in, around and on top of roots very firmly to a depth of several inches. When hole is about two-thirds refilled, fill the depression with water twice. After all water has soaked in the second time, use the remaining dirt to finish filling the hole—but do not pack. Now cut all broken or weak canes and cut back remaining canes, leaving from six to ten inches depending on size of plant. Make cut on a slant just above an outside eye. Any excess dirt may be piled up around the plant, but must be removed when buds start to break. About three days after planting, water again thoroughly; continue to water weekly until good growth is evident.

The name label should be removed from the plant and placed on a separate support. If a large planting is made, a plot plan is advisable. Maintaining correct names will add to your enjoyment.

The placing of the potted rose plant into the permanent bed should be the same as any other potted shrub. Dig the hole slightly larger than pot diameter and to a depth gauged by the dirt height. Plant at the same level as in the container. Cut the container from the soil ball, taking great care not to allow the dirt to fall from the roots. Place in hole and pack the soil snugly around until near top. Now water well twice. After all water has soaked in, fill the remainder to level of bed; do not pack. Keep plant well watered for a week or two.

Feeding. Since the rose bush is a producer of beautiful blooms almost all year long, it must be supplied with food; and because of this long working period, the food cannot all be supplied in one big application. Most of our modern roses are croppers; that is, they are repeat bloomers. Immediately on completion of one bloom-out they will, if food and water are supplied, start another crop. An all-around yearly feeding program consists of an early spring feeding of a complete rose food plus some organics, such as cottonseed meal. This first feeding should be the heaviest. If you mix your own food elements, let the nitrogen content be high. Through the summer use a balanced ration, and in the fall change to low nitrogen. Plants then will not approach winter in a soft, succulent condition. Otherwise, any rose food marketed by a reputable manufacturer will serve well for all-year feeding. Use in amounts as directed. Repeat in more or less regular periods—thirty to sixty days all summer. Some growers use 12-24-12 fertilizer, sprinkling one cup around each bush and watering it in, four times a year: the middle of March, April, June and September.

Foliar feeding, the supplying of food to the plant through the leaves, is not recommended to take the place of soil feeding, but rather to supplement it. The two together will keep the plants vigorous and producing blooms with more substance. Foliar feeding may be done in any manner that puts the diluted solution in contact with the leaves, particularly the undersides for best absorption. It may be incorporated with the fungicide or insecticide spray. It has been found to be compatible with almost all of these materials. The recommended frequency is every other week.

A word of caution—food has to be in solution before it can be taken up by the roots. A thorough watering of the bed before feeding and again after will dilute the strength of the food to the extent that it can be assimilated without a shock to the plants. This deep watering will also tend to carry the food down to the lower root area.

Watering. Roses enjoy an abundance of water. If a rose is not doing well, don't feed—water. It has been said that roses love water more than food, so never feed without watering. Use a soaker hose or attachment and water thoroughly when needed. The bushes require an inch of water each week. An occasional watering from above is desirable during long dry spells; this should be done before late afternoon so foliage will dry before nightfall.

Mulching. A summer mulch is any material that will help hold water, lower soil temperature around the roots, and reduce the need for cultivation. There are many useful results derived from various mulches. For instance, any humus-forming material will aid soil conditioning and supply needed bacteria. Inasmuch as a mulch is almost a necessity for success in growing roses in our area, here are a few good ones:

MANURE: One of the best, if well composted.

BAGASSE (Cane pulp): An excellent mulch for this area, possessing unusual ability to hold water and to disintegrate slowly.

COTTON SEED HULLS: A good soil conditioner. Tends to form a mat. Better if mixed with another type of mulch.

PEAT MOSS: Dries out and crusts over. Excellent if mixed with some other mulch. Acid-forming.

OAK LEAVES and PINE NEEDLES: Both are good. Both are acid-forming. Better if partially broken down in compost pile.

REDWOOD SHAVINGS: Excellent appearance. Slow to disintegrate. Adds little to soil.

MIXTURE: A mixture of any or all above may be used in any amounts at hand, and/or compost.

GRASS CLIPPINGS: May be used green if care is taken to apply only in ½-inch layers. So applied, the grass will quickly dry out without fermenting and heating. Three or four such layers may be applied during the summer and may be turned under the surface in the fall.

Pest Control. There are always rose pests. Very troublesome in warm, humid areas like Houston are Blackspot and Mildew. Both fungus diseases are controllable by several procedures: regular weekly spraying with appropriate fungicides; assurance of sufficient aeration among the bushes by ample spacing and within each bush by keeping it pruned into an open-vase shape, and removal of the foliage up to four or five inches from the ground; buy resistant varieties. Aphids, Red Spider Mites and Thrips are insects which can damage flowers and foliage by sucking out vital juices. Forceful sprays of water, repeated several times, may eliminate many insects. Some growers rely on companion plantings of chives, dwarf marigolds, garlic and parsley as a low ground cover, and spraying with home remedies of chili pepper and garlic solutions. As a last resort, there are insecticides. Some are less toxic to people and wildlife than others. Follow manufacturer's directions and protect yourself from inhalation of the spray material or otherwise touching it. Wash hands and face after using pesticides. During the summer's heat it is wise to use solutions at half strength to prevent burning the foliage; water bed before spraying or dusting. For information on recommended fungicides and insecticides check with your local rose society and garden suppliers as well as your County Extension Agent.

The principal thing is to spray or dust regularly and effectively. The frequency and the amount of material used will have little effect unless properly applied. The whole leaf must be covered, particularly the underside. The underside is far more important than the upperside. This is also true if you use a foliar food. There is greater absorption from the underside, so strive for complete coverage.

Pruning. If we use Webster's definition of pruning, "the removing of superfluous twigs and branches," then the cutting of spent blooms would be classed as such. First-year plants need all the leaves they can produce to help build strong roots and stems. Therefore, remove the first bloom without any leaves. Later on during the year it is permissible to cut down to the first five-leaf leaflet. Flower-producing growth comes only from buds at leaflets of five or more leaves. In fact, this is good practice on all plants except those that are extremely strong growers; the cutting of longer stems helps keep rose bushes in shape. On second-year and mature plants, stems may be cut to the lowest leaf on the branch on occasions only. If at least two sets of leaves are left on the branch, a stronger plant and more blooms will be produced. In addition, keep nonproductive shoots cut off. Remove dead canes down to live wood even if the cane has to be cut back all the way to the bud union.

Depending on the weather, the annual pruning time should be between the middle of January and the middle of February, just before the spring buds break, a difficult date to predict. Early pruners are taking chances. Late pruning is safer but delays spring bloom. The physical operation of pruning should be done in the following order:

1. Cut all dead wood.
2. Cut out all weak or diseased canes.
3. Cut out crossed or rubbing canes.
4. Cut off about one-third of previous year's growth on all remaining canes. Make all cuts on a slant about one-fourth inch above a strong bud, preferably an outside bud.
5. Treat cut ends larger than a dime with orange shellac or wound paint.
6. Clean up all debris—twigs, leaves, etc. —from the bed. Strip all remaining leaves off plants—this is very important to encourage dormancy.

7. Spray canes and bed with a good clean-up spray such as Calsul.

The rose plants are now ready for their first spring feeding and another year of beautiful roses may be anticipated.

Cutting blooms is also a way of pruning. Gather roses late in the afternoon or early in the morning, cutting just above an outside eye (bud) at a five-leaf leaflet. Buds at three leaf leaflets do not produce flowers. Place stems in warm water eight to ten inches deep or almost to the bloom; set aside and let cool to room temperature. Refrigerate at thirty-two to thirty-four degrees for several hours before arranging.

Classification of Roses. The classification of roses is sometimes based on origin of species and sometimes on growth habits, flower form, or some other distinguishing characteristic. With the passing years and continuous interbreeding, many classes have emerged, overlapped, or even disappeared. However, the two main divisions of roses remain: bush roses with upright shrubby growth, and climbing or trailing roses with long canes requiring support. The climbers, vigorous, hardy, and lovely, are used in landscape work to cover fences, trellises, arbors, and banks. Bush roses are subdivided into the following major types:

HYBRID TEAS: (descendents of the true Teas, which bequeathed them the habit of continual bloom). They are distinguished by the long pointed buds, large size, elegance of form, and wide range of color of the blossoms. Favorites of florists, exhibitors, and gardeners alike, they are the most important class of roses. Many are fragrant.

HYBRID PERPETUALS: Vigorous and disease-resistant, they make one large display in the spring and bloom sparsely in the fall. The flowers are large and fragrant, mostly crimson, pink, and white; but they lack the elegant form of the Teas. Two famous hybrid perpetuals are the American Beauty and the pure white Frau Karl Druschki.

POLYANTHAS: Dwarf, bushy plants bearing small flowers in clusters, they are continuous bloomers from April to December. They are excellent for mass effects and low hedges or borders.

FLORIBUNDAS: Produced from crosses of Polyanthas and Hybrid Tea varieties, they grow taller and have larger flowers than the polyanthas. They may be used for hedges or bedding and last remarkably well as cut flowers.

GRANDIFLORAS: a cross between the Hybrid Tea and the Floribunda). These plants have the vigor and the blooming habit of the Floribunda with the flower form of the Hybrid Tea. Among the few varieties so classified is the Queen Elizabeth, which will reach eight feet by the second year.

FLORA-TEAS: These are a recent introduction. They are a cross of Floribundas and Hybrid Teas with good qualities of each.

SHRUB ROSES: A miscellaneous group of wild and hybrid species, they produce mostly single blooms on hardy upright plants. They have fine glossy foliage and bright fall fruits. Some are good as hedges, screens, or in mixed planting with other shrubs.

TREE or STANDARD ROSE: This classification refers to a plant form, not a flower type. Any bush variety and some climbers may be budded at the top of a straight understock two to four feet tall and then trained to a standard. Beautiful in formal or modern gardens or as an accent among other roses.

MINIATURE ROSES: Related to *rosa chinensis*, they are only six to twelve inches high with blossoms less that an inch across. They are effective as edgings, borders, and patio plants. Tree forms available.

OLD-FASHIONED ROSES: Species, hybrids, and varieties introduced more than fifty years ago are classed as "old roses." Familiar among them are the Tea, Cabbage, Moss, China, French, and Damask Roses. Very fragrant, vigorous, and practically disease-free, they bloom profusely in June. They may be used in almost every way in the garden when there is enough space to accommodate their great height and breadth. Complementing the Nineteenth Century charm of the reconstructed Nichols-Rice Home in Sam Houston Park in downtown Houston is an old-fashioned garden featuring old roses.

There are climbing sports of most rose types. Because climbers bloom on new wood they should be pruned immediately after blooming, removing old canes which are now easily recognized. Tie canes in lateral design to force breaks for more bloom.

(See Rose Chart on next page)

SOME NEW AND OLD ROSES NOW GROWN IN THE
HOUSTON AND UPPER GULF COAST AREA

Hybrid Teas

Buccaneer—yellow
Charlotte Armstrong—deep pink, fragrant
Century Two—medium pink, fragrant
Confidence—pink
Dainty Bess—light pink, single
First Prize—pink blend
Garden Party—white
Golden Scepter—yellow
Helen Traubel—pink blend
Lemon Spice—light yellow, very fragrant
Mr. Lincoln—red, fragrant, robust
Oregold—yellow, fragrant
Peace—yellow blend
Royal Highness—light pink
Swarthmore—pink blend, light perfume
Tiffany—pink-yellow blend
Tropicana—orange, fragrant

Grandiflora

Arizona—copper-gold, fragrant
Doctor Eldon Lyle—red

Montezuma—pink orange, fragrant
Mount Shasta—white, fragrant
Queen Elizabeth—pink, fragrant, robust
Scarlet Knight—red, fragrant

Floribundas

Angel Face—lavendar, fragrant
Apache Tears—red blend
Apricot Nectar—blend, fragrant
Europeana—red
Gene Boerner—pink, light fragrance
Ginger—orange
Ivory Fashion—ivory, fragrant
Jazz Fest—raspberry red, fragrant
Leprechaun—small red-yellow blend (no Blackspot), good massed
Rose Parade—pink blend, fragrant
Spanish Sun—yellow, fragrant
Spartan—orange

Polyanthas

China Doll—pink
Margo Koster—coral
The Fairy—pink

Climbers

Blaze—red, vigorous
Don Juan—dark red, fragrant
(Many varieties of other classifications may be had in climbing form)

Miniatures

Beauty Secret—red
Chipper—pink, all year bloom
Cinderella—white
Kathy—red
Jet Trail—white
Judy Fischer—pink
Lavendar Lace—lavendar
Magic Carrousel—red blend
Mary Marshall—orange blend
Over the Rainbow—red blend
Yellow Doll—yellow

Bulbs

The daffodil is our door-side queen;
She pushes up the sward already, to spot with sunshine the early green.

—Bryant

The term "bulb", as generally used, refers to a plant having a thickened underground stem and the common characteristic of food storage. There are five classifications of bulbs. A true bulb is just one type and is of almost round form composed of fleshy leaves or scales that protect an embryo plant inside. (Tulip). A corm is a short fat bulb which stores food in its center instead of in scales and has a bud on top. (Gladiolus). A rhizome has its bud on the end and roots below an underground stem, which may be long and slender or fleshy and thick, of a creeping habit. (Iris). A tuber is an underground stem, thicker and shorter than a rhizome, which bears buds on the mass of food storage tissue. (Caladium). A tuberous root has thick underground food-storing roots with buds at the base of the plant's stem. (Daylily). More and more gardeners appreciate the rich rewards received with minimum effort from this group of plants. Most bulbs require little care, and once properly established, they send up their lovely blossoms with seasonal regularity, increasing in number and beauty through the years.

Most bulbs thrive in a sunny location in a neutral to slightly acid (pH 6-7), porous, crumbly, well-drained soil. They need only two feedings annually, at planting time and after blooming, and their foliage should be left on until completely dry.

The general planting depth, the distance from the shoulder of the bulb to the soil's surface, is three times the diameter of the bulb. Notable exceptions to this rule are lilies, whose stemroots require deep planting to develop anchorage, and iris rhizomes, which should be planted just under the surface. Loosen about two inches of the soil at the bottom of the hole and work in a mixture of sand and one tablespoon bone meal. Cover this with just enough soil to prevent the bulb's touching the fertilizer and place the bulb securely in the hole, covering with soil and firming well to displace air pockets. The spacing of bulbs depends on their size and habit of growth. Small buds may be placed four to five inches apart, whereas those of spreading habit are spaced more widely.

Bulb foliage should never be cut until it has dried because the foliage provides the bulb with food for next year's growth. If the droopy foliage offends your sense of neatness, plant a ground cover of ivy, ajuga, petunias or other such plants to hide it, but do not cut the foliage from the bulb until it is thoroughly dry and brown. Faded flower heads of bulbs should be broken off to prevent the formation of seed pods.

Many bulbs adapt themselves to a location and become naturalized; that is, they come up year after year in ever greater numbers. When the clumps show the effects of crowding by producing smaller and fewer blooms, the bulbs should be lifted and divided. Allow the lifted bulbs to dry, dust with sulphur, label, and store in a cool dry place until planting time next season. When bulbs are to stay in the ground after blooming, they should be fed with a mixture of bone meal and super-phosphate scratched into the soil around the bulbs and watered in to encourage bloom potential for next year. Never use fresh manure around bulbs.

Because they are a permanent investment, it is worthwhile to buy good quality bulbs from reputable sources. New varieties introduced each year allow for pleasurable experimentation in your garden. Try lesser-known species of small bulbs which will thrive in this climate and provide spectacular color when massed in large informal groups (see the "Bulbs, Tubers and Rhizomes" Planting Chart).

Amaryllis Family *(Amaryllidaceae).* This large group includes some of the handsomest plants grown in this area. Hybrid Amaryllis, Amarcrinum, Alstroemeria, Chlidanthus, Clivia, Crinum, Cooperia, Eucharis, Habranthus, Haemanthus, Hymenocallis, Ismene, Leucojum, Lycoris, Narcissus, Sprekelia, Tuberose, Tulbaghia, and Zephyranthes are spectacular-blossoming representatives of this family.

Among the many Amaryllis are traditional favorites and modern hybrids, providing picturesque shapes and exquisite colors for your garden. The Dutch, Sequoia, and Houdyshel hybrids are especially lovely. Amaryllis should be planted with the neck and upper portion of the bulb above the surface of the soil. If in time the bulbs settle, they may be carefully raised and reset on a handful of sand. Amaryllis will bloom well in semi-shade, and they lend themselves to planting alone, in groups or among the shrubbery.

Crinums are an excellent choice because of their fragrant, long-blooming flowers and attractive foliage. The type commonly known as the Milk-and-Wine Lily is a delightful survivor of old gardens. Improved hybrid varieties such as the choice early-blooming white *Powellii,* St. Christopher, Ellen Bosanquet, Cecil Houdyshel, *Rattrayi,* and

the late-blooming *giganteum,* which thrives in deep shade, provide a succession of bloom from spring through autumn.

Amarcrinum Howardii, an outstanding hybrid of *Amaryllis Belladonna* and *Crinum Moorei,* has especially lovely clusters of shell pink flowers and prospers in semi-shade, blooming periodically during the summer.

Tuberoses, Ismene (Peruvian Daffodil), and Hymenocallis (Spider Lily) are dependable favorites, bearing fragrant white blossoms in the summer. Tuberoses, single and double, produce fragrant, wax-like flowers. Ismene boast exotic lily-shaped flowers, with segments extending beyond the petals like small horns faintly veined with green. Hymenocallis take their common name from the spidery appearance of their narrow fragile petals and long stamens.

Clivia, Eucharis, and Haemanthus are tropical plants usually grown in pots or tubs in a shady garden or patio for the summer and in a protected location for winter. They require a potting mixture of sandy loam, bone meal and humus with some charcoal to insure good drainage.

Lycoris have strap-shaped leaves and clusters of funnel-shaped flowers in many colors. There are summer and autumn bloomers. In addition to those listed in the "Bulbs" Planting Chart, the lilac rose *L. squamigera,* the red *L. sanguinea,* and the blush pink *L. incarnata* are beautiful species. The Lycoris and the Guernsey Lily *(Nerine sarniensis)* are similar in appearance. Most of these bulbs naturalize well, but they should not be disturbed unless absolutely necessary because they often fail to bloom for two or more seasons after being moved.

Zephyranthes, Cooperia, and Habranthus are somewhat alike, having grass-like foliage and the habit of blooming intermittently throughout the summer. *Tulbaghia violacea,* with its small orchid clusters, is an almost constant summer bloomer. All these little bulbs are lovely tucked into corners or used as borders.

Other amaryllids providing splashes of brilliant color are the showy *Alstroemeria aurantiaca* (Peruvian Lily), the gorgeous Sprekelia, and the fragrant Chlidanthus, resembling the amaryllis in miniature.

Narcissi or Daffodils. Narcissus is the botanical name of the genus encompassing all species and varieties of daffodils and jonquils. The name daffodil is used loosely, referring both to narcissi with large trumpets and to others. Jonquil is the term commonly used for the rush-leaved *Narcissus Jonquilla, odorus,* and their hybrids. Narcissi are hardy, dependable, and adaptable bulbs, unsurpassed for informal plantings. Since winter in the South is comparable to spring in the North, the early varieties are more satisfactory for the upper Gulf Coast area, giving repeated seasons of bloom. Some, especially the polyanthus or bunch-flowered *N. Tazetta,* will naturalize. The new hybrids are larger and often more beautiful than the older favorites. To increase the blooms in your winter garden add a few new varieties each year. Some of the varieties recommended for this area, listed by the generally accepted classification, are:

TRUMPET NARCISSI
    Yellow:
        Aerolite, early
        Alasnam, early
        King Alfred, mid-season
        Unsurpassable
    White:
        Mount Hood, mid-season
LARGE-CUPPED NARCISSI
    Fortune, early
    Silver Star, early

SMALL-CUPPED NARCISSI
    Pomona, early

DOUBLE NARCISSI
    Texas, early
    Twink, early

TRIANDRUS NARCISSI
    April Tears
    Moonshine, mid-season
    Thalia, early
CYCLAMINEOUS NARCISSI
    February Gold, extra early
JONQUILLA NARCISSI
    Campernelle, early
    Trevithian, mid-season
TAZETTA (Poetaz or Bunch-flowered) NARCISSI
    Cheerfulness
    Chinese Sacred Lily
    Cragford (white petals, gold cup)
    Paper White
    Silver Chimes
    Soleil d'or

POETICUS (Poet's) NARCISSI
    Actaea, early
    Recurvus, early

Many of the unclassified varieties produced throughout the South were named to suit their owners. The survivors have become part of the garden heritage in their locale.

Narcissi accept various soils, but they demand adequate drainage and surface fertilization following their spring bloom and again in the fall. About ½ pound of mixed bone meal and superphosphate for every ten square feet of clumps should be worked lightly around the bulbs and watered in.

Varieties that naturalize may remain undisturbed until overcrowding is evidenced by smaller and fewer flowers; then lift and divide. The early spring blossoms of narcissi make beautiful and fragrant arrangements. They are best cut as opening buds, taking very few of the leaves through which the bulbs attain food for future growth.

Lily Family *(Liliaceae).* The lily family is noteworthy for the showy blooms of its numerous genera: true Lilium, Agapanthus, Allium, Camassia, Chionodoxa, Galtonia, Gloriosa, Hemerocallis, Hyacinth, Kniphofia, Lachenalia, Leucojum, Liriope, Milla, Muscari, Ornithogalum, Scilla, and Tulip.

The term "Lily" is often used in conjunction with common names of many bulbous plants and is more descriptive than accurate. The number of true lilies which thrive in this climate is somewhat limited, but careful planning and planting will provide a succession of bloom in a wide range of color and variety. The Creole, Regal, and Philippine lilies are special favorites in this area, as they are easily grown and naturalized. Other lilies raised successfully are the Speciosums, Croft, Estate, Tiger, Goldband, Centifoliums, Turk's-Cap, Coral, Madonna, and the Bellingham and Green Mountain hybrids.

Good drainage is rudimentary in lily culture. A sandy loam with leafmold added suits most species. All lilies send out roots from the base of their bulbs, but some also develop roots on the stem, above the bulbs. True lilies have loose, fleshy scales that hold

water and decay easily. They must be planted in well-drained soil. Companion plants are beneficial to lilies, as they adsorb surplus water in the soil and shade the area adjacent to the lilies, but the lilies should not be crowded. A loose mulch helps keep the soil and stems cool and moist, makes cultivation unnecessary, and discourages weeds. The flowers of all lilies are excellent for cutting, but only the top part of the stem should be cut off so that the bulb can complete its growth. (For lily diseases, see "Diseases, Insects and Weeds.")

Hemerocallis (Daylilies) are unexcelled for colorful, long-lasting bloom. Daylilies thrive in full sun or partial shade. They require only average soil and, once established, demand little care; however, they respond with continued and better bloom if watered liberally and fed with a complete fertilizer. A careful selection of varietes, including dwarf types, will provide a sequence of bloom from early spring until fall. New varieties are introduced continually.

Hyacinths, especially the Dutch and Roman varieties in delightful shades, are most attractive in groups. Store bulbs in a refrigerator and plant after weather cools. Hyacinths may also be grown indoors in hyacinth glasses. The Multiflora and Borah, in blue or white, naturalize.

In this climate tulips must be refrigerated (not frozen) for at least three to six weeks before planting. Bulbs are usually discarded at the end of the blooming season, except *Tulipa clusiana* and some other species, which may be left in the ground to naturalize. The Cottage and Darwin hybrids, noteworthy for their flower size, length and strength of stem, and beautiful color, do well in this area but do not naturalize.

Called the "harbingers of spring" bulbs, the Muscari (Grape Hyacinth), Scilla (Squill), Leucojum (Snowflake), Ornithogalum (Star of Bethlehem), Chionodoxa, and Milla are hardy, dependable, and indispensable for brightening spring gardens. A light mulch should be used as a winter protection.

Kniphofia (Torch Lily or Red Hot Poker) and Yucca are generally used to add a touch of novelty and give bold accent to summer gardens. They do well in hot sun and require little water. Some smaller hybrids of Kniphofia have more beautiful coloring than the older types, formerly listed as Tritomas. There are a few other summer-blooming bulbs, such as the white-spiked Galtonia, Allium, Liriope. Camassia, and the decorative-flowered Lachenalia.

Gloriosa (Climbing Lily) is an unusual and spectacular plant, bearing brilliant yellow and red flowers, with tendrils on the tips of its leaves. Given necessary support, the climbing plant reaches a height of five or six feet. To grow, each tuberous root must have an eye. They should be watered freely during the growing season and fed generously with applications of liquid manure every two weeks until the buds begin to form.

Iris Family *(Iridaceae)*. The *Iridaceae* family contains over 60 genera and perhaps 1,000 species. They are generally described as herbs having sword-shaped leaves, rhizomes, bulbs or bulb-like rootstocks, and handsome, six-segmented flowers. Southern garden favorites include: Iris, Blackberry Lily, Dietes, Gladiolus, Ixia, Marica, Montbretia, Sisyrinchium, Sparaxis, Tigridia, and Watsonia.

The genus Iris boasts one of the world's most famous flower forms. Different species of iris grow in sundry climates, from cold mountain regions to swamps, sea coasts, and temperate plains. If their needs are met some will flourish and naturalize. Irises are divided into two main root classifications: bulbous and rhizomatous; and the rhizomatous classification is in turn subdivided into: Bearded, Beardless, and Crested, according to their petal forms. The bulbous group includes the Dutch, Algerian *(Iris tingitana),* and the small winter-blooming *I. reticulata.* They are most effective in the garden when planted in clumps and may be interspersed with other spring bulbs. Plant three inches deep on a cushion of sand underlain with bone meal and phosphate. Avoid planting them in a bed which requires summer watering, as they are subject to rotting. They are excellent for cutting.

The beautiful rainbow-hued Bearded Irises do not adapt easily to our scorching summers and mild wet winters, but if their basic requirements are met and if the varieties have been tested in mild climates they may thrive. Varieties "too tender" for northern growers are often just right for us.

Proper varietal selection, plenty of sun, good drainage, and slightly alkaline soil are the keys to good iris culture. Bearded irises cannot share beds with plants needing heavy watering in the summer because the rhizomes' natural cycle demands dormancy and fairly dry soil in the summer. The re-bloomers are an exception to this, if you want fall or winter bloom. Early autumn planting in raised beds of sandy loam sweetened with lime and enriched with bone meal and superphosphate is recommended. Rotted manure or commercial fertilizers may be turned deep into the bed where the feeder roots will reach, but must never touch the rhizomes. Each rhizome, with its roots trailing downward, should be placed on a small mound and barely covered with soil. After blooming and in the fall fertilize with bone meal, either alone or in combination with an inorganic formula. Remember that too much nitrogen in any form produces fine foliage but few flowers. At the first sign of rot, or of growing tips melting away after a prolonged rainy spell, the rhizomes may be lifted and the soft parts cut off. Treat with sulphur, full strength Clorox, or Terracolor before replanting; or on noticing the first mustard-seed-like particles of the fungus at ground level, douse the entire area with a mild solution of Terraclor. This treatment is also good for Spurias and other irises which have contracted bacterial soft rot.

The Beardless types which may be grown in this area include the Japanese, Siberian, Spuria, Algerian (*I. unguicularis*), and the Louisiana natives and hybrids. The spectacular Japanese *I. kaempferi* and its hybrids prefer very rich, lime-free soil and must be kept very wet before early summer blooming and quite dry while dormant in autumn and winter. They may be planted in redwood boxes or tubs, sunk in ponds for flowering, and then removed to a dry situation for their dormant season. The dainty Siberian Iris is an early bloomer which may adapt itself to southern gardens if given a rich soil and plenty of sun and moisture. They are most effective in clumps and do not like to be disturbed. *I. unguicularis,* also called *I. stylosa,* is valuable for its long period of winter bloom. The flowers, which have no real stems, should be gathered in bud and will open in water the next day.

Highly recommended are the stately Spuria Irises, which have handsome sword-like leaves and erect stalks crowned with six or eight blooms in spike formation. They are long-lived as cut flowers and resistant to wind, rain, heat, and cold. The older species *I. ochroleuca* is a favorite for flower arranging because its blooms spiral close around the un-branched stalk in an unusual manner. Plant only in the fall in sunny, well-drained beds, into which any balanced fertilizer or manure supplemented with bone meal has been mixed. Set the rhizome on a mound of soil with roots spread beneath it. The roots must not be allowed to dry out during the purchasing and transplanting process. Barely cover the top of the rhizome with soil and level the bed. Add a little mulch to prevent sunburn. Fertilize in the early fall and again in the late winter. Spurias should not be moved often, so allow a three foot area for the mother rhizome to spread into a large clump. They like wet winters and dry summers but will tolerate more extremes than the Bearded varieties. Should fungus appear, treatment is the same as for bearded irises.

The slender swamp irises of Louisiana are the most indigenous of their family to our area. With a wonderful range of colors, the new hybrid varieties rival in beauty and grace the more difficult Japanese. They will adapt easily to most gardens here, whether sunny or semi-shaded. However, an ideal situation for them is a low bed or pond edge where they may occasionally have standing water in their winter growing season and dry out in summer. Barnyard manure and leafmold are preferred soil conditioners, but others may be used. The rhizomes should be barely covered with soil, and mulched quite heavily in the hot months with any handy dressing. As with other irises, feed generously after blooming and in early autumn with well-rotted manure or a balanced fertilizer. Never put fertilizer directly on a rhizome; scratch it lightly into the surrounding soil, and water.

The Crested or Evansia Irises are very useful in Houston gardens. They make good companion plants for azaleas, as they bloom about the same time and have the same acid soil and shade preferences. *Iris cristata,* with lovely little blue flowers, is a miniature variety of Evansia. It prefers year-round moisture and soil with much humus, but will adapt to other conditions. Transplanting is best done immediately after flowering when new roots are produced. Another Evansia iris which has been proven here is the widely-branched *I. japonica,* which bears numerous pale lavender flowers with orange crests on a single stem. It does better in considerable shade than in sunlight and, like *I. cristata,* needs humus and leafmold. Two beautiful hybrids, Nada and Darjeeling, have frilled white flowers.

A few vigorous Bearded irises have been developed which will give both spring and autumn or winter bloom if continuously fertilized and kept moist all summer. These are called "remontant," or reblooming, and are recommended for this climate; however, they may bloom in only one of these seasons in this area. Few Dwarf, Intermediate or Miniature Tall Bearded Irises have thrived here, but older Intermediates sometimes bloom after a period of years. In selecting bearded irises choose those listed as rebloomers or mild climate irises.

The Beardless irises in the following list after a wide color range and have been grown successfully in this area:

LOUISIANA IRIS

Barbara Elaine Taylor (Levingston)—tall white
Bayou Sunset (MacMilian)—soft rose and gold
Chuck (Arny)—wine red
Charlie's Michelle (Arny)—frilled rosy pink
Dean Lee (Arny)—small bright brown
Dixie Deb (Chowning)—yellow, good garden iris
Eolian (Arny)—light blue
F.A.C. McCulla (Arny)—fine red
Faenelia Hicks (Arny)—large pink
G.W. Holleyman (R. Holleyman)—tall yellow
Ila Nunn (Arny)—tall cream
Katherine Cornay (Arny)—mineral violet
Marie Caillet (Conger)—red purple
Mrs. Ira Nelson (Arny)—large lavender
New Offering (Davis)—blue purple
Queen of Queens (Holleyman)—creamy white
The Kahn (Dormon)—black purple, yellow signal
Violet Ray (Dormon)—purple, white ray
Wheelhorse (Dormon)—bright rose
Wood Violet (Dormon)—low, bright blue

SPURIA IRIS

Arbitrator (Ferguson)—purple and yellow
Archie Owen (Hager)—deep yellow
Baritone (Ferguson)—large brown
Driftwood (Walker)—brown
Elixir (Hager)—orange yellow
Fort Ridge (Ferguson)—good blue
Golden Lady (Combs)—good yellow
Good Thunder (Ferguson)—large yellow
Marilyn Holloway (Hager)—blue lavender
Frost (Ferguson)—ruffled white
Minneopa (Ferguson)—pale blue and yellow
Proverb (Ferguson)—dark blue purple
Wakerobin (Ferguson)—white
Windfall (Ferguson)—cream and yellow
Wadi Zem Zem—pale yellow
I. ochroleuca—white and yellow

DUTCH IRIS

Wedgewood—medium blue, early
Imperator—dark blue, late
Blue Ribbon—vivid blue
White Perfection—white
Golden Emperor—yellow
Le Mogul—bronze
Princess Irene—white and orange

Gladiolus, another major member of the *Iridaceae* family, is available in a dazzling range of colors, although form varies little. They are easy to grow in good garden soil and will provide a succession bloom if planted at two-week intervals in the early spring and late summer. They should be staked. Gladioli give most satisfactory results in garden display and for cutting when selected color blends are planted rather than packaged mixtures, which are usually disappointing and often inferior.

For maximum bloom, gladioli should be fed with a liquid fertilizer once a week from the time the stalk begins to lengthen until the first color shows. This is particularly important when growing flowers for exhibition. Flower spikes should be cut when the two lowest florets open, and not more than one leaf should be cut from each plant. Thrips, gladiolus' worst pest, are easily controlled if a recommended soil and bulb dust or spray is applied weekly from the time foliage is six inches high to flowering. Some gardeners let bulbs stay in the ground, but flowering diminishes each year. Bulbs may be lifted and stored for the winter after foliage has dried. Before storage, remove old foliage and treat corms with an insecticide. The *Primulinus* type, the *Gladiolus tristis,* and the dainty hybrids known as Baby Gladioli are smaller, more graceful plants popularly grown in this area.

The South African Dietes, though not a true iris, has iris-like foliage and blooms on and off all summer. Each flower lasts only a day but is rapidly followed by another. The Oakhurst and *Johnsoni* hybrids are particularly adaptable to this climate. Marica, or the so-called "Walking Iris," naturalizes easily, as the weight of young plants formed on the ends of old flower stalks pulls the old stems down and these proliferations take root.

Montbretias and Watsonias make a brilliant, colorful and decorative display in summer gardens and are desirable acquisitions for the border or for cutting. Their culture is similar to that of gladioli but they may be left undisturbed for several years. The Earlham hybrids of montbretias are very lovely and excellent for cutting. These bulbs may be left in the ground but will be improved by lifting, separating, and replanting every alternate autumn.

The Blackberry Lily, or Belamcanda, is adaptable to any soil, thriving in full sun or semi-shade. The yellow flowers brighten summer gardens and keep well when cut. The seed formation, which resembles a blackberry, may be dried and used for winter arrangements.

Ixia and Sparaxis, both originating in South Africa, have similar small, star-shaped flowers borne on long slender stems above grass-like foliage. Lovely for cutting, the colors run the gamut of the golden tones from cream to scarlet.

Tigridias (Shell Flowers) thrive in southern gardens because they can withstand intense heat. Natives of Mexico, their large, triangular-shaped flowers are brilliantly colored and have a long blooming season. The smallest member of the iris family is the *Sisyrinchium,* or Blue-eyed Grass. Its small, dainty blossoms open one at a time, keeping up a long succession of bloom.

Arum Family *(Araceae).* In the South Callas do best in a light soil to which well-rotted manure, sand, and humus have been added. If desired, the roots may be started early indoors in pots and later transferred to the garden when all danger of frost is past. After blooming, when the foliage has dried, the roots should be dug and stored in dry sand or peatmoss to give them a few months rest. The hardy White Callas may be left in the ground for the summer in order to increase, but they too will benefit by digging in the fall. The yellow variety, *Elliotiana,* with its interesting spotted foliage, is less hardy and requires semi-shade and a slightly acid soil. The shade-loving, evergreen Baby Calla and the Pink Calla, usually grown in pots, are becoming more popular. Rot sometimes occurs in callas and is usually caused by a high soil pH or by using green manure.

Anthuriums are highly prized as pot plants for their beautiful exotic flowers. *A. scherzerianum* (Flamingo Flower) and *Spathiphyllum clevelandi* will bloom in high garden shade or in the house. The shade- and moisture-loving *Arisaema triphyllum* (Jack-in-the-Pulpit), with its calla-like flowers of mottled green and brown, is most effective when planted among ferns or wild flowers.

Caladiums, related to callas, are highly esteemed as bedding plants for their ornamental veined and marbled foliage and brilliant coloring. They like a well-drained, friable, somewhat acid soil, semi-shade and moisture.

They may be used among azalea plantings to provide color during the summer. Tubers may be planted as soon as the ground has warmed. Caladium leaves die back naturally in the fall, when the bulbs should be dug, dusted with sulphur, and stored in dry sand.

Ginger Family *(Zingiberaceae)*. Several varieties of the tropical Ginger family are grown successfully in this area. Butterfly Lilies *(Hedychium coronarium)* bloom in summer and are prized for their pure white fragrant flowers which resemble large butterflies. Ginger Lilies *(H. gardnerianum)*, a more tender variety, have yellow flowers tipped with scarlet and bright green canna-like foliage. After blooming, each hedychium stalk should be cut off near the ground to promote new growth. Pink Shell Ginger *(Alpinia speciosa* or *nutans)* has handsome clusters of pink buds opening into striped yellowish flowers. Hidden Ginger *(Curcuma petiolata)* flowers in a compact spike of pink, yellow, and lavender bracts.

Canna Family *(Cannaceae)*. There are many beautiful Canna hybrids. The two main groups are the orchid-flowered type and the more popular gladiolus-flowered type, which is of dwarf habit and free-blooming. Cannas may be selected according to color and are most effective when planted as bold accents in borders or in large masses. Grand Opera varieties include colors of old rose, salmon, peach-pink, yellowish-pink, and canary yellow. The bronze-leaved varieties are especially desirable for their foliage as well as for their flowers.

Dahlias. Dahlias may be grown successfully in any well-drained soil, but a good garden loam rich in humus is best. They should have an open sunny situation with free air circulation at all times. The tuberous roots should be planted horizontally with the sprout pointing upwards, and they need to be staked at planting time to give support to the plants as they grow. Cultivation should be shallow to avoid damaging the root system. When plants are about a foot high, the top should be pinched out to develop a sturdier, more branching plant. Tall dahlias benefit from disbudding, leaving only the largest and best bud on each branch. The smaller varieties need no disbudding, may be planted closer together, and are more adaptable in landscaping than the larger varieties, especially for the upper Gulf Coast area. They come in a wide range of colors and provide a lavish supply of blossoms, which are long-lasting if cut in early morning or late afternoon and immediately immersed in water to cover most of the stems. The plants should be fed as soon as the flower buds form, using a small amount of commercial fertilizer lightly worked into the soil, but not within several inches of the stem. Feedings may be repeated every ten days during the blooming season. The soil should be well-watered after planting; but during early growth, watering should be just sufficient to keep the plants growing well. The plants require more water after feeding begins. A light mulch of leaves or dried grass cuttings will conserve moisture, keep the roots cool, and make cultivation unnecessary.

Miscellaneous Bulbs. Gloxinias are grown as pot plants. The gorgeous flowers and velvety foliage of the California-grown hybrids are preferable to the Belgian types. Achimenes grow well in loose soil and morning or filtered sun, providing a long succession of summer bloom.

Ranunculi and Anemones are among the gayest and most brilliantly colored spring flowers. They require much the same culture, are ideal for cutting purposes, and are well adapted to this climate. The Tecolote Giant ranunculi range in color from red, pink, yellow to white. Anemones that do well here are the single De Caen and the semi-double St. Brigid types, in shades of red, pink, blue, and white.

Oxalis are hardy low-growing or trailing border plants with an abundance of small buttercup-like flowers and shamrock leaves. The newer strains have more compact growth with flowers held high above the foliage. Bermuda Buttercup *(O. cernua)* thrives here and makes a good ground cover.

Waterlilies bloom in this area from May until frost. They may be grown in tubs or pools, but they must have full sun to bloom freely. When planted in submerged boxes the soil should be very rich, containing a generous amount of manure or bone meal, renewed every second year. Lilies growing in a natural pool may be fertilized by spreading bone meal on the water surface in March. Roots should be divided in April while the plants are dormant. The roots will not freeze in this climate if they are covered with a foot of water. Varieties which are successful here are the Blue Beauty, the Pink Houston Lily, the white yellow-centered Georgia Prince, and the Pink Zanzibar. Lavender Water-Hyacinths and yellow Waterpoppies add interest and color to pools. For large pools or small lakes the native Chinquapin is ideal, as it has huge pale yellow lotus-like flowers.

Pot-Grown Bulbs. Most bulbs may be grown successfully in pots. Many gardeners prefer pot culture, even for hardy bulbs, because potted plants may be conveniently moved and easily protected from sudden drops of temperature. Pots and other containers are used for year-round growing as well as for "forcing," that is, grown out of the normal season for flowering.

There are three methods commonly used for growing bulbs in pots; the first and easiest is using fiber, pebbles or water as the growing medium. Paperwhite Narcissus, Lilies-of-the-Valley, Ismene and others are grown in this manner. When first planted, the bulbs should be kept in a dark cool place until the root system is developed. Moisten fiber thoroughly before placing bulbs in it, then drain off excess water. The bulbs must be firmly placed with fiber closely packed around them. Never permit fiber to become dry. When growing bulbs in water and pebbles, keep the level of water just below the bases of the bulbs. Bulbs grown by this method exhaust themselves in one season and should be discarded after blooming.

The second method, generally used for hardy bulbs such as Ixia and Sparaxis, is that of forcing in soil with preliminary root growth. While some bulbs require special soil formulas, a light, rich, well-drained soil of an equal mixture of loam, sand, and leafmold suffices for the majority. Two tablespoonfuls of bone meal may be added to each 8-inch pot for nourishment. The potted bulbs should be stored outside in a cold place and covered with leaves and peat moss for six or seven weeks. Clay pots should be well-watered before storing. Slightly dampened sawdust may be used if pots are stored under cover. Bulbs which are grown carefully in this manner may usually be saved for another season's bloom. Bulbs should be ripened properly after flowering, by lessening water gradually until leaves turn brown. Leave in pots until fall then plant in the garden.

The third method, generally used for tender bulbs such as Eucharis and Anthurium, is to plant in a sufficiently enriched soil in which the bulbs can make normal growth and development without relying upon the food supply stored within the bulb itself. Many bulbs grown by this method will need replanting only every two to four years.

Garden Flowers

If thou would'st attain to thy highest, go look upon a flower.
—Schiller

Garden flowers bring a feeling of youth and gaiety to a landscape. Perhaps it is their impermanence, but most likely it is the masses of blooms they produce in such riotous abandon. One pansy plant may boast 30 blossoms; a petunia plant, well over 200! No wonder beds of annuals are show-stoppers. Though there are many other classifications of blooming plants, those most often associated with the term "garden flowers" are annuals, biennials, and perennials.

Annuals. Annuals are flowering plants which complete their life cycle from seed to blooming plant and back to seed in a single season, beautifully demonstrating what a miracle a seed is. In their compulsion to reproduce, annuals will bloom and promptly form seeds, unless the cycle is delayed by removing spent blooms, thus extending the flowering season many weeks. Pansy plants can easily be kept blooming from December until June. When annuals do go to seed they employ fascinating ways to scatter it. Most form some sort of seed pod. When the seeds are ripe the pods spring open, casting the seeds many feet away onto the soil where they may lie dormant until the appropriate season, when they again sprout, send down roots and repeat their cycle.

Annuals are of easy culture, needing only a fairly rich, loose soil, sun, water, and a little room to grow. Naturally, they become more productive with fertilization and care. One of the few exceptions is the nasturtium, which thrives in poor soil but tends to produce mostly foliage and few flowers in rich soil. Annuals classified as hardy are reasonably frost-resistant, and their seeds may be sown in open ground in the fall or early spring. If perchance they are frozen they may be resown. Annual seeds are inexpensive. Half-hardy annuals are those sensitive to frost, and they are often started in a cold frame or greenhouse. To go through their normal cycle, annuals classified as tender must not be subjected to cold at any time. Tender annuals are usually bought as small plants at nurseries, though they may also be started in a cold frame. Do not set them out until you are sure cold weather is past.

Annuals can be used in many interesting ways. For a new garden whose permanent plants are still immature, annuals like amaranthus, sunflower, castorbean, and tithonia, which grow to shrub size in several weeks, provide quick flowers or colorful foliage. Annuals make a lovely display sown among bulb plantings, and they hide dying bulb foliage, which must not be cut off until totally dry. Containers or a sunny corner of the garden become beautiful with blooming annuals, and there are numerous annual vines that can shade a window or cover a trellis with flowers for the summer.

In Houston and the upper Gulf Coast annuals often reseed themselves, blooming abundantly year after year. Bluebonnets, cornflowers, feverfew, and marigolds are among these. Because there are so many varieties of annuals, it is exciting to try different ones each year.

Biennials. Biennials are plants that make part of their growth one year, and bloom and die the next. The climate and time of seeding determine the longevity of biennials, and the fickleness of the weather in the Gulf Coast region makes them temperamental. They often follow the cycle of annuals, completing their life span in one year. They sometimes reseed, sending up seedlings the following year. Pinks (Dianthus) are among the few true biennials grown successfully in the South.

Perennials. Any plant that lives more than two years is classified as a perennial. Obviously, that definition could include other plants such as trees and bulbs, but the generally accepted meaning of the term "perennials" refers to blooming plants with fleshy or herbaceous stems as opposed to wood-producing stems. The durability of a perennial's roots distinguishes it from annuals and biennials, and a perennial's inability to store food for the following year's growth distinguishes it from bulbs. Herbaceous perennials die down to the ground in the winter but sprout from the same roots each spring. Hardy perennials can live through the winter and survive long hot summers and high humidity, but the upper Gulf Coast fails to meet a usual requirement of most perennials—a well defined period of cold weather to stimulate dormancy in plants. There are, however, numerous tried and true perennial mainstays adapted to our climate, and many are listed in the "Flowering Plants Grown from Seeds" Planting Chart.

Perennials are easily propagated, and many bloom from seed the first year. Certain perennials multiply and form thick clumps. Among these are blue salvia, chrysanthemum, dusty miller, gerbera daisy, verbena, and violet. They might be called friendly plants, for gardeners exchange divisions from the clumps, creating "Friendship Gardens." (See "Propagation" for details on dividing.)

Location of Flowers. Planning the location of garden flowers is just as important as planning any other element in garden design. The best method is to draw your plan to scale on graph paper. Consider differences in height, spread, leaf size and texture, soil and sun preferences, as well as season of bloom and flower color. Because perennials are long-lived, determine their placement on your plan first, remembering that flowering seasons vary. Although the conventional advice is to keep taller varieties at the back of the bed, there are situations in which this suggestion can be attractively ignored. Experiment until you achieve the effect that pleases you. Plot annuals into the plan, blending their colors, cultural needs, and growth habits with those of the perennials. Do not forget that many garden flowers are fragrant, an additional pleasure. Some gardeners prefer to use just one or two blossom colors in their gardens. Others prefer a casual collage of various hues. Obviously, your color choices depend on the effect you want to achieve and the growing preferences of the plants. If you are dissatisfied with the outcome, move the plants to another spot, taking them up with a spadeful of dirt and transplanting them tenderly. They will need water, preferably with a rooting stimulant, and protection from the sun for a day (see "Propagation").

Culture. Annuals and perennials have their individual soil and sun preferences just as other plants do, but the majority like several hours of sun and well-draining soil. Since annuals and perennials bloom so prolifically, the soil should have ample amounts of compost, manure or other organic matter and complete fertilizer tilled or well mixed into it before planting. This is the time to incorporate a high-phosphorus fertilizer, worked in deep enough to fertilize the area where the roots will be. If it is carefully watered in, a complete fertilizer may be very gently scratched in around the roots during the blooming season, and frequent foliar feeding will also increase the amount of bloom. Cutting the flowers for arrangements and removing the spent blossoms will stimulate continuous flowering. For cutting purposes, annuals are often planted with vegetables or in a separate cutting bed to avoid denuding the flowering border.

Annuals, biennials, and perennials are so adaptable that anyone willing to provide their cultural needs and some tender loving care can have a lavish array of flowers. The hours spent in your garden are restorative, another pleasant aspect of gardening.

The Shaded Garden

Shadows are in reality, when the sun is shining, the most conspicuous thing in a landscape, next to the highest lights.

—Ruskin

A shaded area can easily be transformed into a beautiful garden oasis to which you can retreat from the summer sun. The amount of shade is one of the primary considerations in selecting suitable plants, but there are numerous plant materials from which to choose, even if the shade is dense.

As in all garden planning, consider first the drainage and the soil. Shaded beds need better drainage because there is less sunshine to evaporate the moisture, but poor drainage is not an insurmountable problem. Modifying the soil itself, laying tiles to carry excess water away, or raising the bed a few inches by use of bordering material are all possibilities. The "Drainage" and the "Soil and Soil Improvement" chapters can help you with any of these procedures. The soil must be slightly acid, loose, and friable with about 30% organic matter worked into it.

Often the degree of shade can be altered. If trees are responsible for the lack of light, most can be thinned to allow sunlight to filter in. The chapters on "Pruning" and "Trees" provide suggestions. If the planting bed is built over the roots of a tree, take care to keep the soil very loose and no more than three inches above normal soil level to avoid suffocating the root system. Leave two-thirds of the tree root area uncovered by the extra soil.

When trees are close to a flower bed their surface roots may rob the garden plants of moisture and nutrients. Roots may be pruned with a sharp spade, but only a few at a time, to protect the tree from shock. Shove the spade full depth into the ground, between the tree and the planting bed, staying as far away from the tree trunk as you can. If you root prune every year there should be no problems for either tree or plants.

There is no difficulty finding plants that can adapt to a filtered shade environment. Some of our handsomest plants originally grew in forests. Azaleas, camellias, lycoris, violets, vinca, and brunfelsia are all blooming plants which appreciate partial shade. St. Augustine grass also grows well in partial shade.

Even if the shade is dense you still have a wide selection. All aucubas need shade, and the variety "Gold Dust," with its golden-spotted foliage, gives shadows the appearance of being illuminated by sunbeams. Though they need protection from freezing temperatures, rice paper plant and aralia, with their stunning large lobed leaves, are dramatic in combination with other background shrubs and plants. Ferns prefer shade and, given the type of soil they love, will thrive in a shaded bed (⅓ sand, ⅓ organic matter, and ⅓ loam make a good fern soil). Feed lightly with slow-acting organic fertilizer. One of the most ancient families of plants, ferns offer varying leaf shapes. (See he "Ferns" Planting Chart.) Many ground covers also adapt well to shade.

Shaded beds offer an excellent opportunity to create a monochromatic garden picture with shades of green, arranging plants with pleasing contrasts in texture and size and shape of foliage. As a rule, shade-loving plants do not need as much fertilizer as those in sun. So, with drainage and soil properly handled, a thick loose mulch, and occasional watering, a shaded garden is a low-maintenance one.

If you want to add summer color, caladium bulbs are available in many shades and striations of leaf. Potted blooming plants may be sunk in the ground and removed as their flowers fade. You may find your shaded garden area becoming your favorite.

The Planting Charts denote many plants which tolerate shade, but since there is great variance in the amount of light, filtered or indirect, in individual gardens, you should experiment until you find the plants which thrive in your garden. The listed plant material will add interest to garden areas in fairly dense shade.

Ajuga	Elaeagnus
Aspidistra	Euonymus
Aucuba	Fatsia
Azalea	Fatshedera
Begonia	Ferns
Bulbs	Forget-Me-Not
Amaryllis	Hypericum
Butterfly Lily	Hydrangea
Caladium	Impatiens
Calla	Ivy
Crinum	*Osmanthus illicifolius*
Iris, bulbous	Pittosporum
Lily	Mahonia
Liriope	Nandina
Lycoris	Nicotiana
Narcissus	Shrimp Plant
Oxalis	Strawberry Begonia
Roman Hyacinth	Spathiphyllum
Scilla	Sweet Olive
Zephyranthes	Viburnum
Dogwood	Vinca

The Fragrant Garden

With fragrant breath the lilies woo me now,
And softly speaks the sweet-voiced mignonette.
—Julia C.R. Dorr

A fragrant garden has an ineffable charm. Design and color are certainly enjoyable visual pleasures, but fragrance adds a romantic dimension to a garden's appeal. Somehow it evokes memories—or creates them. Surely no garden is complete without fragrant plants, nor need it be, for numerous aromatic plants are available.

Science attributes the degree of a fragrance to atmospheric moisture; scents are keener in warm, moist, fairly still air. Walk in your garden after a summer shower; flower and leaf perfumes are then at their peak. Hot dry weather seems to dissipate most flower fragrances. Some flowers, however, apparently bestow their fragrances to the air only in full sunshine; others become much more fragrant at dusk and are a joy placed near outdoor sitting areas.

Nature's purpose for fragrance is to attract pollinating insects. Such flowers as jasmine, honeysuckle, and narcissus, all habitually pollinated by moths and butterflies, are sweet scented. According to experiments, bees have a keen appreciation of perfume, but hummingbirds show no sense of smell and are attracted to bright-colored but odorless flowers. The theory of companion planting is partially based on the fact that certain insects are repelled by certain plants. This is probably why plants recommended as insect repellants have a strong leaf and stem fragrance.

Fragrant flowers are most often white or pastel-tinted, and in decreasing order red, yellow, purple or blue. Exceptions immediately come to mind. There are fragrant roses of every color, and bluebonnets are quite sweet-scented. But that brings up the very nature of fragrances. People have varying sensitivities to scents. A flower may be fragrant to one person but not to another. Since the petals of flowers produce the scent, the most heavily scented blooms have thick waxy petals or numerous petals. Butterfly lilies, Cape jasmine, hyacinths, tuberoses, Sweet Olive, loquat, magnolia, and pittosporum are examples.

Plants that are related botanically have similar odors, yet the scents of related species are seldom identical. Flowers may be more or less perfumed at different stages in their development.

Leaf fragrances also make the garden more pleasurable, and scents range from aromatic to spicy to pungent. Pick a leaf of any geranium, rub it a moment and savor its fragrance. A garden seems incomplete without the enticement of fragrance. Try the mints, lemon-verbena, eucalyptus, roses, lemon grass, herbs and a host of others. Their fragrances will heighten your enjoyment of your garden.

The Tropical Garden

Nature was here so lavish of her store,
That she bestowed until she had no more.

—Brown

The term "tropical" brings to mind lush, verdant vegetation, swaying palm trees, exotic flowers, and sweet fragrances drifting through the air. Gardeners along the upper Gulf Coast can use the information herein and the plants listed to create just such an effect in their own gardens.

To obtain successful results in tropical gardening there are many variables to consider, the most unpredictable being the weather. Although our region generally enjoys a mild, even temperature, this can be disastrously interrupted by thrusts of cold arctic air which bring our frosts, some six or so in most years. Although the average first frost date is December 10 and the last is February 10, it is necessary to keep abreast of weather reports from November at least through March, particularly with tropical plantings in your garden. If a freeze is predicted, water your garden. (Please see "Winter Protection.")

Plant the more tender vegetation in protected locations such as south or southeast exposures near a building, near a protected swimming pool, especially a heated one, or next to doors and windows, which readily transmit heat from the home.

Finally, and of utmost importance, keep all plant materials in a healthy condition by proper fertilizing, watering, and pruning. For maximum growth apply granular fertilizer three times yearly. In March apply a high-nitrogen ratio like 15-5-5, following in June with a balanced ratio, 12-12-12. Fertilize no later than mid-September with a low-nitrogen fertilizer; the phosphate and potash help harden the plants for winter, but nitrogen encourages rapid growth subject to frostbite. Use organic-based, complete fertilizers containing trace elements. Never fertilize dry soil, and *always* water a fertilizer in.

Keep plants evenly moist through the spring and summer to avoid the stress of being too dry during hot weather. In September and through October, gradually decrease the amount of water; rainfall usually provides sufficient moisture during this season. Dryness in plants induces dormancy, making them resistant to winter frosts. (Also see the "Pruning" chapter.)

All good gardens start with good soil. Unless you are lucky enough to have fast-draining sandy loam or can amend your soil to be well-drained, raised beds are the best means of assuring drainage and aeration. (See "Soil and Soil Improvement" and "Drainage.") The most economical way to modify the black gumbo clay frequently found in Houston is to add to it sand and generous quantities of organic matter.

Part of the fascination of gardening is the continual change in evolving landscape.

To create a tropical garden begin by planting hardy shrubs and trees. Tender plants may also be interplanted with hardier ones. For the desired effect, shrubs should be planted in masses, and bed outlines should have gradual contours. A cross section of a typical bed would show the hardy material in the center with perennial-type tropicals such as bananas, gingers, and rice paper plants to the back. This way, when the tender tropicals freeze in the winter, you can trim them below the line of vision, hidden by sheltering evergreens. Allow enough space in front of the shrubs for masses of seasonal color with copper plants, lantana, caladiums, coleus, impatiens and similar dependable summer plants.

There are numerous plants which are effective in the tropical garden. The following list includes only some that are usually available, dependable, and require a minimum of special attention. You can observe many of the plants listed at Houston's Hermann Park Zoo and Busch Bird Park, the latter having over 1,000 species of plants, including more than 30 species of palms and cycads.

SHRUBS FOR BACKGROUND

ARALIA PAPYRIFERA, Rice Paper Plant (*Tetrapanax papyriferus*): Leaves toothed lobes 1' across. Tall stalks of creamy flowers.

ARALIA SIEBOLDI (*Fatsia japonica*): Native of Southern Asia, grows more slowly and finer quality than *A. papyrifera*. Hardy to 15°. Palmate leaves, white flower panicles, black berries. Decorative in pots. Shade and good drainage.

CARICA PAPAYA (Papaya): Tropical bush-like tree, dramatic foliage, cream-colored blooms, bright fall fruit. Fast-growing; semi-hardy.

CARISSA GRANDIFLORA (Natal plum): South Africa. Very branched, spiny. Fragrant, large, white, star-shaped flowers; plum-like red fruit. Tolerates pruning. Sandy, well-drained soil, sun, tender.

CITHAREXYLUM SPINOSUM BERLANDIERI (Fiddlewood): 4-6'. Clusters of black, green, and red berries. Foliage has bronze cast. Fibrous loam, well-drained.

CLEYERA JAPONICA: Thea family. Culture similar to camellia. Slow growth; may be pruned tree-like. New growth reddish. Hardy. Fertile, slightly acid loam. Scale-resistant.

DRACAENA DRACO (Dragon Tree): Name attributed to blood red sap of mature tree. Grey-leaved, symmetrical growth, 3'-4' in diameter; survived the blizzard of 1951 with temperatures approaching 15°.

ERIOBOTRYA DEFLEXA (Bronze Loquat): 5-8'. Asiatic. Beautiful, bushy, small shrub. Ideal for small gardens. Sun or semi-shade. Hardy. Well-drained loam. Excellent in pots.

LEUCOTHOE CATESBAEI (Drooping Leucothoe): Beautiful broad-leafed evergreen. To 5', with arching branches of large shining leaves, bronze autumn color on new growth. White flowers in clusters along stem, resembling Lilies-of-the-valley. Protect. Moist sandy loam. Will not tolerate winter drying.

MAHONIA FORTUNEI (Chinese Mahonia): 5-6', erect, woody, bamboo-like stems. Rosettes of long pinnate leaves. Clusters of yellow flowers, blue berries. Shady north exposure. Sandy, well-drained rich loam.
    M. BEALEI: (Leatherleaf) and *M. LOMARIFOLIA* (Burmese): Orange flowers, powdery blue berries. Partial shade, rich soil.

PIERIS JAPONICA (Andromeda): 6'. Fast-growing. Handsome form, lustrous leaves delicately tinted when young. Upright panicles of white flowers. Sheltered position in sandy loam with peat or leaf mold. Requires good drainage.

SARCOCOCCA HUMILIS: 3-5'. Good drainage; tolerates shade and drip of trees. Glossy green leaves. Clusters of small white flowers April until June.

SCHINUS TEREBINTHIFOLIUS (Brazilian Pepper-Tree): Bushy, 5'-15' high. Freezes but comes back more shrub-like. Striking in shrub borders. Bright red fruit. Sun.

SMALLER SHRUBS FOR FOREGROUND PLANTING AND ACCENT POINTS

ACALYPHA WILKESIANA (Copperleaf): Ornamental foliage and showy bracts. 3'-5'. Needs sun for vivid leaf color, variegated copper, bronze, red and purple.

ACANTHUS MOLLIS (Bear's-breech): Perennial old world thistle-like shrub; decorative leaves provided pattern for capitals of Corinthian columns. Semi-hardy, full sun in rich, well-drained soils. 2' tall with large spineless leaves. Protect.

AUCUBA JAPONICA nana: Asiatic. 18"-2' high. Hardy, dwarf evergreen; waxy, dark green leaves. Clusters of bright red berries fall and winter. Must have male and female plants to produce berries. Shady, moist, humus soil with good drainage.
    AUCUBA JAPONICA, variegata (Gold-Dust Tree): 3'-5'. Form and culture similar to above, leaves larger, longer, with golden yellow spots.

CARISSA GRANDIFLORA, dwarf ('Boxwood Beauty'): to 2'. Compact upright growth. No thorns; tolerates pruning. White star-like flowers, red fruit.

HEDERA CANARIENSIS (Algerian Ivy): Hardy to 17°. Leaves 5″-8″ wide. Lobes more widely spaced than English Ivy. Moisture and semi-shade. Fine wall or ground cover.

IXORA COCCINEA (Jungleflame): Tropical evergreen. Handsome woody plant, bushy growth. Tender. Fibrous loam with peat and sharp sand. Prune after flowering. Light shade. Flowers.
I. acuminata: white.
I. chinesis: red to orange.
I. fulgens: scarlet.

JACOBINIA CARNEA: 2-3′. American shrubby plant of Acanthus family. Rosy-pink flowers most of the year if in protected sunny location; good loamy soil. Excellent for color.

SKIMMIA JAPONICA ('Dwarf Female'): Asiatic. Dwarf shrub of slow growth. Moist loam, partial shade. Healthy and hardy. Fragrant, creamy flowers. Male and female plants necessary to produce scarlet berries.
S. Reevesiana: To 2′. Flowers; dark red berries.
S.R. variegata: White-edged leaves.

ZAMIA INTEGRIFOLIA, (Coontie—Cycad): in species. Dwarf, 2′-3′, wide leaflets, stiff and leathery. Palm-like. Sandy moist loam, well-drained. Shade or semi-shade. Hardy.

TROPICAL AND SEMI-TROPICAL PLANTS FOR POTS, TUBS AND PLANTING AREAS

CARISSA, var. 'Minima' (Dwarf Natal-plum): 1-1½′. Full sun. Superior foliage.

CHAMAEROPS HUMILIS (Mediterranean Fan Palm): North Africa. Dwarf. Hardy, satisfactory low-growing palm. All fronds come from base of plant, giving desirable shape for container or ground planting. Fibrous loam with well-mixed leaf mold and sand. Palms must be watered freely in summer, not allowed to dry in winter.

CODIAEUM VARIEGATUM, dwarf varieties also (Croton): Extensively grown in warm or protected regions. Ornamental foliage varies in form and color. Mass in sunny place for tropical summer effect. Rich, fibrous loam with leaf mold and sand. Some shade in heat of day to prevent leaf burning. Gradually move indoors for winter; feed monthly, bright light, keep moist.

CORTADERIA SELLOWIANA (Pampas Grass): Low maintenance, 3′-5′, excellent for noise abatement. Showy fall plume. Drought resistant. Sun.

CROSSANDRA INFUNDIBULIFORMIS (Crossandra): India-Malaya. Deep green, waxy leaves. Dense terminal spikes of salmon-colored, funnel-shaped flowers. Protect.

CYCUS REVOLUTA (Sago Palm): Ancient, primitive plant. Good outdoor specimen. In tubs thrives in good sandy loam, with drainage and abundant moisture in the growing season. Stiff, evergreen leaves in rosette form on strong trunk.

DION EDULE (Chestnut Dion): 2′-5′. Graceful, gray fern-like leaves from a pineapple-like trunk. Leaves rigid, leaflets sharp-pointed. Light shade, well-drained soil. Plant away from passing traffic to prevent bruising leaf points. Hardy to 15°.
D. SPINULOSUM (Mexican Cycad): Slimmer, taller trunk and longer leaves than *D. Edule.* To 5′ indoors, generally below 10′. Less hardy but same culture as *D. Edule.* Protect below 26°.

ERYTHEA ARMATA (Mexican Blue Palm): Beautiful powder blue fan leaves. Arching flower stalk. Slow growth to 25′. Very hardy. Best with green background.

FATSHEDERA LIZEI: A true hybrid between *Fatsia Japonica* and English Ivy. Leaves dark green 3″-5″ lobes like large ivy. Needs support. Shape by pinching and pruning.

LIVISTONA CHINENSIS (Chinese Fan Palm): Shade. Weeping effect. Medium size. Very hardy. Needs good drainage.

PAUROTIS WRIGHTII (Everglades Fan Palm): Native. Clustering form with slender 4′-6′ trunk up to 30′ tall. Slow-growing.

PHILODENDRON SELLOUM (Philodendron Tree): Large leaves. Interesting trunk pattern, unusual roots; primeval. Tender under 20°. Semi-shade, very moist soil mixture of loam, leaf mold and sharp sand. Very tropical effect.
P. SELLOUM JUVENILE: Same as above but smaller growth pattern.
P. 'EVANSII': Giant wavy-edge leaves to 6′. Rapid growth with ample water. Also dwarf form.

PHOENIX CANARIENSIS (Canary Island Date Palm): Large, fast growth to 75′. Dark green feathery leaves. Huge trunk. Good drainage.
P. RECLINATA (Senegal Date Palm): Picturesque leaning trunks. Very hardy, any good soil, requires good drainage.

PLUMERIA (Frangipani): Shrub or small tree, deciduous. Long pointed wide leaves. Fragrant 2″ waxy flowers. Sun. Tender.
P. RUBRA: Pink to bright red flowers.
P.R. ACUTIFOLIA: White or pink flowers.
P. ALBA: Yellow to white flowers.

POLYSTICHUM SETOSUM: Feathery fern; new fronds develop from crown. Rich, moist loam in shade. Tender under 30°.

RHAPIS HUMILIS (Slender Ladypalm): 4′-6′ clustering stems. A reed-like oriental palm of ancient genus. Excellent in tubs or protected areas in beds. Well-drained, rich sandy loam. Protect.

SABAL TEXANA (Texas Palmetto): Attractive trunk and leaves, to 50′. Hardy and robust. One of the best sabals.

ERENOA REPENS (Saw Palmetto): A dwarf palm with silvery foliage forming clumps. Good for shade. Very hardy. Keep moist.

OLANDRA GUTTATA (Cup of Gold): North Africa. Strong climbing evergreen, huge golden funnel-shaped flowers. Large, glossy green leaves. Rich soil kept damp. Beautiful pruned to tree shape in container. Tender.

S. G. DWARF: Same quality as above, but compact mass of flowers at early age. Tender.

TRELITZIA REGINAE (Bird-of-Paradise Flower): South African, 3'-4'. Banana-like foliage. Blooms bright orange and blue. Good drainage, rich sandy loam. Plenty of moisture as growth starts, but keep fairly dry during dormancy. Sun, southern exposure. Semi-hardy.

S. NICOLAI (giant variety): Rapid growth. White flowers, large banana-like leaves. Tender below 22°.

S. PARVIFOLIA: Shorter leaves, bright orange flowers, green bracts edged with red.

TABERNAEMONTANA GRANDIFLORA (Carnation of India): Asiatic. 4'-5'. Foliage similar to gardenia, but resistant to white fly. Flowers small, double, white, fragrant. Acid soil, some sun, much water. Tender.

T. CORONARIA: Smaller leaves, more compact.

TRACHYCARPUS MARTIANUS (Windmill Palm): to 50'. Slim trunk, devoid of fibers; more graceful than *T. fortunei.* Slow growing, hardy, desirable.

T. TAKIL: Neat dwarf. Slow-growing, to 6'. Hardy, rare.

WASHINGTONIA FILIFERA (Desert Palm): Very hardy. Trunk to 3' diameter, 60' tall. Common, easy. Plant in clumps of assorted heights.

ZAMIA: Very good for pots. Tolerates cold weather, attractive on terrace for winter. Organic matter in soil, regular watering key to success here. Prune in spring. Remove dead leaves.

MISCELLANEOUS TROPICAL PLANTS

AGAVE AMERICANA (Century Plant): Long, stiff leaves forming rosettes from which rise tall, bar flower stems. Native of semi-arid regions of America. Porous soil, good drainage. Many varieties.

CYPERUS ALTERNIFOLIUS (Umbrella Plant): Cultivated Sedge, long stems with large palm-like heads. Very good for patios and in pots. Grows in water or in dry places.

PHORMIUM TENAX (New Zealand Flax): Makes striking groups. To 15', with long, narrow leaves and numerous dark red flowers clustered on long stems. Showy color forms, variegated reddish-purple foliage.

P. COLENSOI: To 7', less rigid leaves, yellow flowers.

BAMBOOS

Bambusa multiple. (Hedge Bamboo): Fern-like leaves—long, glabrous, deep green, silver cast beneath; forms clumps to 10' in height.
B. multiple. nana (Dwarf Bamboo): 3-4'. Woody, hollow, green purplish grass-like canes.

Phyllostachys Niger (Black-Jointed Bamboo): 8-10'. Black cane, sparse, medium-sized leaves, delicate growth pattern. Hardy to 15°, moist soil.

Sasa Pygmaea (Pygmaea Bamboo): Rarely over 8'', creeping rootstock, dense clumps. Small, leathery leaves, deep green. Excellent ground cover; moisture.

BANANAS*

Musa ensete (Abyssinian Banana): Very large ornamental; leaves originating from base of trunk. Dark red veins on mature leaves. 12'-15'. Semi-shade and moisture. Any good soil.

Musa rosacea (Pink Banana or Indian Banana): 8'-10' tall. Large, pink flowers all summer. Semi-shade and moisture.

Musa paradisiaca sapientum (Plantain or Common Banana): India. Tree-like; to 25'. Spiralling leaves, yellow flowers, purplish bracts. Edible fruit; the stem dies after fruiting but is replaced by new suckers. Fairly rich soil with moisture.

Musa Sumatrana (Sumatra Banana): Semi-dwarf. Leaves long and narrow, reddish-brown underneath, green and brown spots on top. Well-moistened, fibrous soil, semi-shade, 4'-6'.

HARDY TREES FOR SUN

Bauhinia corniculata (White Orchid Tree) Small tree with bloom summer to late August. Protect when young. Any soil. Grows in shade or sun.

Calliandra Guildingi (Trinidad Flame Bush): Small tree related to mimosa. Bright red flowers cover entire plant in spring and fall; scattered bloom in summer.

Camphor officinanum (Camphor Tree): Beautiful, slow-growing evergreen with bright green leaves, fragrant foliage and flowers. Best as multi-trunked specimen. Do not plant near paved area.

Viburnum japonicum: Large, bright green leaves and clusters of small white flowers. Fast-growing. Excellent small, multi-trunked tree. Many other viburnums available.

Xylosma senticosa: Excellent small tree. To 20'. Shiny bright green leaves. Spines on branches make it good barrier plant.

SEMI-HARDY TREES

Cupaniopsis anacardioides (Carrotwood Tree): Fast-growing, to 40'. Pinnate-leaved tree, tolerant of wet soils or poor drainage. Very attractive foliage.

Grevillea robusta (Silk Oak): Fern-like, dark green foliage. Fast-growing. Hardiness increases with age.

Laurus nobilis (Grecian Bay Tree): The bay leaves for cookery come from this tree. Fragrant, light green magnolia-like foliage. Requires excellent drainage.

Stenocarpus sinuatus (Firewheel Tree): Large, shiny, dark green oak-like foliage. Circular, bright red-orange flowers.

PLANTS FOR THE SHADE

Alsophila cooperi (Australian Tree Fern): Rapid-growing; 20 to 30'. Hardy to 32°. Good organic soil and even moisture. Excellent in container.

Dicksonia antarctica (Tasmanian Tree Fern): Slower than above, but much hardier. Protect under 20°. Good organic soil and even moisture. Fine in containers.

Tibouchina semidecandra (Brazilian Spider Flower): Large shrub or small tree with velvety leaves and purple flowers. Spectacular. Almost evergreen; rapid-growing. If frozen will sprout from base. Excellent as single trunk standard in container. Slightly acid, well-drained soil with roots in shade, top in sun. Pinch for bushiness.

---

*All members of the banana family may be damaged by freezing but put on new growth next spring.

Container Gardening

If eyes were made for seeing,
Then beauty is its own excuse for being.
—Emerson

You can decorate your home with a wide variety of plants attractively arranged, from collections of tiny cacti to indoor gardens complete with pool or fountain, choosing some plants for lush foliage, others for bloom. Since potted plants have individual requirements, each must be provided with a micro-climate best suited to its particular needs. Although this may limit flexibility of placement, potted plants can be interestingly positioned nonetheless, keeping in mind the proportion of plant form and leaf to the surroundings.

Massed plants enjoy the humidity obtained by the proximity of many leaves and damp soil, yet they may be watered, fed, turned, or removed according to individual needs. The amount of shade or light can usually be controlled by proper placement in the group.

Success with potted plants depends on several factors: light, temperature, air, growing medium, moisture, container, and how well these are combined.

Exposure: The best temperature for potted plants is 72°, but indoor plants must be able to live in the normal temperature of the house, whatever their native preferences. As long as the temperature stays between 50° and 100°, plants can adapt. The placement of a potted plant to receive its proper amount of light is of primary importance. Without it photosynthesis cannot occur.

Flowering plants and cacti need as much light as possible, at least three hours of sun each day in a south or east window. Most foliage plants—the philodendrons, dieffenbachias, draceanas etc.—thrive in the bright light or partial sun of north or west exposures. However, there are plants, such as spathiphyllum, ferns, and some bromeliads, which do well in diffused interior light. Most tropical plants need 50 to 90% of direct sun filtered as through sheer curtains. Regardless of location, all should regularly be turned a quarter to keep growth straight and balanced. Artificial light, either from an incandescent 100-watt bulb or a fluorescent tube, may supplement sunlight or entirely supplant it. Plants that have become spindly and lustreless through lack of light may be rejuvenated by a summer in the garden, but take care to accustom them to sunshine gradually.

Hardy plants thrive in ordinary garden beds; others need bottom pot protection from marauding insects. Layers of charcoal and/or gravel serve this purpose. In our mild climate, the out-of-doors may be used as both hospital and nursery most of the year, making possible more luxuriant growth and a much wider selection of potted plants.

Watering. The amount and frequency of watering depends on the size and type of plant and container, the stage of growth, and the humidity. A plant putting out new growth needs more water than it does during its resting period. Furnace heat in winter and air conditioning in summer draw moisture from the plants, necessitating more frequent watering. However, too much water is as harmful as too little and will soon kill the plant. It is said that more potted plants are killed by overwatering than by anything else, for the water fills the air spaces in the soil and depletes the oxygen that roots require. When the surface soil seems light and dry, it is time to water. Rainwater is ideal when available. Using tepid water, especially during winter, avoids shocking the plant. Occasionally allow the pot to stand in water just long enough to soak the soil thoroughly. Additional moisture must be supplied by misting once a week or by putting the plant out in a warm, gentle rain.

Smooth-leaved plants may be cleaned gently with a detergent, skimmed milk or dry milk in solution, followed by clear water. Never use oil and never leave a filmy deposit on the leaves. Dust the foliage of hairy-leaved plants with a pipe-cleaner or small paint brush. If a plant becomes waterlogged, repot it immediately in fresh soil. A white crust on the outside of the pot may be due to a salt build-up. Flood the soil by watering thoroughly about ten times in succession and clean crust off container.

Feeding. A newly purchased plant usually has sufficient food for about a month. Apply a water-soluble plant food every month thereafter, sufficient to soak the soil entirely, not just the surface. Commercial preparations are popular, using the concentration recommended on the label for indoor plants. Frequent application of a weak feeding solution is more beneficial than an occasional heavy dose. Plants grown entirely under artificial light require only $1/3$ the amount of fertilizer used by similar plants growing in natural light.

Repotting. Even with adequate food the soil's fertility diminishes, so most plants need to be repotted every few years. Check by holding upside down and tapping pot until plant slides out. If the roots are a solid mass it is time to repot. The new pot should be only slightly larger than the old one. Always use clean, scrubbed pots. Soak the pot thoroughly, cover drainage hole with concave pieces of broken flower pot, and add a layer of crocking (small chips or gravel). Follow with a layer of coarse compost material or sphagnum moss, and lastly some fresh soil. Graduated layers assure good drainage, and they will vary in thickness with the size of the pot. Gently rub old dirt and chips from the plant ball, and set it in the pot so the top of the ball will be about 1 inch below the rim to allow room for watering. Firm new soil around the sides, keeping the same soil level as before, and water thoroughly. A good general potting soil mixture contains 2 parts loam to 1 part rough leaf mold (or peat moss), 1 part coarse sand and $1/2$ part manure and bone meal, but other mixtures are also used.

Based on ten years of research, the Texas Agricultural Experiment Station recommends the following growing medium for potted plants grown indoors:

$1/2$ bushel peat moss
$1/2$ bushel horticultural grade perlite
2 ounces 20% superphosphate
2 ounces dolomitic limestone
2 ounces gypsum
4 ounces slow-available complete fertilizer with a 1-2-1 ratio.
(1 bushel = 8 gallons)

To be satisfactory any potting mixture must support the plant mechanically, allow circulation of air throughout, and retain adequate moisture. The recommended mixture meets these requirements and more: it weighs about 50% less than most soil-containing mixtures; the ingredients are easily obtained, uniform in grade, inexpensive and sterile; it is disease resistant, drains well, and neither shrinks nor expands with continuous watering. The mixture can be prepared and kept available until needed.

When a plant has reached a desirable size its growth may be slowed down by tapering off both water and food to a subsistence level, and by pinch-pruning new growth tips. If repotting is indicated, yet a larger pot would be unwieldy, the top soil may be redressed, or some of the bottom roots pruned away to make room for fresh soil in the same pot. Root pruning must always be balanced by top pruning.

Hanging Baskets. Hanging baskets offer an engaging way to add vertical accents and movement to your garden. They are especially useful to gardeners with limited space, and they lend a decorative touch to patios, terraces, and decks. The choice of plant material is extensive. Emphasize color, interesting form, cascading habit, or texture of foliage.

The intended location is the first consideration in plant selection. Will the basket hang in total shade, filtered light or sun? Will it be above or below eye level? Will it be subject to strong breezes?

SUGGESTIONS FOR BASKETS

Flowering Plants in Sun: marigolds, periwinkle, cascading petunias, dwarf chrysanthemums, verbena, lantana, ivy geraniums or perhaps trailing nasturtiums, Snow-on-the-Mountain (*Euphorbia marginata*).

Flowering in Filtered Light: Achimenes, impatiens and begonias.

Attractive Foliage in Shade: Caladiums (upright growth), Swedish ivy (*Plectranthus australis*), air plant (*Chlorophytum*), ferns and ivies.

Foliage Plants for Sun: coleus, velvet plant (*Gynura aurantica*), copperleaf (*Acalypha wilkesiana*), chenille plant (*Acalypha hispida*) or wandering jew in various forms.

Edibles: thyme, mint, cherry-type tomatoes and strawberries.

Plants grown in hanging baskets require more water than those grown in other containers because they are exposed on all sides to wind and evaporation. Thus they also need more frequent feeding because the nutrients tend to be leached out by the water. The soil must be fertile and well-draining yet moisture-retentive. Do not fertilize a newly planted basket until the plants begin healthy growth after the shock of transplanting. A suggested soil mixture is 2 parts organic matter (peat moss, fine pine bark mulch, compost) and 1 part mineral matter (soil, sand, perlite, vermiculite). Another popular mixture is equal parts of sand, peat moss, and loam. To each of these mixtures add a small amount of time-release fertilizer. The light-weight planting medium recommended earlier in this chapter is helpful for baskets.

Several types of containers are usable as hanging baskets. Each has advantages and disadvantages. Galvanized wire or plastic baskets of open design must be lined with damp sphagnum moss (with the green side facing outward) thick enough so that no light shows through, and then filled with soil. With these baskets you can set plants on all sides to provide a very full effect, but they require more frequent watering and have less space for soil because of the necessary thickness of the moss. Or you can line the basket with clear or milky plastic just inside the moss; fill and plant; then perforate plastic for drainage. Nylon net is another possibility as a liner.

Clay or ceramic containers are porous, so these, too, need frequent watering, though not so frequent as the moss baskets, but they are heavier. Plastic baskets need less water and afford more space for growing medium.

Water the selected plants prior to composing a hanging basket, so they will slip out without injury to the roots. Set gently in place, allowing enough space around them for future growth. Firm the plants in the soil, and water to settle the root system. Keep them out of the sun for several days until the plants appear to have recovered from the move.

Feed about every two weeks with a light, water-soluble fertilizer suitable for potted plants. The soil in the basket should be moist, never dry, before feeding. To keep plants in hanging baskets lush and symmetrical, frequently pinch off tips of each lateral.

Though hanging baskets do require more care, they provide such unusual effects that gardeners seem not just willing but eager to meet their needs.

Terrariums. Terrariums are clear, transparent containers holding miniature gardens for pleasurable viewing in the home. The container should have a removable top or a piece of clear glass or even Saran wrap to use as such. The cover is kept on most of the time to provide moisture in the container. Wash the container thoroughly and rinse with hydrogen peroxide, lest the residue from the former contents prove harmful to plants. Use about ½ inch of gravel sprinkled with activated charcoal as the bottom layer. Mix 9 parts potting soil to 1 part activated charcoal and use as a 1-inch layer over the gravel.

Water the plants you are going to use so the soil will be damp when you place them in the terrarium. Gently remove most of the soil, taking great care to avoid injuring the roots, trying to leave a little soil ball around the roots. Do not overcrowd your tiny garden; the plants must have room to grow. Dig a hole barely large enough to insert the little plants' roots. Place the plants and cover firmly but tenderly with soil. Water just to moisten the roots. Water can be added, but not subtracted. Overwatering is the terrarium's worst enemy. Just two or three teaspoons of water, or a quick misting, is sufficient for a small terrarium about six inches in diameter. Now add any decorative items such as pebbles or figures.

Plants that bloom require more sun than those that do not, with a few exceptions like spathiphyllum. Annuals and perennials can bloom in the house if they have adequate sun. A plant brought into flower outside may be enjoyed for a few days in the house, but probably will not flower again until given adequate sunlight outside.

SOME PLANTS COMMONLY GROWN IN CONTAINERS

AFRICAN VIOLET, in variety, (*Saintpaulia*): Small gesneriad, 4″-6″ tall, with rosettes of hairy, green-to-bronze leaves, forming plant about 10″ broad; flowers in single or double forms, from white through pinks to purples. Bright, indirect or filtered light. Water just enough to keep evenly moist, not wet. Misting cleans leaves. Feed monthly. Pot in equal parts loam, peat moss, sand.

AIRPLANE PLANT *(Chlorophytum)*: Long thin green or variegated leaves in bushy plant with drooping racemes which bloom and then produce plantlets at ends. Medium to strong light. Moist but not wet. Feed monthly. Easy.

ALUMINUM PLANT *(Pilea cadierei)*: Small plant to 12″, leaves with puffy design of metallic-gray color, resembling watermelon markings. Average light. Keep barely moist. Feed half-strength every two months. Normal potting soil. Dwarf form *P. cadierei minima,* and *P. crassifolia; P. involucrata; P. pubescens; P.* 'Silver Tree'.

ARALIA ELEGANTISSIMA *(Dizygotheca)* or FALSE ARALIA: 3-5′ plant of upright growth with leaflets of long thin jagged leaves like fingers of a hand. Foliage begins coppery, turning black-green as it unfolds. Bright to medium light, average humidity; keep soil barely moist. Propagate from stem cuttings spring or summer.

ARAUCARIA, in variety
(A. excelsa) NORFOLK ISLAND PINE: Symmetrical tree with branches of evenly whorled dark green leaves of fine texture. Beautiful Christmas tree (without lights); good patio tree. Long-lived. Bright indirect or filtered light. Keep soil on dry side or barely moist. Mist foliage. Fertilize sandy soil with organic matter, well-drained. Feed twice during growing season.
A. IMBRICATA (Monkey Puzzle Tree): Hardy outdoors; prickly branches twist and turn in tortuous fashion.
A. BIDWILLI (Bunya-Bunya): glossy green-leaved Australian tree with sharp pointed leaves.

ASPIDISTRA ELATIOR or A. LURIDA (Cast Iron Plant): Leathery, dark green shiny, long leaves arching from base. Survives with neglect, but thrives with care. Likes shadowless north window light, with soil barely moist at all times. Feed monthly, spring through early fall. *A. elatior variegata* has white stripes on leaves that disappear if plant is fed too much. Never place in sun.

BROMELIADS, in variety: All bromeliads grow outside in Houston in warm weather, but it is essential to accustom them to sunshine gradually or their foliage will burn. Bromeliads grown as house plants should be kept in bright light. Any well-draining growing medium which anchors the roots, such as osmunda, fern bark, or a mixture of equal parts of peat moss, perlite and sand is recommended for bromeliad culture. Some bromeliads can be attractively attached to a tree trunk, a wood slab, or a piece of driftwood by tying with strips of nylon hose or by gluing. Used this way they need frequent misting. Water in cup of plant until it overflows around roots. Do not overwater. Feed with ¼ strength balanced, water-soluble fertilizer; pour around root system, not in cup. There are about 40 genera and hundreds of species of bromeliads, each with its own stylistic form and fascinating coloring of leaves, bracts, and flowers. Though each plant blooms only once, it will remain attractive for years if given proper care. Bromeliads form pups which can be removed from the mother plant and potted when at least half the size of the mother. Need winter protection.

BULBS, in variety

CALADIUM: Variegated, colorful foliage, moderately rich, loose soil with good drainage; shade or part shade; moist, but not soggy. Water every day in summer heat. Plant 2″ deep. Pinch off blooms; they rob plants of food needed to produce leaves. Very colorful summer patio or garden plant until cool fall nights.

CLIVIA: See "Bulbs" Planting Chart. *C. CYRTANTHIFLORA* and *C. MINIATA* (both called Kafir Lily): Waxy strap-like, dark green leaves arching from bulb; clusters of flowers on single tall 14′ stalk; lily-like flowers orange to red with yellow throats. Allow to become crowded before repotting.

EUCHARIS GRANDIFLORA or *E. AMA-ZONICA* (Amazon Lily): Fragrant, waxy white flowers 2″ across, in clusters on stalks 1′ tall, several times a year. Shade outside; low bright light inside. Potting soil with sharp sand or perlite, kept very moist; withhold water for few weeks in winter to force bloom. Feed balanced fertilizer during growing season.

CACTUS, in variety: Most are native to America. Similar to succulents. Usually leafless with ability to store water in their stems (cylinders, joints or pods). Evaporation is lessened by thick skin, and spines discourage foraging animals. Bright flowers and interesting forms. Feed and water well in hot weather. Encourage dormancy by tapering-off feeding.

CALATHEA zebrina: Bold vigorous plant to 3′, with magnificent deep velvety leaves, having mid-rib and lateral veins yellow, palish green above, purple beneath. Good medium light. Keep evenly moist, but very well drained. Rich soil. Grouping around larger plants increases needed humidity.

CHINESE EVERGREEN *(Aglaonema commutatum)*: Large, dark green lanceolate leaves emerging closely from stalk to 24″ tall. No direct sun, but bright light. Good soil kept evenly moist. *A. treubi* is variegated form with arrow shaped leaves; needs medium to bright light. Both grow in water.

CHRISTMAS CACTUS *(Zygocactus truncatus or Schlumbergera bridgesii)*: Epiphyte to 2′ across; branches arching; red flowers at joint ends.

CRAB CACTUS *(S. truncata)*: Smaller plant with varying color flowers. Medium to bright light; 6-8 weeks of lower light and short days to bloom. When buds form move plant gradually into brighter light. Keep evenly moist. High-phosphate food monthly.

CRASSULA ARGENTEA (Jade Tree): Many species, native of South Africa. Long-lived. Medium to bright filtered light. Do not overwater. Tree form to 3′ with small fleshy leaves on branches. Leaves store water and show need for it with wrinkled look. Water only when necessary. Pinkish-white bloom about Christmas. Feed lightly each month with complete house plant fertilizer. Can stand heat and drought. Pot in very well-drained mixture of 2 parts loam, 1 part sand and charcoal or wood ashes with a little ground limestone.

CURCULIGO CAPITULATA (recurvata): Stemless plant from Java, of Amaryllis family, with cluster of attractive foliage almost hiding yellow flowers. Leaves have ribbed or plaited look. Medium light, warm humid atmosphere, about 75°. Soil: good drainage in mixture of sand, loam, peat moss with a little limestone and bone meal.

DEVIL'S IVY, POTHOS *(Scindapus aureus)*: Tropical vine adapting well to low light and humidity. Green and white heart-shaped leaves. Any soil or in water. Easy and attractive.

DRACAENA, in variety: Bright indirect light, 65°-85°. Keep soil moist but never allow to stand in water. Average potting soil. Do not fertilize recently purchased or potted plants; feed at six month intervals. Varieties differ in appearance.

D. DEREMENSIS ('Janet Craig'): Strap-like, shiny, long dark green leaves.

D'WARNECKI': Sword-like stiff leaves 7-12″ long, white stripes on gray-green leaves.

D. FRAGRANS MASSANGEANA: To 6′ with leaves almost 30″ long and 3″ wide, having yellow stripe down middle, called Cornstalk Plant.

D. MARGINATA To 8′ tall. Looks like Spanish dagger with clusters of 14″ thin pointed leaves.

DUMB CANE (Dieffenbachia): Upright growth of large 14″ leaves, variegated, emerging from stalk. Leaves arch gracefully as plant grows, but lower leaves finally drop off leaving tall snake-like stalk. Adapts to medium-low light. Don't water until soil is dry. Feed monthly. Dieffenbachias are poisonous when eaten and can paralyze vocal cords. Protect children.

ECHEVERIA, in variety: American succulents with rosettes of fleshy leaves which retain water. Flowers in panicles, spikes or racemes. Good light. Easy on water; allow to dry thoroughly. Soil of ½ sand, ½ compost, and a little bone meal. Easy to propagate.

EUPHORBIA SPLENDENS (Crown of Thorns): Orange red blooms on spiny gray-green stalks to 12″. Bright light, average potting soil.

E. LACTEA CRISTATA: Distorted spiny growth of compact form, 2-3′ tall.

E. TIRUCALLI-Pencil Tree or Cactus.

FERNS, in variety: One of oldest plant forms with a multitude of species, most of similar culture: rich, loose organic soil, lots of peat moss, kept evenly moist with high humidity and part to full shade. Lower temperature than most plants. Keep dead fronds cut off and protect from injury. Feed lightly. Sun bleaches and burns ferns. Springeri (Asparagus), in variety, is kept moist to dry, and is exception because it will take sun, though it bleaches. Light green needle-like leaves on vining or branching thin stalks. Develops little tubers on top of soil when pot-bound; repot. Cascading habit.

ASPLENIUM NIDUS (Bird's Nest Fern): Attractive rosette of broad upright leaves, to 30"; reduce humidity during winter.

PLATYCERIUM BIFURCATUM (Elk or Stag-horn Fern): Epiphyte; grows attached to another object, but not a parasite. Native to rain forest in Asia. Fairly bright light. Fibrous moss to which plant is attached must be kept moist. Water twice weekly. Feed fish oil monthly, after watering; can be hung on wall in winter, or on tree in summer.

NEPHROLEPIS EXALTATA, 'Bostoniense' (Boston Fern): Classic parlor plant. Graceful arching fronds. *Whitmannii* and *Rooseveltii* are more feathery and finely cut. Cool north light. Water when dry.

FICUS BENJAMINA (Weeping or Benjamin Fig): Tree with branches weeping from dense head on trunk, dark green small, shiny, laurel-like leaves. To 15'. Bright light but no direct sun. Evenly moist. Rich garden loam with compost or potting soil. Condition to any change gradually. Will drop leaves if moved too suddenly, in too dark an area or in draft as from air-conditioner vent. Mist. In proper location, very attractive small tree for house.

FICUS ELASTICA (Rubber Tree): Grows to 15' in sprawling habit; very large dark green oval-long leaves from stalk. Good filtered light half day at least. Keep evenly moist in average, well-drained soil. Wipe off leaves and mist. Sudden temperature change may cause leaf drop.

FICUS LYRATA (Fiddle-Leaf Rubber Plant): Large oblong dark green prominantly veined leaves from upright trunk. Good in dark corners; burns in sun. Wants high humidity, but do not water until completely dry. Sponge leaves for humidity. Needs good drainage. Overwatering signified by large black spots on leaves.

FITTONIA ARGYONEURA: Silver-veined strong mosaic pattern; *F. verschaeffeltii* has red veining. Creeping plants for very warm, humid area. 2-4" leaves are unusual in patterning. Low light of north window or in terrarium. Placing pot on pebbles in water-filled saucer keeps humidity high. Average potting soil. Keep soil moist and feed monthly with half-strength fertilizer, very lightly.

GRAPE IVY *(Cissus Rhombifolia):* Shiny green leaves in threes. Filtered sun for medium light. Standard potting soil. Keep moist. Roots in water. Good for hanging baskets. Ivy does not grow very well in house unless it is placed outside in shade frequently, but grows well in containers in shade. English Ivy (Hedera Helix), Hahn's Ivy are good varieties.

KALANCHOE: Succulent. Small flowers in flower heads red, yellow, orange-red, orange. Leaves fleshy, to 3", oval. Dwarf form available. Needs good, airy light but no noonday sun. Likes short days to bloom. Keep out of drafts. Don't stand in water, but keep evenly moist. Allow to dry out. Average potting soil on gritty side with good drainage. Feed monthly, when growing and blooming.

LEOPARD PLANT *(Ligularia tussilaginea aureo-maculata):* Large rounded leaves, blotched cream and yellow; yellow daisy-type flowers. Any garden soil. Bright light.

NEPHTHYTIS *(Syngonium podophyllum):* Arrow-shaped leaves, very dark green on vining-type plant. Adapts well to low light and low humidity of house. Grows in water and is good for totem pole. Average soil.

ORCHIDS: Thousands of species some from hot jungles, others from cool mountains, not easily grown in Houston except in greenhouse. The terrestrial varieties grow in loose, moist soil rich in organic matter like humus; require continuing supply of food and moisture as well as sun; Cymbidiums, their hybrids and dwarf forms are in this category. The epiphytics grow perched on tree branches, getting their food from air, rain and any decaying organic matter they can reach with their roots; Cattleyas, their hybrids and dwarf forms belong in this cateogry. Phalaenopsis and Vanda are among most tolerant of house conditions. Orchids must have ample circulation of humid air, temperature from 60° to 80°, no direct noon sun, but good light. Experiment to find proper location in your home for these beautifully-flowering plants.

PALMS: A large diversified family with some producing foliage at top of bare trunk while others put out fronds in clusters. Most come from tropical or sub-tropical areas. Some of the hardier types are listed in "The Tropical Garden." Indoors, palms like to be in good average potting soil, very well-drained, in a not too big container in bright indirect light.

RHAPIS EXCELSA (Lady Palm): 5-12" tall, slow growth, tolerant of poor light and drought, responds to good light and feeding; hardy to 22 degrees.

RHAPIS HUMILIS (Bamboo Palm): Tall to 15', bamboo-like stalks of grace and charm; likes east window filtered light. Feed lightly to retard rapid growth. Water weekly or bi-weekly.

ARECA *(Chrysalisdocarpus lutescens):* Feathery, yellow-green arching fronds with yellow stems; needs light (6-8 hrs.). Keep evenly moist and mist foliage. Fertilize monthly with organic food. Prefers to be outside in light, but not sun. Iron and nitrogen feeding and outdoor light may revive it after a stint indoors.

HOWEIA, in variety: *H. belmoreana (Kentia belmoreana),* sentry or curly palm; *H. forsteriana (K. forsteriana),* flat, thatch-leaf or paradise palm. Both are fine for indoors. Slow growth, graceful feathery arching leaves with slender leaflets. Sentry spreads in habit; Paradise attains vase-shape; both have single trunks, but 2 or 3 may be placed in same pot for effect of multiple trunks.

PONY TAIL or ELEPHANT-FOOT PALM *(Beaucarnea recurvata* or *Nolina recurvata* or *N.*

tuberculata): Tall-growing, with slender drooping leaves at top of bare stalk emerging from huge bulbous swelling of trunk at soil level which serves as water reservoir; direct sunlight at least 4 hours daily or very bright indirect light. Allow soil to dry out between waterings. General purpose potting soil. Feed established plants only once annually.

CARYOTA MITIS (Fishtail Palm): Name reflects shape of leaves on stems rising upwards before branching from center; likes small pot with bright light, wet soil, and monthly feeding spring until fall.

C. URENS (Wine Palm): Tall with solitary trunk, broad dark green leaves, very long. Warm, moist air. Not too wet during winter.

NEANTHE BELLA *(Chamaedorea elegans):* Dwarf form, growing in clusters of dark green fronds to about 2' tall. Fine table plant with medium light; also outdoors in part shade in summer.

SANSEVIERIA THYRSIFLORA (Common Snake Plant): Tropical succulent of lily family; erect stiff, pointed, basal leaves, variegated or mottled in green, and yellow or white. Very easy. Low sunlight. General potting soil kept moderately dry. Feed every 3 or 4 months while growing.

SCHEFFLERA *(Brassaia actinophylla):* Large glossy green leaves in bushy form to 12' tall. Good filtered light most of day. Avoid air vents. Sandy fertile potting soil, well-drained. Feed once or twice monthly when growing. Medium moisture and misting but leaves turn yellow with overwatering.

PEDILANTHUS TITHYMALOIDES VARIEGATUS, also *EUPHORBIA T.V.* (Redbird Cactus): To 3'. Stems have zigzag effect bending slightly at each leaf; pointed leaves variegated green and white with pink edge; flowers small, red, appearing at tips of stems. Bright indirect light, average potting soil kept barely moist. Feed only spring through summer at 2- or 3-month intervals. CAUTION: Milky juice in stems is caustic and irritant.

PEPEROMIA, in variety: Low-growing table plants with foliage of varying designs. *P. arifolia argyreia* (Watermelon Plant), *P. caperata* 'Emerald Ripple' with dark green, very wrinkled leaves on red stems. Average to bright light. Allow soil to dry out between waterings. Feed every 3-4 months with half-strength house plant food.

PRAYER PLANT *(Maranta leuconeura):* Name derives from fact leaves move upward at dark as though in prayer. Table plant; grows well under lamp. Light makes leaves move back into normal position. To 9" tall. *M.l. kerchoveana* has grayish green leaves that have, when young, reddish spots resembling animal tracks. *M.l. massangeana's* leaves have fishbone patterned veins and purple undersides.

PHILODENDRON, in variety.

P. PERTUSUM: Sold as Split-Leaf Philodendron, is actually *Monstera deliciosa,* an evergreen vining plant with very large leaves needing filtered shade outdoors, rich soil, ample water and a stout support. Must have good drainage. Protect from freeze. Indoors same culture; keep leaves clean.

P. OXYCARDUM (Heartleaf): Name describes leaves which are small, medium green and vining, usually grown on a support.

P. SAO PAOLO: Vigorous with deeply frilled leaves.

P. EICHLERI: Very large, hardy, self-heading hybrid, resistant to sun.

P. GLORIOSUM: Rosette form with ivory ribs.

P. IMBE: Vine with dark red spots.

P. SODIROI: Vine with silvery gray spots and red stems.

P. SELLOUM: Hardy, bold, to 4' tall, spreading to 6', with short trunk and handsome leaves, long and wide, deeply cut. The *P.s. 'Lundii'* is more compact. Excellent plant.

SPATHIPHYLLUM (Closet Plant): Glossy green, elliptical and pointed erect leaves rising direct from soil. Compact habit. Low to medium light, but sun burns leaves. Feed lightly when indoors. Likes to be potbound. Puts up white spathe flower resembling calla lily, slightly fragrant. Pot in equal parts potting soil and sharp sand or perlite.

SUCCULENTS, in variety: Fleshy stems which retain water, as cacti do, making them drought resistant. Leathery, coarse or spiny foliage that suspends growth like yuccas do. Least demanding of all container plants. Give them sun, dry air, minimum water, and quick-draining, gritty soil. Propagated by seeds, cuttings or graftings.

TI PLANT *(Cordyline terminalis,* variety 'Ti' or minima 'Baby Ti'): Long narrow stems arising from single trunk, to 3-6'. *C.t. bicolor* has red edged leaves; *C.t. tricolor* has green, pink, red and white variegated leaves. Needs good bright light, good potting soil and even moisture.

YUCCA FILAMENTOSA FLACCIDA: Bluish sword leaves in bold rosette. To 2½'. Sandy loam; good drainage; open exposure.

ZEBRA PLANT *(Aphelandra),* in variety: Favorites in Victorian times. Leaves heavily veined in white. Flowers yellow to scarlet. High intensity light makes white stripes wider. Needs bright light and high humidity, but must not be over watered. Never stand in saucer with water. Allow to dry out, but not to wilting point, before watering thoroughly. Feed balanced food such as 20-20-20 or 20-10-10. After bloom, cut to one or two pairs leaves for bushiness. Loose, well-drained potting soil.

The Vegetable Garden

Who loves a garden still his Eden keeps,
Perennial pleasures plants, and wholesome harvests reaps.

—Amos Bronson Alcott

Growing vegetables is soul-satisfying. There is something about producing one's own food that fulfills a basic human need. A food garden can be attractively incorporated into the overall landscape design, right on stage with the flowers, as many vegetables and herbs are ornamental. Europeans have grown "mixed gardens" for centuries, and to great advantage.

Over-zealous beginners commonly make the mistakes of attempting too large a bed and not allowing time to prepare the soil properly. Start small. Remember, the summer sun gets very hot, and the chores of weeding, watering, and watching for insects continue throughout the season. A 100 square foot bed filled with rich friable soil, well-drained and sunned, can supply plenty of vegetables. It is more satisfying if you can keep a garden well tended, and with better care the plants will reward you with a bigger harvest. As for timing: allow a minimum of four weeks to get the soil ready for planting. If you are in a terrible hurry to get started, plant in containers while waiting for the big bed to settle and weather.

Vegetables require excellent drainage, a minimum of six hours of sunlight, and a loose, rich soil. They do not like to compete with the roots of large trees and shrubs nearby, so an open area is best. The water supply should be conveniently located, vegetables need water. Though most varieties prefer a slightly acid soil, some prefer neutral or even slightly alkaline soil. Try to learn the needs of your varieties.

In selecting the location of the vegetable bed remember that vegetables can be grown year-round along the Gulf Coast, so there should be ample sun in the winter as well as in summer. Excellent drainage is imperative; without it vegetables will not thrive. Dig several holes about 14 inches deep at various locations in the proposed site, then fill them with water. If the water drains out within 20 minutes, drainage is good. If it takes as long as an hour, corrective measures are necessary. Refer to the "Drainage" chapter for remedies.

Soil. "Don't guess, have a soil test," is good advice. Soil analysis, fertilizers, spraying, water management, variety selection, and other assistance is available from your County Extension Agent's Office and from the Soil Conservation Service of the U.S. Department of Agriculture. Do not hesitate to call them, for they are able and willing to help you. Reading the chapter on "Soil and Soil Improvement" will advise you of procedures for soil testing. Few gardeners are lucky enough to begin with an open sunny site and well-drained loam. Yet you can make sand and clay soils productive. A heavy black clay, called gumbo, is often found in the Houston area. It can be trying, but with perseverance it can be transformed into very useful soil. Never work soil when it is wet, for it will dry out harder than ever. After scraping off surface groundcover, spade the soil to a depth of at least ten inches and rototill it once or twice. Spread a minimum of two inches of organic matter (a mixture of humus, compost, manure, peat moss, and pinebark mulch) and two inches of sand over the soil. For every 100 square feet of surface area sprinkle about 15 pounds of gypsum and five pounds of superphosphate. Add five to ten pounds each of bone meal, blood meal, potash, and 100 pounds of sheep or steer manure. Rototill several times until the clods are broken up. The soil must be thoroughly mixed with all the amendments to form a homogenous mixture which will be hospitable to seeds and small plants. Water. Allow the bed to weather and settle for at least three weeks and rototill or hoe-cultivate again until the soil has a fine texture. Rake smooth. Now the vegetable bed is ready to plant.

Organic gardeners may prefer ground rock phosphate to the superphosphate, and other gardeners may choose a complete fertilizer such as 13-13-13 or 6-24-24 instead of the meals. If a soil test has shown an alkaline reaction, add one to two pounds of agricultural sulphur or iron sulphate (copperas) for every 100 square feet of surface area. If the soil is too acid, add lime carefully and according to the manufacturer's directions. If you are planting primarily fruiting crops such as eggplants and tomatoes, a high phosphate additive is helpful. All fertilizer should be used with care, following directions. More is never better than just enough. Organic fertilizers stay in the soil longer, but chemical fertilizers give quicker results. A combination of the two seems reasonable. Your vegetables will appreciate a soil in which they can grow at maximum speed, and your reward will be a harvest of maximum flavor—and vitamins!

Planning. Planning for planting is a must. Rows running north and south allow all plants to receive equal sunshine. Taller vegetables planted on the north side will not shade small ones. Plant what will be eaten and enjoyed, perhaps slipping in one or two new kinds to educate your palate. If you cannot find unusual varieties in the nurseries, check the many tantalizing ones listed in seed company catalogues, but try to select those that will do well in the climate of the upper Gulf Coast.

County Extension Agents, garden articles, and nurseries have information on new and improved varieties of vegetables. Hybridizers are striving to make plants more disease- and insect-resistant, more tolerant of weather, stronger, and more prolific. Consult them. Plan the spacing of plants according to variety and mature size, allowing ample room for growth and for adequate aeration to discourage diseases and insects (see "Diseases, Insects and Weeds").

Transplants. Most transplanted vegetables make stronger plants. Sow seeds in a small corner of the big bed or in flats or other containers. Use a very loose, sand soil or disease-free vermiculite. Transplant outdoors on a cloudy day or late in the afternoon to avoid scorching the little plants. Otherwise, provide a sunshade for them and water carefully and well. Placing hotkaps over seedlings will speed their growth. Avoid setting plants too deep, for they will die.

Some growers plant tomatoes very deep, but others have found that a tomato plant laid on its side in a two- to four-inch deep trench with the top of the plant gently curved upward above the soil surface will develop a much stronger root system and therefore be more productive. (See the chapter on "Propagation" for suggestions.)

Mulching. Mulching is of great importance to vegetable plants because it keeps the soil at an even temperature, protects from heat and cold, discourages weeds, adds nutrients to the top soil, improves the soil's texture, keeps produce clean, and allows more water penetration and better aeration. To avoid packing use mulches composed of a mixture of various materials like peat moss, pinebark mulch, bagasse, old hay, pine needles or manure. Black plastic or newspapers held down by bricks or soil may also be used, but they do not serve as many useful purposes as an organic mulch (see "Soil and Soil Improvement").

Fertilizing. Vegetables have better flavor and less time to be attacked by insects and diseases if they grow rapidly. To hasten growth after plants are established and growing, side dress every month with rotted manure, 8-24-24 or a nitrogen fertilizer used according to manufacturer's directions. Do not allow fertilizers to touch the plants. The ground should be moist before fertilizing and must be watered after applying the fertilizer. If you are careless the chemicals can burn the plants. Fresh manure may also burn; it should be well decomposed.

Planting Techniques. Many growers feel that diversity in planting and "companion planting" are very helpful in avoiding excessive insect damage. Insects are attracted to certain plants and not to others; some plants seem to repel certain insects. Hence the basis for companion planting. With diversification there is less chance of having a whole crop decimated by an insect attack.

Some companion plants are: beans with carrots, cucumbers, cabbage, potatoes, and herbs; cucumbers near corn, beans, radishes, sunflowers; lettuce near carrots and radishes; garlic and onions near beets, strawberries, tomatoes, and lettuce; parsley and basil near tomatoes, asparagus, chives, onions, marigolds, nasturtiums, and carrots. The tomato is the most popular vegetable planted in the United States, but it is susceptible to many diseases and insects. Try planting one basil and one marigold plant to every four tomato plants for protection (See "Diseases, Insects, and Weeds").

Intercropping, succession, and rotation are terms commonly used in vegetable gardening. Intercropping is the practice of planting rows of quick-growing crops, such as lettuce, spinach or radishes, between widely spaced slower-growing crops, such as peas, tomatoes and celery. Succession cropping is the growing of two or three crops on the same soil in one season; for example: early peas followed

by later planting of beets, carrots or cabbage. Waste is avoided by making smaller and more frequent sowings, and as each crop matures start another. This method of planting is particularly desirable where space is limited, but it requires an abundance of soil nutrients and water. Rotation is the practice of changing the location of different vegetables from year to year; so plant root vegetables where leaf crops had formerly grown.

Containers. Many vegetables adapt readily to growing in containers. Tomatoes grow especially well this way. Place a thick layer of gravel or vermiculite, from three to eight inches (depending on the size of the container), on the bottom of the container, and cover with a loose, rich soil. Suggested is a bushel each of vermiculite and shredded peat moss with one and one fourth cups of ground dolomitic limestone, one half cup each of superphosphate and 12-24-12 fertilizer. Mix thoroughly, fill pots with this mixture. Water and allow to drain to the real moist, but not wet condition before planting.

The Circle of the Year suggests vegetable varieties suitable for planting each month. At your request, the County Extension Service will send you a chart of suggested vegetable varieties with planting tips.

Vegetable growing is fun and healthful. Give yourself an opportunity to experience the satisfactions that come with it. Once you have tasted the harvest from your own vegetable garden you will realize just how worthwhile a "hobby" it is.

Herbs. Gardeners nostalgic for old-fashioned flavor and nose-tingling aromas will enjoy a herb garden. Herbs may be grown in pots, as a border, interspersed in existing flower beds, or, elegantly reminiscent of Colonial days, as a formal division of the vegetable garden.

Herbs are easy to grow because their requirements are so average. Nearly all prefer light, slightly alkaline soil, good drainage, and plenty of sun. Some need a great deal of water, while others are drought-resistant. Too much fertilizer stimulates foliage growth but stifles flavor and scent. When partially cut down, many perennial herbs will send up fresh tops for further cutting. Throughout the long growing season the lilting aroma and taste of freshly snipped herbs will add a delightful dimension to your garden and certainly to your cuisine.

A minimum list would include the two bland herbs, parsley and chervil, which blend in seasoning with the more pungent rosemary, savory, tarragon, and sage. Other milder but enjoyable choices might include basil, oregano, borage, mints, dill, sweet marjoram, and fennel. There are numerous flavors and varieties of several of those listed. Garlic and chives, both actually bulbs, would complete a well-balanced herb collection, but there are many more kinds to consider. The more aromatic herbs have been found to protect other plants from certain insects and even disease, and these are used in companion plantings with garden flowers and vegetables.

Before autumn comes you may harvest your winter supply. Those which are to be used for their leaves should be cut just before the flowers open, when the essential oils are heaviest. Cut them in the dew of the morning on a dry sunny day. Wash throughly and shake dry; pick over for bad leaves and cut off flower heads. Spread them out, each type separately, on wire mesh trays or large papers in a warm, dry room. Turn them every day until they are thoroughly dry, then strip the leaves from the stems and store them in sealed jars. Gardeners with home freezers may have fresh herbs all year round. Simply wash in small bunches, shake well, and put in plastic bags sealed with tape or bands. Whichever method is used, be sure to label carefully.

At the end of the fall season, all perennials should be cut down to within three or four inches from the ground and mulched to live through the winter. Most perennials have a given life-span, however, and when their time has elapsed they must be replaced. (See the "Herbs" Planting Chart.)

$\mathcal{P}$ropagation

To own a bit of ground, to scratch it with a hoe, to plant seeds, and watch the renewal of life—this is the commonest delight of the race, the most satisfactory thing a man can do.

—Charles Dudley Warner

Propagation of plants is the producing of new plants from parent stock by one of various methods: from seed or by the vegetative processes of divisions, cuttings, layering, grafting or budding.

Seeds. Propagation from seeds is a very common method of obtaining new stock, as most plants produce seed, and some species reseed themselves freely. The factors essential for the successful raising of plants from seed are: properly prepared fine soil, good fresh seed, and the requisite amounts of sun, shade and moisture. Pretreated seeds are available that are resistant to "damping off" or seeds may be dusted, before sowing, with a special disinfectant preparation available at garden shops.

Seeds should be planted thinly in moist soil, usually twice their depth, with the soil pressed firmly above them. Extremely fine seed should be mixed with sand and pressed lightly but not covered. A common fault is to sow seeds too deep and too thick.

Germination of many seeds may be hastened by dusting them with hormone powder. Hard-coated seeds and seeds which are naturally slow to sprout, such as sweet peas and parsley, should be soaked in tepid water, and planted before they dry out. Bluebonnet and Texas bluebell seeds should be planted when ripe, otherwise they will become hard and need to be soaked. The growth of certain hard seed such as canna, coralbean, and mountain laurel can be accelerated by clipping off an end of the hard seed coat, permitting moisture to enter the inner part of the seeds without delay. The seeds of many flowering shrubs germinate in the first year after sowing, but there are numerous garden shrubs and trees which commonly require two years or more before the seeds germinate. Nuts, if not planted as soon as ripe, should be stratified (stored in moist peat moss or sand) to simulate the usual conditions under which they sprout. (The Planting Charts give approximate germination periods for this latitude.)

Although seeds of bulbs take three or four years to bloom, a single choice bulb yields dozens of fertile seeds. Agapanthus, hybrid spurias, and hybrid amaryllis may be produced in great quantity by planting the seeds. (To insure true color of amaryllis, tie cheesecloth or a paper bag around bud before it opens and pollinate artificially.) Allow the seed pods to ripen and dry on the stalk. Fertile seeds contain a kernel. Fill a wooden box four to six inches deep with friable soil. Press each seed into soil one inch apart, bearing down strongly with finger. Sprinkle ¼ inch of soil over entire surface, but do not press down. Place four sheets of newspaper the same size as the box directly on soil, and weight the edges with narrow strips of wood. Wet paper thoroughly, then cover all with a pane of glass. Place the box in semi-shade, and sprinkle the paper lightly whenever it seems to be drying out. After a few days, when the sprouts are ¼ inch tall, remove the paper and replace the glass. Keep soil moist but not sopping. Seedlings may be planted in the open ground when seven to twelve inches tall. Too much shade makes spindly seedlings. Correct fertilizing and watering will bring them to earliest possible bloom.

Open Beds. Open beds should be carefully prepared by having the soil worked thoroughly and fertilized. Beds should be watered sufficiently before sowing so that no further watering will be needed until the seeds germinate. Seeds of bedding plants, especially those which do not transplant easily (such as poppies, phlox and larkspur) may be broadcast where they are to bloom. Seeds of edging plants, (as sweet alyssum) may be sown in shallow drills. When planting in open beds, mix the seed with sand to insure thin sowing and to reduce the labor of thinning out excess plants. Newly planted seeds may be protected from hard rains by covering with cheesecloth or burlap.

Flats. Flats are generally used to sow seeds for transplanting, as they are easily handled and protected from rain and extremes of heat and cold. Flats may be purchased ready-cut or made at home. The usual dimensions are three inches deep, 12 inches wide, and 18 inches long. Because some seeds require a longer time to sprout than others, it is advisable to plant in the same flat those which take about the same time to germinate.

Old flats should be whitewashed to destroy fungus and preserve the wood. Pots used for seed planting should be scalded and scrubbed or washed in a chlorine solution. An inch layer of gravel or broken flower pots should be spread over the bottom of the flats or whatever receptacle is used. Flats should be filled to the top with light porous soil in a mixture of one part good garden loam to supply food; one part coarse sand to improve drainage; and one part peat moss to retain moisture. The soil may be sterilized by heating as an extra precaution against damping off. A layer of vermiculite spread over the soil or used alone is an excellent sterile medium for starting seeds, with maximum germination. The best method of watering pots is to set them in water until the soil becomes moist. Overwatering is injurious.

Flowers and vegetables that are needed early may be started under glass, in flats placed in coldframes or hotbeds, and covered with lath, newspaper or clean burlap. This covering may be gradually lifted on sticks as the tiny plants develop and are ready for full light. Essentially, a coldframe is a bottomless box with a sloping glass or plastic-glazing top which sheds rain and conserves heat. A hotbed is of similar construction, but is heated so that seeds may be started in it during cold weather. Electricity is sometimes used, but manure or leaves, or a mixture of both, are commonly used for heating hotbeds. Raising or lowering the sash of the coldframe or hotbed permits circulation of air and control of temperature. Water as necessary with a fine-spray nozzle.

Transplanting. When the small seedlings have from two to four or more "true" leaves, they should be carefully "pricked out" with a knife or sharp stick and transplanted to stand farther apart in other flats or be set in permanent beds. The flats should be well watered before seedlings are removed to new soil, which should also be moist. Some species, pansies for instance, do better if reset and transplanted twice, to develop stronger root systems and sturdier plants. Seedlings that grow too quickly need to be thinned out before they become leggy so that the plants may develop shorter, stronger stems and a well-balanced top growth.

In any transplanting, pressure of the soil against the roots is necessary to anchor the plant and bring the roots into closer contact with the soil so they can absorb moisture and food. Many plants have highly developed taproots, as well as a system of fibrous roots. Great care should be exercised to prevent injury and breakage of the root system. Handling the seedlings by the leaves and stem avoids injury to the roots. Bare-rooted plants may be dipped in a rooting hormone solution to speed growth. The roots should be spread out to their natural position, and bits of earth kept clinging to them to avoid tearing-off hair roots. To prevent decay, badly bruised roots should be snipped off with shears.

If plants are transplanted on a cloudy day or late in the day they will not wilt easily and will take almost immediate hold in their new surroundings. If transplanting is done in sunny weather, wilting may be avoided by inserting sprays of evergreens among the plants to provide shade. Summer transplanting is generally considered dangerous, but it can be done safely if the plants are well-encased in a ball of earth, watered liberally, and provided with temporary shade.

Division. Vegetative propagation without using seed is carried out by dividing into sections those species which form bulbs, corms, tubers, rhizomes or crowns. Varieties which do not reproduce seed, or do not reproduce true to color or form because the seed-producing flowers have been cross-fertilized, are perpetuated by this reliable method.

Many of the bulbous plants, such as narcissi, tulips and hyacinths, propagate naturally by the division of the bulbs into smaller bulbs or bulblets. When naturalized, these should be separated when they become crowded. Some other species, such as the Tiger Lily, form aerial bulblets in the leaf axils. These may be planted in the same way as the bulblets produced on the underground parts.

Scaly bulbs, such as those of many lilies, may be propagated readily by removing the loose outer scales and planting them in the same way you plant seeds.

Corms are bulb-like structures popularly classed as bulbs. They proliferate in much the same way as bulbs, by producing one or more tiny corms, known as cormels, on top of the parent corm. Gladioli form cormels around the base of the new corm. Cormels are planted in essentially the same way as seeds. If properly cared for by transplanting when they become crowded, they will grow into corms of flowering size in one to four years.

Tubers are thickened stems with eyes below the soil, such as potato and Jerusalem artichoke. Tubers are easily propagated by planting whole or cut in sections, each possessing an eye, from which a new plant will sprout. Tuberous roots have eyes in the stem. Dahlias and daylilies are examples. For propagation purposes the roots should be cut with a portion of stem attached to each division.

Rhizomes are underground or partially underground stems which, if cut into portions, each bearing a growth bud, rapidly increase the plants producing them. Usually, such divisions are made when plants are dormant (cannas, for example), but in the case of Bearded Iris most gardeners prefer to do this soon after the plants have bloomed.

Runners are slender shoots that run along the surface of the ground, rooting and developing into a succession of new plants. These may be separated from the parent stock and set in new locations. The strawberry is propagated by this means.

Stolons are underground suckers or trailing branches peculiar to some species. They take root when they come in contact with the soil. Stolons may be severed with attached roots and transplanted. Some azaleas and many grasses, such as St. Augustine, may be propagated in this manner.

Many garden plants form crowns that may be broken apart with the hands or cut with a sharp spade into root-bearing sections which, when replanted, form new plants. Clumps should be lifted and divided at intervals if the plant's vigor is to be maintained and new plants secured. Crowns must be planted slightly above soil level.

Layering. Several methods of layering are used to multiply new stock from plants which are difficult to propagate by other means. Simple layering is the easiest method. Strong, young branches, notched on the underside, may be pegged firmly to the ground, preferably at a joint or near an eye. The cut portion should be buried about two inches deep so that calluses will form at the cuts, on which roots will develop. When layering woody or semi-woody plants, strong shoots should be slit part way and a wedge or pebble inserted to keep the cut open. Layers are usually made in the early spring, in order that roots may develop by fall, when they may be severed from the parent plant and transplanted. Many plants, including jasmines, pink magnolias, holly, dogwood, and most hardwood shrubs, may be easily propagated in this way.

When serpentine or continuous layering is employed, several plants may be obtained at the same time from one long flexible shoot, as grapes, ivy, and some roses. In serpentine layering a long shoot is undulated and the lower loops are covered with earth. In continuous layering the long shoot is pegged down and covered lightly with earth along its length.

In mound layering the parent plant should be cut back to promote the production of quantities of young shoots near the ground. A layer of earth is mounded over the center of the plant until the stems root. These rooted shoots are cut off at normal ground level and planted. The parent or mother stock plant is then allowed to produce another crop of shoots that are in turn mound layered. This method is used mainly with low bushy shrubs, such as azaleas, hydrangeas, Japanese quince, and spirea.

Trees and shrubs whose branches cannot be conveniently brought into contact with the earth may be propagated by air-layering, often called Chinese-layering. A notch should be cut in the branch or the bark girdled and kept open at the point where root formation is desired. A ball of well-saturated sphagnum moss should be bound firmly with plastic over the wound. The moss will stay moist until sufficient roots have formed, when the rooted branch may be severed and planted. This method, commonly applied to rubber plants, crotons, dracaenas, and similar foliage plants, causes the old plant to leaf out and become more shapely.

Cuttings. Cuttings are sections of plants that are rooted in shallow boxes or pots of sand, soil, peat moss or one of the patented root growth mediums. There are several methods of taking cuttings of most shrubs and trees, both deciduous and evergreen, from roses and many perennials. Cuttings of root, leaf or stem may be made at any time of the year, but the early spring months are considered best.

Cuttings may be soaked in root-inducing chemicals for better propagation. Synthetic plant hormones, marketed under various trade names, are proving very successful in stimulating root growth of plants heretofore considered difficult to propagate. With any chemical, follow directions explicitly, as success depends mainly upon the correct strength of the solution and the proper duration of treatment for each particular plant. Fungus attacks on cuttings, which often cause them to rot, may be prevented by dipping the ends in a mixture of one part Fermate and nine parts hormone powder.

Stem cuttings, the type usually employed by amateur gardeners, are made of non-flowering shoots of either half-ripened wood (softwood cuttings) or of dormant shoots (hardwood cuttings). Make all cuttings with a sharp knife, just below an eye or bud, into lengths containing three or four eyes. Cuttings should be stripped of all surplus leaves except the upper two, which should be cut in half. Important factors in the success of cuttings are: a good rooting medium, adequate shelter from wind and sun, and sufficient moisture. The roots develop from a callus formed on the cut surface, and when the roots are about an inch long the cuttings should be repotted or placed in good garden soil.

Although hardwood cuttings usually take longer to form roots than those of softwood, they may be rooted more successfully in the open ground. Hardwood cuttings of shrubs and trees may often be rooted where they are to remain, if planted in holes the size a posthole digger makes, filled with a rooting medium. If kept constantly moist, the roots of the cuttings soon go through the medium and into the soil, making transplanting unnecessary. When cuttings are taken in quantity in the late fall they may be tied in bundles for convenience, buried completely in moist earth or sand, and mulched. In the early spring the majority will have callused or rooted, and these may be planted in beds for further development. Some cuttings, as those from oleander and willows, root easily in jars of water.

Heel cuttings are made so that a small portion of the older stem is left at the base of each cutting. Although this type of cutting is more damaging to the parent plant, they root more readily than when cut off below the node.

Leaf cuttings taken from certain plants, generally those that are fleshy or succulent, soon form roots and new plants. Rex begonia leaves should be cut across the larger veins and pegged down in damp sand, while leaf sections taken from sansevieria plants should be simply cut into sections and stuck in moist sand.

Root cuttings are the easiest of all in the case of crapemyrtle, blackberry, and many trees and perennials. When cut into sections and covered with earth the roots soon form new plants.

Grafting and Budding. The word "graftage" is used to include both grafting and budding. The difference between the processes is slight; both are used to unite the growing tissues of two plants which are botanically related. Many varieties of citrus fruits are rendered hardier by being grafted or budded on the native orange stock known as *Citrus trifoliata,* which becomes dormant and practically frost-hardy in winter. Many varieties of ornamental trees and shrubs are grafted or budded on stocks having a very strong root system.

In grafting, the base of the shoot, known as the "scion," is shaped and inserted into a previously prepared incision in the stem or branch of a rooted plant, known as the "stock." Good contact between the soft outer tissues or cambium layers of scion and the stock is essential. The two are bound tightly together to maintain the close contact, and the graft is often covered with a grafting wax to insure that the juncture does not become dry before the union is established. Shoot roots growing from below the point of grafting continue to produce their own characteristic leaves, fruits, and flowers. To give all possible strength to the new and desirable growth all suckers coming from below the point of union should be cut off. There are numerous types of specialized grafting practiced by experienced gardeners, mainly cleft, whip, bark, splice, saddle, veneer, side, and shield grafting.

Budding involves the same essential processes, except that the scion consists merely of an axillary bud together with a small portion of the outer tissues of the stem on which it was borne. The practices of grafting and budding require accuracy and skill, and there is much to learn from authoritative writers and nurserymen.

Clones. A clone is the original selected plant and the aggregate of the plants descended from it by vegetative (asexual) propagation. Most so-called "varieties," "cultivated varieties," "horticultural varieties," "named varieties," and "garden varieties" are clones. Clones may be selected from species, varieties, or forms of species. Plants grown from seed are not identical as are members of a clone, but if you raise a plant grown from seed and propagate it, then that plant and all the individuals descended from it form a clone. "Clone" is a horticultural rather than a taxonomic term.

Pruning

When love and skill work together expect a masterpiece.
—John Ruskin

Pruning is the removing of part of a plant to improve it and keep it healthy. No phase of gardening maintenance is more important, and knowledge of plant structure and growth is a prerequisite for successful pruning. Study the natural habit of each plant as it grows in your area before trimming, even before purchasing. The necessity for pruning may be considerably reduced if you think ahead. Do not place a large plant in a small space. Do not try to turn a tall-growing tree into a short one, or a wide-spreading shrub into a narrow one. Dwarf varieties are often more suitable for home landscaping.

Plants grow in their predestined size and shape. No amount of pruning will actually succeed in changing them, and in the attempt you will exhaust your time and patience and probably ruin the beauty of the plant.

Plant growth comes from the terminal bud at the tip of each branch. The removal of a tip bud forces other buds along the stem to develop, and bushiness results. The top bud of a tree controls its shape, so do not tamper with it unless you know exactly what you are doing. The removal of the top bud of some palms, for example, may kill the tree. Buds incline in the direction which the growth will take, so we often prune just above a bud pointing the way we want the branch to grow. There is a balanced one-to-one ratio between the top growth of a plant and its root system. Too heavy a pruning at any one time may throw this balance off. If drastic pruning is necessary, do it a little at a time over a period of weeks or even years. Since plant food is manufactured in leaves by the process of photosynthesis, it follows that a plant's root system can seldom survive the removal of too great a quantity of leaves. An exception is the transplanting of a deciduous tree, when foliage is often stripped to give the root system time to recover from the shock of the move. An example of balancing this ratio is the planting of bare-rooted shrubs like roses; not only the injured roots are removed but other roots are usually tipped to balance with the pruned top canes.

The fundamental purposes of good pruning are to control undesirable growth habits, remove old, diseased, and surplus wood, shape, increase quality and quantity of the flowers, and to promote growth. Judicious pruning will often accomplish wonders, while improper pruning can irreparably injure plants. This is particularly true for shade trees and evergreens. No attempt should be made to prune a tree suffering from decay or major injuries. Such treatment requires the skill of a trained tree surgeon. Proper pruning for power line clearance is best done by reliable tree surgeons, and many utility companies employ professionals for this purpose.

Pruning cuts should be on a slant, preferably made at a joint or crotch, or flush with the trunk. All pruning cuts larger than an inch in diameter should be covered with special paste-type pruning paint to facilitate healing and waterproof the wound. Avoid leaving stubs, for decay and disease often result. Cut out dead or useless wood at any time of year. Before you start pruning, study the plant until you have a mental picture of the way you want it to look. Take your time. A severed limb cannot be reattached. As you prune stop periodically; survey your work from every side. If in doubt do not cut. Wait a few days and try again.

Pruning tools should be carefully selected for the work they have to perform, and kept sharp to minimize injury to the plant tissues. Do not try to force-cut a branch of a larger diameter than will fit into the blades of the half-open tool. Tools should be cleaned, disinfected with alcohol, and oiled after each use.

Try to cut the branches of shrubs just above a bud or joint pointing in the direction you want the bush to develop. When ornamental shrubs are carefully chosen for their location they seldom require heavy pruning, but they may need systematic trimming to maintain their characteristic habit of growth. When removing an obtrusive branch, cut well inside the shrub, perhaps even at the base, as with nandinas and others of the same growth habit. Top and root pruning have a retarding effect on growth and are sometimes practiced on shrubs that are apt to grow out of scale. Root pruning involves cutting around a plant with a sharp spade about two feet from the stem or trunk. When wisteria has ceased blooming it will often rebloom after a severe root pruning, which discourages excess new growth and stimulates blooms on old wood. Root pruning several months before the move is particularly advantangeous when transplanting shrubs. With skillful pruning, you can transform shrub-trees such as crapemyrtles, ligustrum, and althea into small, beautifully sculpted trees by reducing the numerous shrubby canes to one or perhaps three in number and keeping the lateral buds rubbed off to allow the canes to branch out at the top.

The removal of old, diseased or cold-injured parts improves the appearance of woody plants and frequently saves the lives of sick ones. Burn diseased wood immediately after removal, and sterilize tools with a household disinfectant to prevent spread of the infection. Cutting half-dead or cold-damaged shrubs to the ground and incorporating manure and compost into the soil around them serves to stimulate new growth.

Prune ornamental shrubs at the proper season, according to their time of blooming and the age of the wood on which they bloom. Dormant pruning refers to pruning during that time of year, usually winter, when plant growth is suspended or at least diminished. Shrubs that produce their flowers on new wood during the summer should be severely pruned when they cease producing new wood or when flower and foliage quality is inferior. Prune these in winter so they can make abundant new wood before blooming time. When necessary, prune most evergreens, fruit trees, and shade trees during dormancy.

We frequently cut evergreens in December for holiday greenery. This is also a type of pruning, and properly done, it keeps the plants in better conformation with greater density. To force evergreens to spread out cut the top buds or shoots; to force upright growth tip the lateral branches. Conifers need little pruning, but you may pinch out the terminal buds to insure symmetry and promote bushiness before new spring growth starts. If the leader (the strongest and longest bud or shoot) is destroyed, bind the next most likely branch in an upright position to take its place.

Most spring-blooming shrubs flower on wood that is at least one year old. Prune these immediately after bloom or during flowering for arrangements. Cut from the most crowded part of the bush, or cut branches which are spoiling the plant's natural beauty. Always cut on a slant, using a sharp garden knife or pruners; never break off a branch. If you prune spring-blooming shrubs too late, the plants may lose vitality, or they may not have enough time to produce sufficient wood for next spring's flowers.

Pruning to shape shrubs and trees in formal plantings is best begun when plants are young and pliable. Clipped hedges are an example. They need frequent shearing to preserve the precision essential to formal design. To encourage overall bushiness in hedge plants clip them in an almost triangular form, making the top narrower than the base. This shape allows sunshine to reach all portions of the plant, and fosters even, proportionate growth. Topiary pruning, the close shearing of plants into ornamental or unusual shapes, was known in Rome during the first century, but reached its height of popularity in sixteenth century English gardens. It requires constant clipping to be attractive. Yews and arborvitae need frequent light shearing to maintain their form. Prune camphor trees once or twice each spring to encourage their characteristic rose-tinted foliage. Espaliering is the training of branches flat against a wall or other support so that they form a distinct pattern. This is a difficult technique, requiring almost constant pruning of the side shoots. Train the leaders as desired. The evergreen pear, *Pyrus kawakami,* and pyracantha are often espaliered.

Disbudding, or finger pinching, is a very useful kind of garden pruning. Pinching off the main stem of young plants forces the development of side buds in the axils of the leaves. The flowering period may be delayed, but the reward is stocky, compact plants with many more blooms. When annuals like sweet alyssum and *Phlox drummondi* have passed their peak of bloom, shear them back to within two inches of the ground to obtain another crop of flowers. Removing all blossoms from annuals as soon as they fade prolongs their bloom season by discouraging their natural inclination to form seed.

Pruning of azaleas, camellias, and roses is discussed in the chapters so entitled.

Shrubs and trees to be pruned while dormant in winter or early spring are:

Abelia	Flowering fruit trees*
Althea*	Hibiscus
Beautyberry (Callicarpa)	Oleander*
Butterflybush*	Parkinsonia*
Buttonbush*	Plumbago
Chaste tree (Vitex)*	Poinciana*
Crapemyrtle	Pomegranate
Elderberry	Salt-cedar*
	Willow, flowering*

Shrubs and trees to be pruned immediately after flowering, before blossom buds have formed for the next year:

Bottlebrush	Japanese Flowering Quince
Cape jasmine	Jasmines
Climbing roses*	Mockorange
Deutzia*	Photinia
Dogwood	Pittosporum
Haw, Black	Redbud
Honeysuckle, Bush	Spirea
Huisache	Viburnums
Hydrangea*	Weigela

(*Should be pruned to increase blooming.)

Winter Protection

*The melancholy days are come, the saddest of the year, of wailing winds,
and naked winds, and meadows brown and sere.*
—Bryant

There is no such thing as a "typical" winter in the upper Gulf Coast region. Though there are average dates for the first and last frosts, a quick freeze earlier or later comes as no real surprise to experienced gardeners. Because Gulf Coast winters are so fickle, and because plants have no chance to attain real dormancy, weather-wise gardeners take precautions to help their plants survive the difficult alternate freezings and thawings of our winters.

Keep your garden soil moist, with occasional deep, thorough waterings, especially if the autumn has been dry. Deep moisture encourages deep root growth, which provides protection from cold, and the water replaces air in the soil, thereby preventing rapid cooling. All plants withstand freezes much better when wet than when dry. On the other hand, precautions should be taken to assure good drainage; roots in standing water will rot, whether hot or cold. Never use high-nitrogen fertilizers and never prune severely in the fall. Both encourage quick, soft, succulent growth that is very susceptible to freeze injury. Instead, use fertilizers high in potash to harden the plants for winter.

Know the cold hardiness of your plants, and place the tenderest of them in the higher, more sheltered areas of the garden. Cold, like water, settles in low places, and this is why only the lower parts of a shrub may sometimes brown from cold damage. In raised beds, even tender foliage may escape cold damage, while hardy shrubs in low areas do not. Young plants need more protection from cold than do older established ones.

Be prepared to move tender tropical plants into a closed garage or greenhouse, either for the winter or before a predicted frost. You may have to do this on short notice for our "blue northers" take devilish glee in blowing in unannounced. If you are using a greenhouse, remember to open or ventilate it as soon as the sun shines on it, because the temperatures rise very rapidly in a closed greenhouse.

Plan ahead for coverings for those plants that need protection. Do not allow plastic to touch the foliage for it will burn it. Keep in mind that strong winds often accompany northers, so coverings must be firmly secured. A three to four inch mulch of materials allowing good aeration and water penetration are excellent over the roots of shrubs and young trees. Seedlings may be covered with mounds of leaves, pine needles or loose soil, but these must be pulled back from the plants as soon as warm weather returns to avoid burning them.

Freezes are usually of short duration in Houston and the Gulf Coast, with warm, strong sun the next day. In such cases a sprinkling of water on frost laden foliage before the sunlight strikes it might prevent or at least diminish injury. The frozen tops protect the remainder of the plant, so do not be too quick to remove apparently frozen foliage or plants. Wait until frost danger is definitely past, then cut away the injured foliage gradually and carefully down to firm vigorous portions. There you may find fresh green growth, demonstrating once again the eternal cycle of the awakening of the plant world.

Diseases, Insects and Weeds

How nature delights and amuses us by varying even the character of insects; the ill-nature of the wasp . . . the volatility of the butterfly, the slyness of the bug!

—Sydney Smith

Diseases, insects, and weeds are part of our world and always will be. All members of our vastly complicated, interdependent ecological system are necessary and important, but it is often difficult to appreciate whatever benefits diseases, insects, and weeds afford in view of the plant injuries they cause. Continual widespread use of chemical sprays as a preventive and control does not seem to be the answer. Species may adapt and become immune to a chemical. Spraying and dusting kill beneficial insects and plants along with the harmful ones, and as natural predators of harmful insects and bacteria are decimated by careless chemical attacks, the injurious ones multiply even more rapidly than usual. The solution appears to be to employ natural and biological controls first. Then, if absolutely necessary, resort to poisonous or toxic materials with the greatest caution, reading and following label instructions to the letter.

General Suggestions. Healthy plants are the best defense against diseases and insects. Since many insects carry disease, discouraging one reduces the other. Follow sensible garden practices.

Correct any drainage problems. Build and maintain a fertile soil. Cultivate and till it to remove pests overwintering in the soil and weeds serving as host plants to the pests.

Grow a diversity of plants rather than all of one species, and avoid planting the same kinds of plants in the same location each year; their enemies build up in the soil. Plant resistant varieties whenever feasible. Plants native to your locale are often the most resistant. Interplant aromatic herbs and other pungent plants. The multitude of odors confuses the pests.

Keep your garden clean—cleanliness is just as important in the garden as in the home. Gather and burn diseased foliage. Entice birds to your garden. The good they do in consuming insects usually outweighs any damage they may cause. Do not kill toads, frogs, lizards, and non-poisonous snakes; they all eat insects. Learn to distinguish the poisonous snakes from the non-poisonous. Some diseases *not* harmful to plants can be used to kill others that are destructive: *Bacillus thuriengensis* and milky spore disease are often so used, especially in greenhouse culture.

Use your imagination: slugs come to drink and drown in saucers of beer; if replaced often, wood ashes, sharp sand, diatomaceous earth, flour, and other materials sprinkled around young transplants have proven helpful in discouraging worms and caterpillars. Burying unburned tobacco in soil, and watering in, will help control underground pests. Sprays of soapy (not detergent) water, a strong force of water, repellent sprays of red peppers, garlic, onions, etc. Try to catch infestations in the early stages so that less pesticide is required. Companion planting also seems effective. The "Vegetable Garden" chapter lists some combinations.

Recent studies confirm the wisdom of using insecticides less frequently to allow the natural predators of damaging insects to accomplish their beneficial purpose.

Beneficial Insects and Diseases. The *glow worm* or *firefly,* a beetle identified by a light on the terminal segment of its body, together with its larvae, is a voracious eater, feeding especially on slugs, cutworms, and snails.

The *lady bug,* or lady beetle, is one of the most effectively beneficial insects. It is small (about ¼-inch long), almost spherical in shape with a convex back. Though there are numerous varieties, those commonly seen here are the red, the spotted, and the convergent lady beetle. The latter has 12 small black spots on reddish wing covers and 2 convergent white lines on the thorax. Other lady bugs are red or tan with black spots, or black with red spots. Their larvae, also helpful predators, are flat, carrot-shaped with a warty grayish-black coloring and blue or orange spots. Eggs, usually orange, stand on end in large clusters attached to a leaf. Lady bugs and their larvae eat aphids, mealy bugs, and scales.

The *lacewing* has gauzy green or brown wings. Its larvae, called aphidlions, are ⅓-inch long, yellow or gray mottled with brown or red, and have flat bodies tapering at both ends. They suck juices from aphids, cottony-cushion scales, mealy bugs, thrips, and mites.

Praying mantis and its relatives are beneficial insect predators. Their name is derived from their habit of holding their front legs in a praying position as they eat their prey.

Caterpillar hunter beetle, which serves the purpose its name suggests, is an iridescent ground beetle which cannot fly but scurries rapidly along the ground.

Trichogramma wasps lay eggs which become minute parasites inside the eggs of other insects, especially caterpillars. Most wasps are beneficial predators.

Bacillus thuringiensis, a nonharmful bacterium, paralyzes and kills insects eating it. Sold as Dipel, Biotrol, or Thuricide, it is particularly successful in controlling caterpillars and worms.

Milky spore disease, a bacterial organism known commercially as DOOM, is a fatal disease in some grubs, particularly that of the Japanese Beetle, a terrible pest.

Chemical Pesticides. The mild climate which allows gardeners of the upper Gulf Coast to enjoy beautiful gardens all year is also, unfortunately, inviting to diseases and pests. Gardeners in this area may have more reason to use poisonous materials as controls, but that decision each gardener must make himself. Some chemicals are at present approved by the appropriate authorities as safe, when properly used according to label instructions. From time to time even some of these may be found inadvisable. If registered chemicals are used as directed by the manufacturer there should be no harm to the user nor to the environment.

No endorsement is intended of any product mentioned in this book.

If chemicals are used the following precautions are of extreme importance:

1. Use the product specified for your purpose. It may lose its effectiveness with age.
2. Read all the directions on the label and follow them to protect both yourself and the environment.
3. Wash any portion of your body that has been exposed to a chemical.
4. Keep all poisons out of reach of children.
5. Make certain of the advisability of using any poisonous product on or near food crops.
6. Dispose of empty containers safely.

7. Alternate chemicals periodically in case insects have become immune to a particular one.
8. Dusting may be quicker, more economical, and less injurious to plants, but a protective mask should be worn to prevent inhalation. A mask is advisable with liquid chemical sprays as well.
9. Drift or run-off of chemicals can result in a hazardous residue.

Some materials are systemic, that is, they enter the structure of the plant and the soil. Be cautious about these. If you have doubts ask the County Extension Agent. Because there are differing opinions as to the safety of using certain chemicals in disease and insect control, it is your decision as to the control method you use; but whatever you decide, correct identification of the problem is always the first step.

Following is a list of descriptions and symptoms of some diseases and insects most often found in the Gulf Coast area. If you still cannot identify the problem, gather damaged foliage, twigs or plants, place in closed plastic bag, and take to your nursery or County Extension Agent for assistance. It is a waste of time, effort, and money, as well as an unnecessary stress on the plants involved, to treat an unidentified pest with a chemical in a hit or miss fashion.

Diseases. Fungi, bacteria, viruses, and lack of certain soil nutrients are the most common causes of plant diseases. Fungi often cause leaf-spotting diseases. General purpose fungicides (benomyl, chlorothalonil, maneb, and maneb in combination with a zinc compound, dusting sulphur, and others) may be used for spraying.

Azalea petal blight is a fungus disease symtomized by small brown spots on white azalea blossoms and white spots on colored flowers. (See "Azaleas" for additional details.)

Blackspot, a fungus disease, causes small black spots on foliage which gradually become larger, yellowing and killing the leaf. It spreads quickly and, if uncontrolled, defoliates the entire plant. The plant cannot effectively manufacture its food without foliage, and it may die. There are several preventive measures: good air circulation by ample spacing of plants and by keeping each bush in an open vase shape, picking off foliage at the first sign of disease, using disease-resistant varieties, and removing and burning all fallen foliage. Avoid excessive moisture on leaves. Morning sun will dry foliage quickly. Regular spraying with a fungicide such as benomyl is a preventive. An insecticide such as Black Leaf 40 may also be used.

Botryitis blight, a fungus disease, produces brownish-red spots on foliage, flower, and stem which may become watersoaked and discolored; blossoms may be covered with thread-like gray mold. Spray with appropriate fungicide (perhaps Bordeaux mixture) when the disease becomes a problem, adding a spreader-sticker to the solution. Remove and destroy infected leaves. Mites spread the disease. Spacing plants for sufficient air circulation, avoiding high humidity and low light intensity are controls. The Madonna lily is more susceptible than the Croft and other Easter lily types.

Brown patch, a fungus disease, shows itself in circular discolored areas in lawn grass. Usually only the leaves are damaged, but the disease can spread over an entire lawn when uncontrolled and encouraged by poor drainage and excessive moisture. A fungicide such as terrachlor is effective. Healthy lawns are not as susceptible. (See "Lawns".)

Camellia Die-Back, a fungus disease, is most destructive of young growth, but it may attack old wood and roots as well. The symptoms are browning or blackening, followed by death of a stem or branch, beginning at the tip and progressing downward toward a larger branch. (See "Camellias" for further details.)

Chlorosis, yellowing of leaves, is not really a disease. It is usually due to a deficiency of iron in the soil; however, deficiencies of nitrogen, sulphur or manganese may also be the cause. Poor drainage, lack of ample aeration, or virus diseases may also cause loss of leaf color. Using iron sulphate (copperas) or iron chelate, as the manufacturer directs to spray or incorporate into the soil, or both, is the recommended remedy. Avoid spraying in the heat of the day. Do not apply fertilizers for at least a week after treatment. Chlorosis is prevalent in alkaline soils. A simple way to acidify the soil is to spray the plant and ground generously with a solution of one cup of cider vinegar to one gallon of water. (See also "Azaleas.")

Conifer blight is a fungus disease attacking especially Arizona cypress, junipers, arborvitae, and native cedars, causing browning of foliage. Zineb or Bordeaux are fungicides.

Damping-off, a fungus disease, seems to attack all types of plants, causing seedlings to rot at soil level. Sterilize the soil and treat seeds with a fungicide; carefully follow the label directions, and eliminate excessive soil and plant moisture. Avoid planting susceptible plants in the same location in succeeding years. Do not water at night. Some growers fumigate new beds with products designed for the purpose, but before using on food crops take great care to read everything on the label of the product. Small amounts of soil can be baked for three or four hours in a 160° oven to sterilize.

Fire blight, a bacterial disease, rapidly discolors and kills parts of the foliage and stems, giving the plant a burned appearance, especially pear trees. The infection is spread by insects and rain. The bacteria overwinter in the bark, so for control, prune out all infected canker areas down to healthy wood during fall or winter. Apply fungicidal sprays, such as Bordeaux mixture or zineb, when 10% of blooms are open. Continue applications weekly until three or four applications have been made. Plant only resistant varieties.

Gall or *grown gall,* another bacterial disease, usually occurs on roots but may appear on above-ground parts. The bacterium enters through natural openings or wounds in the plant; it appears as a large, ball-like woody swelling. Younger plants may die; older ones may live, though stunted and unhealthy. There is no known cure. Prevent by careful selection of healthy stock. Soil may be fumigated carefully to prevent infection of new plants.

Mildew, a fungus disease, causes powdery white mold-like growth on leaves, buds and young twigs, stunting growth and often resulting in loss of foliage and flowers. Crapemyrtle and rosebushes are particularly susceptible. Spray weekly as needed with a fungicide containing sulphur, or dust moist foliage with sulphur early in the morning. Sulphur may burn foliage in high temperature. Plant resistant varieties.

Mosaic, a virus disease, causes varied symptoms of light green mottled foliage, twisted leaves, and deformed flowers. Certain insects spread it. The disease pervades the plant tissue, so the only recourse is to destroy the plant. Plant resistant varieties.

Rust, a name given to any of several fungus diseases, usually causes rusty brown patches or pustules on leaves, stems and buds of a wide variety of plants. The disease is spread by wind and insects, and its growth is encouraged by warm humid weather. It can be checked by dusting or spraying with sulphur. Plant rust-resistant varieties.

Sucking Insects. The sucking group of harmful insects includes aphids, chinch bugs, iris borers, leaf miners, leaf hoppers, rollers and borers, lacebugs, mealy bugs, tarnished plant bugs, red spider mites, scale, thrips, white flies and others. Sometimes repeated strong sprays of water, soap, pepper, garlic, onions, etc. discourage these insects. When resorting to an insecticide, use one that is specifically for sucking insects. Malathion and diazinon are general garden insecticides. Use with care. Malathion is injurious to ferns, petunias, and crassulas.

Aphids, plant lice, are tiny, usually green or brown, soft-bodied insects which suck juices primarily from new growth, excreting a honeydew which attracts ants and forms a medium for a fungus in the form of a black sooty mold. They spread fire blight, mosaic, and other virus diseases. Strong sprays of water are an effective control. Nicotine sulphate and malathion are possible insecticides.

Chinch bugs, small black insects, usually attack St. Augustine grass in hot dry weather, killing patches of grass. Irregular patches of brown in lawn may signal their presence (see "Lawns"). Chemical controls are: aspon, diazinon, ethion, or dursban.

Borers, in numerous varieties, are caterpillars or grubs (larvae of moths and beetles) which invade herbaceous or woody tissues. They are especially destructive to newly planted or weakened trees. Sunscald, injuries to leaf or bark, drought, poor soil and drainage are all deleterious to the health of trees, making them particularly susceptible to attack. Prevention is always more effective than a cure. Keep trees and plants healthy. Protect trees from injury. Symptoms of borers' presence are in holes, and residue of pitch or sawdust on the bark. Immediate attention is required, preferably by a professional tree man who may be able to cut borers out. Malathion, methoxychlor or dimethoate may prove helpful once there is an infestation.

Iris borers become larger as they feed. The larvae crawl up leaves, making pinpoint holes, and work their way down to the rhizome on which they feed, leaving a water-soaked and ragged appearance on leaf tissues. Clean up all old foliage, stalks, and debris. The borers introduce into the plants a bacterium which causes a vile-smelling soft rot. Sometimes the borers may be killed while on the leaf by pressing the leaf between thumb and finger; they are otherwise difficult to eradicate.

Stalk borers are slender, striped caterpillars, about an inch long, that work inside the stems of plants. They winter on grasses and weeds as gray-ridged eggs. In early spring they hatch and work first on the grass and then move to larger plant stalks, entering at the side and working their way up inside the stalk. The small grayish-brown, white-spotted moths which lay the larvae appear in late summer, and this is the best time for control. By the time the plant withers it is too late. Clean up weeds. A spray or dust such as methoxychlor destroys borers on the move.

Lacebugs, only ⅛-inch long, tan with clear gauze-like wings, suck sap from underside of leaves leaving them with a brown excrement, draining the plant of vigor. They attack azaleas, pyracantha, and chrysanthemums, giving leaves a mottled appearance. Malathion 50 is a chemical control.

Leafhoppers, small, ¼-inch long, feed on all types of foliage, sucking from undersurface, hopping away quickly when startled. Their sucking often causes yellowing and a white stippled look of the leaf. They carry many diseases. Lady bugs feed on leafhoppers; Bordeaux mixture controls them.

Serpentine Leafminers (many species) are yellow maggots, larvae of tiny black and yellow flies, which feed under the epidermis of leaf surfaces making long white serpentine tunnels. Control promptly with malathion when the flies are swarming. Once the miner is in the leaf and the tunnels are visible the only remedy is removal of the affected leaves. Each day remove the leaves or portions of them before the miner takes over the entire plant.

Leafrollers are caterpillars that feed while protected in a rolled-up leaf, cutting slits in it. Infestation can prevent formation of pods. Control with thuricide, dipel, or Fertilome Biological Spray.

Mealy bugs, soft scales, are small oval-shaped sucking insects covered with white powdery wax. They cluster in axils and on undersides of leaves, multiplying rapidly. Plants indoors are especially susceptible. A vacation outdoors, a strong water spray, or touching each insect and each axil with a cotton tip dipped in alcohol may control them. Repeat the treatment and give the plants air circulation. Malathion may be used. If the temperature is between 45° and 85°, a dormant oil may be mixed with the spray.

The *tarnished plant bug* adult is a small insect about ¼ inch long with yellow, white, and black blotches and a yellow triangle with one black dot on each side; nymphs are small, greenish yellow, with five black dots. They cause various deforming or discoloring injuries to numerous plants, vegetables, and fruits. They overwinter in debris. Prevent by keeping a clean garden. Sprays such as malathion 50 are controls.

Spider mites, often red, are microscopic insects found usually on undersides of leaves which take on a gray or dry-straw, mottled appearance. They can be knocked off with repeated sprays of strong water. The miticides chlorobenzilate and Kelthane 35 are controls, but they are harmful to gardenias, schefflera, and neantha belle palm.

There are various *scales* which damage plants by sucking leaf juices. They feed on underside of leaves, causing typical yellow spots on top sides; leaves eventually drop off. The most common variety is the armored scale, which secretes a waxy house over its body. They are ⅛ to ¹⁄₁₆ inch in diameter, almost any color, and of oval, circular or oblong shape. Newly hatched crawlers feed on young succulent growth. Because they multiply rapidly, start control quickly. Scales excrete a honeydew in which a black sooty mold grows. White oil or summer oil emulsion sprays are often used, sometimes combined with an insecticide such as malathion. Oil sprays will damage foliage, even to the point of defoliation, if used when temperature is over 85° or under 40° within 48 hours following spraying. Spray in late winter or very early spring before new growth begins, and again ten days later to kill in crawler stage.

Thrips are small, slender, barely visible insects that scar fruit and foliage with their scraping mouth parts, piercing flowers and fruit. Some eat harmful mites, but most are very injurious to plants. Rosebuds turn brown and either fail to open or open in a deformed way, with brown edges on the petals. Thrips seem to prefer light or yellow flowers. Because they live in tree and grass flowers and come out when rosebuds form, thrips are difficult to eradicate. Remove infested buds and blooms at once. No insecticide has been thoroughly successful.

Whiteflies are small sucking insects that fly out in clouds when an infested plant is shaken or disturbed. They are especially bothersome to citrus, gardenias, hollies, lantanas, privet, ligustrum, virburnum and, sometimes, boxwood. They secrete a honeydew on which a repulsive-looking black sooty mold feeds and grows. Repeated application of an insecticide such as malathion is a chemical control, but frequent forceful sprays of water applied underside of leaves will discourage them.

Chewing Insects. The chewing group of insects includes caterpillars, rose bugs, worms, some beetles, and any other insect which chews on leaves, flowers, and fruit. Hand picking is an effective control. Stomach poisons such as Sevin or diazinon applied to cover the foliage are chemical controls.

Bark beetles are very harmful to trees, especially weak ones. Proper watering and fertilizing keeps trees healthy and resistant. Woodpeckers feed on tree beetles. Spraying should properly be done by tree experts.

June bugs are large brown or black beetles, an inch or more long, usually appearing in April, May, and June, flying at night to feed on ornamentals. They are attracted to lights, but remain hidden under debris during the day. They enter the soil to lay eggs, and their grubs hatch in two or three weeks and damage grass badly. They eat the roots of grass, and the injury is often not apparent until spring. Use yellow insect lights as a preventive. The grubs are thick, white, repulsive wormlike insects. Periodically cut portions of the grass from the soil, and roll back. If there are more than three or four grubs visible per square foot there is a dangerous infestation. If the grass is left rolled back a few hours birds may eat the grubs. The only control is a poison such as diazinon. There are numerous other harmful beetles.

Rosebugs or rose chafers are ½-inch long tan beetles with reddish-brown heads, long spiny legs, and wing covers softer than those of most beetles. Appearing in swarms, they feed on numerous plants for three to four weeks before breeding. The grubs are white, up to ¾-inch long, and feed on roots. They overwinter in the soil. Handpicking, a temporary cheesecloth fence, and cultivating the soil are alternatives to insecticides such as carbaryl or methoxychlor.

Caterpillars are the worm-like larvae of moths and butterflies. There are thousands of kinds. Most have soft cylindrical bodies, sometimes hairy or spiny. They eat foliage voraciously. Wood ashes, sharp sand or diatomaceous earth (the skeletal remains of microscopic algae) sprinkled on ground around plant will deter these insects. *Bacillus thuringiensis* (BT) paralyzes and kills caterpillars when the eat it. Fertilome Biological Spray, dipel, and thioride kill caterpillars and are considered harmless to people and pets.

Cutworms are caterpillar larvae of various species of night-flying moths. They are fat, smooth, soft, and repulsive-looking. The surface cutworms are the most damaging to home gardens, feeding on foliage and cutting off plant stems at the ground. Some climb up the plant; others remain in the soil, feeding on roots. A stiff cardboard collar placed around the stem and pushed an inch or two into the soil, onions planted nearby, and a light mulch of wood ashes often deter cutworms. The only other control is cutworm bait or diazinon dust.

Bagworms are caterpillar-like insects that carry baglike homes which they attach to a twig by a silken thread when they stop to eat. Remove by hand, and burn. Trichogramma wasps are an effective enemy. If necessary, use a spray such as malathion or diazinon.

Migratory Insects. Included in this group are: ants, earwigs, grasshoppers, sowbugs, and slugs and snails.

Ants are harmful because they spread aphids. They may be controlled by tanglefoot banding on plants, by steamed bone meal sprinkled on the ground, a pepper spray, or tansy planted nearby. Diazinon may be effective.

Earwigs, identified by the pincers on their rears, hide by day and forage at night. Set out shallow tins of water to drown them. When necessary, use a chemical such as diazinon.

Grasshoppers are controlled by many varieties of birds, by turning soil to destroy their eggs, by growing ground covers on soil

to prevent them from laying eggs, and by suitable poisons such as diazinon.

Sowbugs, or *pillbugs,* are small oval gray insects which usually curl up into a ball when touched. Remove their favorite hiding places like boards or logs covering damp dirt. Frogs are their natural predators. A sprinkling of lime repels them. Diazinon may be used as a poison.

Slugs and *Snails* are mollusks. A slug is a snail without a shell. They are similar in appearance, about an inch long, with thick slimy bodies. They are attracted to saucers of beer in which they drown. Both feed at night by rasping holes in foliage. Eliminate their dark damp hiding places, and scatter wood ashes or sharp sand on soil. Flour will kill them by coating slime by which they move. Salt will also kill them, but used in excess will damage plants and roots.

Nematodes are small eel worms that feed inside the root fibers, causing an irritation that produces root knots. The plants become stunted and wilted. Marigold roots poison nematodes; lime and fish fertilizer repel them. A small amount of sugar worked into the soil, and watered, is helpful. There are also chemical controls. Severely infected plants must be removed and burned. Consistent use of compost and fertilizer in the soil is said to eliminate nematodes.

CRABGRASS

Weeds. "One man's weed is another man's flower." The saying has truth in it, yet it is inconceivable that some of our weeds could be considered desirable by anyone. Crabgrass is one of these. It is persistent to the point of driving a gardener to herbicides. Even digging

CHICKWEED

or hand pulling may fail to eradicate it because buds remain in the ground even after the weed is pulled out.

You do not have to be able to identify each variety of weed in order to dig it up, but it is helpful to recognize the enemy. Weeds are divided into two categories: the broadleaf and the grassy. Broadleaf weeds include those that usually invade lawns: chickweed, henbit, spurge, buckhorn, clover, dock, mustards, dandelion, and plantain. The grassy weeds include: crabgrass, Johnson grass, sandbur, nutgrass, annual bluegrass, goose grass and Dallis grass.

DANDELION

Light cultivation with hand and hoe remains the safest method of weed eradication. Herbicides and weed killing chemicals should be used only as a last resort, and even then with great caution and according to directions because the chemicals are poisonous to many desirable plants and can be harmful to people and wildlife. Herbicides remain in the soil up to 18 months. Most herbicides are harmful to ornamentals, and few are recommended for use on St. Augustine

grass or centipede grass. Neither herbicides nor any other weed killing chemical should be used on or anywhere near food crops. If herbicides are used, follow directions explicitly.

Weeds should be removed from a garden because they steal nutrients and moisture from garden plants. They offer shelter to insects and harmful disease spores. Tall weeds prevent smaller plants nearby from getting their share of the sunlight. If permitted to go to seed, weeds multiply manyfold and present an even more exasperating problem to the gardener.

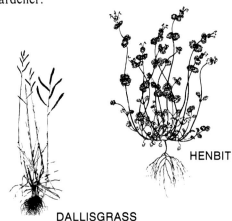

HENBIT

DALLISGRASS

When you are confronted with a large weed-filled space, as is possible when you are about to begin the preparation of a new bed, hoeing, scraping or tilling will help—with the exception of Bermuda grass, in which case you must try to take it out root and all. If an area is small enough for hand digging and pulling, make your plans in advance. Water the ground thoroughly two or three days before weeding. Be sure to wear your gardener's gloves! Use a pointed trowel or long

CLOVER

thin forked tool called a weeder to dig each weed out. The dampness of the soil allows the roots to come up with less disturbance to surrounding soil and plants. A narrow pointed hoe may be used, but do not cultivate deep enough to expose roots of garden plants to drying wind and sun. Carefully cover with soil any accidentally exposed roots. It is best to work on a cloudy day or late in the afternoon, so there will be less possibility of injury to garden plants.

Once a bed is weedfree, mulch the ground at least two inches deep to suffocate future weeds (see "Mulching"). If they do grow through the mulch they will be much easier to pull out. Try to pull weeds when they are still very small, before their root systems get widespread.

A sterilized fertilizer may prevent weeds to some extent, but it is an expensive prevention and may not last for long, since birds, animals, and wind scatter and spread weed seeds anyway. The truth is that there is no complete escape from weeds. Think of weeding chores in a positive way. Enjoy the exercise, the fresh air, and the sure knowledge that you are helping your garden thrive.

Poisonous Plants. Common Poison Ivy (*Rhus radicans* or *R. toxicadendron*) is a native vining plant which is poisonous on contact. It may be identified by its three-part leaflets and its small, white berry-like fruit. Poison Oak (*Rhus diversiloba*) is a similar species with similar effects. Sometimes smoke from a fire in which poison ivy is burning will also be irritating. A good home remedy to employ very shortly after you have touched the plant is to smear a paste made of cheap laundry soap on the affected area. If the irritation has already begun, consult a physician. A related plant with an even more poisonous effect is Poison Sumac (*Rhus vernix*). It is a tall shrub with reddish twigs and leaflets of seven to thirteen leaves with small white fruit. Treatment is the same as for Poison Ivy. To eradicate wear thick gloves and clothing that covers you well, and dig up its deep roots. Salt placed in the heart of the plant will kill Poison Ivy, but it may severely injure other plants nearby.

Do not eat any part of any plant with which you are not completely familiar—many are poisonous.

POISONOUS PLANTS

Jimsonweed (*Datura Stromonium*)—all parts are deadly
Delphinium, larkspur—foliage is poisonous
Poinsettia (*Euphorbia pulcherrima*)—juice is dangerous
Carolina Jasmine (*Gelsemium sempervirens*)—juice is poisonous
Oleander (*Nerium Oleander*)—all parts are very dangerous, do not use for firewood or for barbecuing sticks
Redbird Cactus (*Pedilanthus tithymaloides*)—juice is irritant, emetic, caustic
Rhododendron—foliage of all species

If symptoms of headache, nausea or convulsion appear, see a physician and try to take part of the plant with you.

$\mathcal{P}$lant $\mathcal{N}$omenclature

To know the names of the forms of life is one of the keenest of satisfactions; it brings one into relationship with living things, in endless variety; it multiplies the contacts.

—L.H. Bailey

Early in the history of horticulture it was realized that plants must be named in a universal language. Latin was chosen as the common currency amongst all civilized peoples. One Latin name for each plant serves as an internationally understood term; whereas the numerous colloquial or common names referring to the same plant would lead to complete confusion. Most garden literature, catalogs, and nurseries rely on the Latin names, so you should become familiar with the proper nomenclature. For the purposes of discussion or purchasing, this knowledge is essential. The names serve as far more than mere labels, often describing the appearance, structure and/or the original habitat of the plant.

Yet common names should not be forsaken entirely. They offer another enjoyable facet of garden knowledge, since they are sometimes interwoven with picturesque folklore.

The methods of naming plants derive from the work in the eighteenth century of the Swedish botanist Linnaeus, often called the "Father of Modern Botany." Linnaeus proposed a binomial nomenclature system of identifying each plant with a generic name and a specific name, always in that order. The genus refers to a more or less closely related group of plants. The species indicates plants resembling each other more than any other plant, all within the same genus. Later the system came to include families composed of genera which closely resemble each other in general appearance or technical characteristics. The family may include only one genus or many. For the everyday gardener these family names are not really necessary, but as interest in plants increases it is helpful to know features of families to assist in identifying an unknown plant. A simple example: most salvias have square stems, and so do menthas, or mints; so you can surmise that the two belong to the same family, which they do. Though there are exceptions, family names are usually composed of a genus name plus the suffix "aceae," meaning "belonging to." Rosa becomes Rosaceae, the family to which the genus Rosa belongs.

In some cases the generic name has also become the common name from frequent usage, such as Begonia, Iris, Petunia and Magnolia. The generic name may refer to some features characteristic of the genus; Oxalis, for example, is derived from the Greek word meaning acid or sour-juiced and here referring to the taste of the leaves. Some generic names were chosen to honor botanists. The Gardenia was named for Dr. Alexander Garden, a Charleston physician-gardener friend of Linnaeus.

A genus may contain over a thousand species; thus the importance of the specific name becomes even more obvious. Just as species names may indicate some identifying characteristic of the plant they may also be derived from a person's name, perhaps the person who introduced the species. *Phlox drummondii,* named for Drummond, or the *Rosa Banksia* for Lady Banks. Specific names may designate color of leaf or flower, some particular feature of the plant, its native habitat or, perhaps, the growing conditions it prefers. Several specific names may be used for the same plant, as *Salvia azurea grandiflora* for "Salvia, blue, large-flowered."

The term "hybrid" is sometimes listed along with a binomial name and indicates, in its historic application, the product of a cross between two or more species. "Variety" refers to a member of a group within a species usually restricted to a limited geographic area. The abbreviation "var." is often used. Varieties which originate under cultivation are "cultivars," applying to named varieties of garden plants as distinguished from those in the wild.

It is a worthwhile effort to tag named varieties of plants in the garden with permanent labels, or else keep a chart of the plants, their names, and placement in the garden for future reference.

L.H. Bailey wrote that "The naming of plants under rules of nomenclature is an effort to tell the truth. Its purpose is not . . . commercial. Serving the truth serves everybody. In the end, nomenclature rests with the plants rather than on printed regulations."[1]

As for the pronunciation of the Latin botanical names, it is safest to consult an encyclopedia, for there are exceptions to all the rules, but the following general ones usually apply:

1. Usually the vowels are long
2. When there are two syllables, accent the first
3. With three syllables, accent the middle (many exceptions to this)
4. With four syllables, accent the second
5. If five or more syllables, accent next to last

6. A final *e*, preceded by another vowel, and sometimes by a consonant, is pronounced as a separate syllable.

Some of the Most Commonly Used Specific Names[2]

(The gender of the specific name agrees with that of the generic name)

aggregatus (ag-reg-gáy-tus)—clustered
alatus (al-láy-tus)—winged
alba (ál-ba)—white
albi-plenus (al-bee-pléen-us)—double white-flowered
alternifolius (al-ter-nif-fóh-lee-us)—with alternate leaves
angustifolius (an-gus-tif-fóh-lee-us)—narrow-leaved
arborescens (ar-bor-reśs-ens)—becoming tree-like, woody
argenteus (ar-jeńt-ee-us)—silvery
aurantiacus (aw-ran-týe-ak-us)—orange-red
aureus (aẃ-ree-us)—golden
australis (ost-ráy-liss)—southern
azureus (az-yéw-ree-us)—sky blue
baccatus (bak-káy-tus)—berried
bellus (béll-us)—handsome
biennis (bye-eń-niss)—biennial, living two years
botryoides (bot-rye-oý-deez)—in clusters, grape-like
bullatus (bul-láy-tus)—swelling, puckered
caeruleus (see-réw-lee-us)—dark blue
campanulatus (kam-pan-yew-láy-tus)—bell-shaped
canescens (kan-eśs-sens)—downy gray
cernuus (sér-new-us)—bent, nodding
chinensis, (chin-nén-siss) also *sinensis*—of China
chrysanthus (kriss-ańth-us)—golden-flowered
ciliatus (sil-ee-aý-tus)—hairy fringed or margined
coccineus (kok-sín-ee-us)—scarlet
contortus (kon-toŕt-us)—twisted
cornutus (kor-néw-tus)—horned
crenatus (kren-náy-tus)—scalloped
deciduous (des-síd-yew-us)—with parts falling (as leaves)
dentatus (den-táy-tus)—toothed, dentate

---

[1] L.H. Bailey, *How Plants Get Their Names,* © 1933 by Dover Publications.

[2] From *The Self-Pronouncing Dictionary of Plant Names,* by Ralph Bailey for the 10th anniversary of The American Garden Guild Book Club. © The Literary Guild.

digitalis (dij-it-táy-liss)—finger-form
dioicus (dye-oĥ-ik-us)—having male and female flowers on separate plants
divergens (div-veŕj-ens)—wide-spreading
elatus (ee-láy-tus)—tall
exoticus (ex-ót-ik-us)—foreign, not native
ferox (fée-rox)—very thorny
filicifolius (fil-iss-if-fóh-lee-us)—fern-leaved
flavus (fláy-vus)—yellow
floribundus (floh-rib-buńd-us)—flowering profusely
foetidus (feét-id-us)—ill-smelling
fragrans (fráy-grans)—fragrant
glabrus (gláy-brus)—smooth
glaucus (gláw-kus)—"bloomy," grayish
gloriosus (gloh-ree-oĥ-sus)—superb
gracilis (gráss-il-iss)—slender, graceful
grandiflorus (gran-dif-flóh-rus)—large-flowered
guttatus (gut-táy-tus)—spotted, speckled
herbaceus (her-báy-see-us)—fleshy stemmed, not woody
hirtus (heŕt-us)—hairy
horizantalis (hor-i-zan-táy-lis)—dwarf
humilis (héw-mil-iss)—low-growing, dwarf
ibericus (eye-beér-ik-us)—of Spain or Portugal
ilicifolius (il-iss-if-fóh-lee-us)—holly-leaved
inermis (in-eŕr-mis)—thornless
japonicus (jap-pón-ik-us)—of or from Japan
labiatus (lay-bee-aý-tus)—lipped
lancifolius (lan-sif-fóh-lee-us)—pointed-leaved
latifolius (lat-if-fóh-lee-us)—broad-leaved
leucanthus (lew-kańth-us)—white-flowered
longifolius (lon-jif-fóh-lee-us)—long-leaved
macranthus (mak-rańth-us)—large-flowered
macrophyllus (mak-roh-fill-us)—larged-leaved
microphyllus (mye-kroh-fill-us)—small-leaved
nanus (náy-nus)—small, dwarf
niger (nýe-ger)—black
nocturnus (nok-tuŕn-us)—night-blooming
nudiflorus (new-dif-flóh-rus)—naked-flowered
odoratus (oh-dorr-aý-tus)—fragrant
opacus (oh-páy-kus)—pale
palustris (pal-luśt-riss)—marsh-loving
parviflorus (par-vif-flóh-rus)—small-flowered
patens (páy-tens)—spreading
phlogiflorus (floj-if-flóh-rus)—flame-flowered
plenus (pléen-us)—full, "double" (denoting many petaled flowers)
polyanthus (pol-ee-ańth-us)—many-flowered
praecox (prée-cox)—very early
purpereus (pur-peẃ-re-us)—purple

quercifolius (kwer-sif-fóh-lee-us)—with leaves like an oak
racemosus (ras-em-móh-sus)—with racemes as compared to panicles, spikes, etc.
radicans (rád-ik-anz)—rooting (along stem)
repens (reép-ens)—creeping (also *répttans*)
reticulatus (ret-ik-yew-láy-tus)—netted, net-veined
roseus (róh-zee-us)—rose-red
rotundifolius (roh-tun-dif-fóh-lee-us)—round-leaved
rubens (róo-bens)—red or ruddy
rubrus (róo-brus)—red
sempervirens (sem-per-výe-renz)—evergreen
serratus (ser-ráy-tus)—saw-toothed
sessifolius (sess-if-fóh-lee-us)—stalkless-leaved
stellatus (stel-láy-tus)—star-like
stenophyllus (sten-oh-fíl-us)—narrow-leaved
striatus (strye-aý-tus)—striped
sylvestris (sil-veśt-riss)—of woods and forests
tardiflorus (tar-dif-flóh-rus)—late flowering
trifoliatus (trye-foh-lee-aý-tus)—three-leaved
umbellatus (um-bell-láy-tus)—with clusters of flowers whose stems rise from a common point
vegetus (véj-et-us)—vigorous
versicolor (ver-sik-kól-or)—variously colored
virens (výe-rens)—green
viridis (víhr-id-iss)—green
xanthocarpus (zanth-oh-kaŕp-us)—yellow-fruited

Often Used Prefixes and Suffixes

Prefixes		Suffixes	
semper-	always, ever	*-carpus*	fruit
pauci-	scanty, few	*-ferous*	bearing
multi-	many	*-florus*	flowered
atro-	dark	*-folius*	leaf
leuc-	white	*-phyllus*	leaf

Books for continuing the fascinating study of plant names are available in libraries and bookstores. Suggested here are only three:

A Gardener's Dictionary of Plant Names by A.W. Smith, revised by William T. Stearn.
How Plants Got Their Names by L.H. Bailey.
The Self-Pronouncing Dictionary of Plant Names by Ralph Bailey.

Garden Jargon

ACIDITY, ALKALINITY: Referring to the soil's chemical reaction, or to the type of soil condition a particular plant needs. See pH.

ANNUAL: A plant that completes its entire life cycle within one year.

B&B (Balled-and-Burlapped): Shrubs and trees dug with a ball of dirt around the roots, wrapped in burlap, and tied to hold together, thus protecting roots.

BIENNIAL: A plant that usually completes its life cycle in two years.

BONSAI: Japanese term for training plants on a miniature scale, usually in containers.

BRACTS: Modified leaves that turn a showy color and seem to be flowers (*e.g.,* poinsettia, bougainvillea, shrimp plant).

BUD: A small projection or swelling on a stem, from which growth develops.

BULB: Generally used to refer to any thickened underground stem, but a "true bulb" is only one type of such stem, which is almost round, and is made up of fleshy leaves or scales that store food and protect an embryo plant inside (*e.g.,* Tulip).

CAMBIUM: The very important thin green layer of living tissue just beneath the bark. It channels food to leaves and roots, and produces protective covering for wounds.

CHILLING FACTOR: The degree and the number of hours of cold weather certain plants need for dormancy to develop flowers and fruit properly. Gardeners in mild winter areas should select plants, especially fruit trees, that do not require long cold winters.

CHLOROPHYLL: The substance in leaves which makes them green. It is necessary for photosynthesis.

CHLOROSIS: Referring to the yellowing of leaves, signifying that the plant is unable to absorb the elements necessary to make chlorophyll. May often be corrected by adding iron chelate, a combination of iron and a complex organic substance which allows the plant to absorb the iron in the soil. Acidifying the soil with one part agricultural sulphur and two parts copper- as sprinkled lightly around plant and immediately watered in may also free iron to the plant's roots.

COMPLETE FERTILIZER: Plant food containing the three necessary nutrient elements: nitrogen, phosphorus and potassium, listed in that order, with the percentage of each in numeric form. 12-24-12 signifies 12% nitrogen, 24% phosphorus (phosphate), and 12% potassium (potash), making 48% of the total. The other 52% might consist partially of important so-called trace elements including: iron, manganese, copper, zinc or boron, with any remaining percentage of the whole being a filler for easy mixing and spreading. It is wise to use various fertilizers with varying percentages of the elements, from different sources, combining ample organic materials. "Balanced fertilizer" is a common but ambiguous term, probably referring to a mixture balanced for the needs of certain types of plants.

COMPOSTING: The practice of heaping healthy garden refuse to speed its decomposition for use as a soil additive or a mulch. See "Soil and Soil Improvement."

CORM: A type of short fat bulb which stores food in its center rather than in its scales (*e.g.*, Gladiolus).

DECIDUOUS: Plants that shed all their leaves at one time each year.

DIOECIOUS: Types of plants having male and female flowers on separate plants, often requiring planting one of each for fertility to produce blooms and fruit.

DIVIDING: Digging up and pulling apart the developing roots and top growth of clumps of plants.

DRIP LINE: The imaginary circle drawn around a tree under its outermost tips.

EPIPHYTES: Plants, like orchids and bromeliads, which grow on other plants, perching on trees to attain light and moisture. Since they do not take food from the host plant, they are not parasites.

EVERGREEN: Plants that do not lose all their leaves at one time, though they shed the old leaves intermittently as new leaves come out.

EYE: A growth bud, as on a cutting or a tuber, that eventually produces new growth.

GUMBO: A heavy black-brown clay soil often found in Houston. Though difficult to break up, it is usually productive when properly handled. See "Soil and Soil Improvement."

HARDY: Indicating a plant's tolerance to freeze or frost.

HEAVY SOIL: A dense soil, such as clay, made up of tiny particles which pack closely, preventing aeration and penetration of water, and even of roots. See "Soil and Soil Improvement."

HERBACEOUS: A soft, fleshy plant such as an annual, perennial or bulb, as opposed to a woody plant such as a tree or shrub. The term may also refer to a "herbaceous perennial," which retains leaves all year.

HEELING IN: A method of temporarily storing plants by covering their roots with soil or mulch to prevent their drying out before planting.

HORTICULTURE: The art or science of growing plants.

HUMUS: A soft black or brown substance from completely decomposed animal and/or vegetable matter. In common usage it may refer to incompletely decomposed matter such as pine bark mulch.

HYBRID: A result of crossing two species or varieties of plants.

LEACHING: Repeated watering of plants to drain out and remove excess salts.

MONOECIOUS: Plants with male and female flowers on same plant, though separate.

MULCH: Loose porous material, usually organic matter, to cover soil. See "Soil and Soil Improvement."

NATURALIZE: Acclimating a plant to an environment to which it is not indigenous (native); to become established and grow as its kind does in its native habitat. Also to plant so as to give the effect of natural wild growth.

NITROGEN: An element which increases growth of stem and foliage, gives green color, and stimulates rapid growth.

NORTHER (or Blue Norther): Strong cold north wind which may cause the temperature to drop to freezing or below within a few hours. Characteristic of the upper Gulf Coast area.

ORGANIC MATTER: A general term referring to animal and vegetable materials in any state of decomposition. It is not only beneficial, it is essential to every soil. See "Soil and Soil Improvement."

PERENNIAL: A plant that lives more than two years, but which may die down each winter and grow again in the spring.

pH: A scientific term denoting the hydrogen ion concentration, by which soil acidity or alkalinity is measured on a scale of 14, with 7 being neutral, below 7 acid, and above 7 alkaline. A soil test is necessary to determine the pH rating. Generally, sulphur increases acidity and lime increases alkalinity. See "Soil and Soil Improvement."

118

PHOSPHORUS (phosphate): An element which stimulates root growth, gives plants a vigorous start, promotes greater seed and flower formation, and hardens plants to cold weather.

PHOTOSYNTHESIS: A process, yet to be duplicated by man, by which plants combine chlorophyll, sunlight, air, moisture, sugars, and starches in their leaves to make food for themselves.

PINCH-PRUNING (also called finger-pruning): The pinching off, with thumb and forefinger, of tender new growth at tips of branches to increase growth, promote greater bushiness, and, often, more blossoms.

POTASSIUM (potash): An element that strengthens plants, enabling them to resist diseases, insects, and cold damage; it promotes production of sugar, starches, and oil for food.

RHIZOME: Thickened underground stem, sometimes long and slender, or fleshy and thick, which spreads by creeping (*e.g.,* Iris).

STANDARD: A plant trained into tree form.

STOLON: A runner or horizontal branch, growing either above or below ground from the base of a plant, producing new plants from buds at the tip (*e.g.,* Strawberry Plant).

SYSTEMIC: Anything introduced into the system of a plant by application to the soil or by spraying.

TAPROOT: The main anchoring root growing straight down.

TENDER: Indicates a plant's lack of tolerance to frost or freezing temperatures.

TERRESTRIAL: Plants growing in soil, as contrasted to epiphytes, which grow in the air perched on other plants.

TILTH: The quality of a soil attained by tilling and amending it with organic matter until it has a texture to make it hospitable to plants and seeds.

TUBER: Underground stem, thicker and shorter than a rhizome, which bears buds (*e.g.,* Caladium).

TUBEROUS ROOT: A root that is a thick underground storage structure, with the growth buds at the base of the plant (*e.g.,* Daylilies).

The Circle of the Year

Winter

Spring

Autumn

Summer

The unique Gulf Coast region lends itself to outdoor gardening all year. To enable you to enjoy the benefits of this temperate zone we offer the Circle of the Year. For each month, we make suggestions of seeds to sow and plants to set out, accompanied by hints for successfully growing numerous varieties of plants, from Aspidistra to Zinnias. Included is a list of plants that bloom every month. If you especially desire colorful flowers for a certain month, turn to that month to make your selections; then consult the Planting Charts immediately following the calendar for appropriate directions on the particular plants you choose. By cross-referencing the calendar with the planting lists we think you can enjoy growing flowers, shrubs, trees, and vegetables throughout the year. Even more information is available in the special chapters on various garden subjects.

January

Come ye cold winds, at January's call,
On whistling wings, and with white flakes bestrew the earth.

—Ruskin

SEEDS which may now be sown in flats *(f)* or open ground *(o)*

Ageratum, *f*	Cleome, *o*	Godetia, *o*	Poppy, Shirley, *o*
Alyssum, Sweet, *f* or *o*	Coreopsis, *f* or *o*	Hollyhock, *f*	Queen Anne's-lace, *o*
Arctotis, *f* or *o*	Cornflower, *f* or *o*	Larkspur, *o*	Salpiglossis, *f* or *o*
Babysbreath, *f* or *o*	Daisy, African	Lobelia, *f*	Salvia, Blue, *f* or *o*
Blanketflower, *f* or *o*	Golden, *f* or *o*	Lupine, *o*	Scabiosa, *f* or *o*
Bluebonnet, *o*	Feverfew, *f* or *o*	Mallow, *f*	Snapdragon, *f* or *o*
Browallia, *f*	Forget-me-not, *f* or *o*	Nicotiana, *f*	Stock, *f* or *o*
Calendula, *f*	Four-o'clock, *o*	Petunia, *f* or *o*	Strawflower, *f* or *o*
Candytuft, *o*	Gayfeather, *o*	Phlox, Drummond, *o*	Sweet Pea, *o*
Chinese Forget-me-	Gerbera, *f*	Pinks (Dianthus),	Sweet Sultan, *f* or *o*
not, *f*		*f* or *o*	Sweet William, *f* or *o*
			Verbena, *f* or *o*

PLANTS which may now be placed in the open ground

Alyssum, Sweet	Delphinium	Petunia	Shrubs
Arctotis	Forget-me-not	Phlox, Drummond	Snapdragon
Bluebonnet	Four-o'clock	Louisiana	Stock
Calendula	Gerbera	Perennial	Sweet William
Candytuft	Hollyhock	Physostegia	Trees
Coreopsis	Honeysuckle	Pinks (Dianthus)	Verbena
Cornflower	Larkspur	Queen Anne's-lace	Viola
Daisy, English	Lupine	Roses	Violet
Michaelmas	Nicotiana	Salvia	Wallflower
Shasta	Pansy	Shrimp Plant	

BULBS, TUBERS, RHIZOMES which may now be placed in the open ground

Agapanthus	Cooperia (Rain Lily)	Ismene	Oxalis
Allium	Crinum	Kniphofia (Torch Lily)	Ranunculus
Alpinia (Ginger)	Crocus	Liatris	Scilla
Alstroemeria	Freesia	Lily-of-the-Valley	Sprekelia
Amarcrinum	Gladiolus	(pots)	Tigridia
Amaryllis	Hedychium	Liriope	Tulbaghia
Anemone	(Butterfly Lily)	Marica (Walking Iris)	Tulip
Blackberry Lily	Hemerocallis (Daylily)	Montbretia	Zephyranthes
Canna	Hyacinth, Dutch	Ornithogalum	(Fairy Lily)
Calla	Iris, Bulbous		
Chlidanthus	Louisiana		

VEGETABLES which may now be sown in flats *(f)* or open ground *(o)*

Asparagus roots, *o*	Chicory	Kale, *o*	Potatoes, Irish, *o*
Beets, *o*	(French endive), *o*	Kohlrabi, *o*	Radish, *o*
Broccoli, *o*	Chinese Cabbage, *o*	Lettuce, *o*	Rhubarb chard, *o*
Brussels sprouts, *f*	Collards, *f*	Mustard, *o*	Rhubarb roots, *o*
Cabbage, *f*	Cos (Romaine	Onion, seeds, sets,	Roquette, *o*
Cantaloupe, *f*	lettuce), *o*	plants	Salsify, *o*
Carrots, *o*	Cress, *o*	Parsley, *o*	Spinach, *o*
Cauliflower, *f*	Cucumber, *f*	Parsnips, *o*	Squash, *f*
Celery, *o*	Eggplant, *f*	Peas, English, *o*	Tendergreens, *f*
Celtuce, *o*	Endive, *o*	Pepper plants, *f*	Tomatoes, *f*
Chard, Swiss, *o*	Horseradish roots, *o*	Peppers, *f*	Turnips, *o*
Chervil, *o*			

Soil is the basic element of growing any plant. Study "Soil" chapter before beginning any bed preparation.

Arbor Day is the third Friday in January in the Gulf Coast area to encourage planting of trees.

Azaleas: Plants may be moved. Keep moist to lessen cold weather damage.

Birds: Provide food and fresh water. More birds die from lack of water than from lack of food.

Camellias: Plants may be moved. Pick up and burn all old blooms.

Cultivation: Changes in design may now be made, new beds dug and old ones rebuilt. Correct defects in drainage. Incorporate gypsum into heavy soils; repeat in three weeks. Dig granite dust and rock phosphate deep into soil, and add quantities of organic matter. Allow time for settling before planting.

Fertilize: Daylilies, spuria, Louisiana and bearded irises with complete fertilizer. Give strawberries 1 teaspoon ammonium sulfate, keeping six inches away from plant.

Fruits: Plant fruit trees. Mulch figs with grass or straw to prevent freeze damage to crown.

House Plants: Water only when surface soil is crumbly dry. Wash dust off leaves. Mist often. Inspect for diseases and insects.

Pests: Spray azaleas and camellias for petal blight prevention as flowers open. Spray for scale with dormant oil solution if temperature will be above 35° and below 85° for next 48 hours. ALWAYS read and heed manufacturer's directions BEFORE spraying.

Propagation: Ivy cuttings root easily this month and next. Root cuttings of shrubs in mixture of loam and coarse sand; keep damp and semi-shaded until rooted.

Prune: Fruit trees in advance of new growth. Remove dead wood from trees and shrubs before spring buds swell, but do not prune spring bloomers. Prune crapemyrtles now. Prune nandinas and others of similar growth habit by cutting unwanted canes out at base of plant.

Roses: Plant bare-rooted. Annual pruning should be between middle of January and the middle of February, just before the spring buds break. In the old beds, to prevent the later appearance of disease, gather all dead leaves from bush and ground and burn.

Transplanting: January is one of the best months to transplant woody plants, both evergreen and deciduous, especially trees. Energy will be expended on roots instead of foliage. Learn ultimate size, and cultural needs of tree or plant before buying. Consider dwarf varieties to avoid crowding later. Group plants of similar cultural needs. Do not work wet soil. Assure good drainage.

Vegetables: Prepare beds, preferably raised for drainage, with about 50% humus, including manure.

Winter Protection: Expect freeze any time; plan for protection of tender plants. Water. Remove coverings, particularly plastic, when temperature rises. Protect low plants with dry leaves, pine needles or soil mulch, but remove when weather warms.

PLANTS WHICH BLOOM IN JANUARY

t—Tree   *s*—Shrub   *v*—Vine   *b*—Bulb, Tuber or Rhizome   *e*—Evergreen

d—Deciduous   *p*—Perennial   *bn*—Biennial   *a*—Annual

Azalea, *s e*	Forget-Me-Not, *p*	pubescens, *v e*	Quince, Japanese
Alyssum, Sweet, *a*	Gerbera, *p*	Lachenalia, *b*	Flowering, *s d*
Arctotis, *a*	Holly, *s e* and *d*,	Lantana, *s d*	Rice Paper Plant, *s e*
Babysbreath, *p*	berries	Magnolia, Pink,	Roses
Bouvardia, *s e*	Honeysuckle,	*s* or *t d*	Salvia, *a*
Calendula, *a*	fragrantissima, *s d*	Narcissus, *b, spp*	Shrimp Plant, *p*
Calla Lily, *b*	Horsechestnut,	Oxalis, *b, spp*	Spirea, thunbergii, *s d*
Camellia,	Dwarf, *s d*	Pansy, *a*	Sweet Olive, *s e*
japonica, *s e*	Hyacinth, *b*	Pear, *t d*	Sweet Pea, *v*
Sasanqua, *s e*	Iris, unguicularis, *b*	Pentas, *s e*	Turk's Cap, *s e*
Candytuft, *a*	Jasmine,	Pinks, *a* and *bn*	Verbena, *p*
Daisy, English, *a*	nudiflorum, *s d*	Plum, *t d*	Viola, *a*
African Golden, *a*	primrose, *s e*	Poinsettia, *s d*	Violet, *p*

February

A February face, so full of frost, of storm, and cloudiness.
—Shakespeare

SEEDS which may now be sown in flats *(f)* or open ground *(o)*

Alyssum, Sweet, *f* or *o*	Coreopsis, *f* or *o*	Globe Amaranth, *f*	Pinks (Dianthus),
Arctotis, *f* or *o*	Cornflower, *f* or *o*	Godetia, *o*	*f* or *o*
Babysbreath, *f* or *o*	Cosmos, Early, *f* or *o*	Hollyhock, *f*	Salpiglossis, *f* or *o*
Blanketflower, *f* or *o*	Dahlia, Dwarf, *o*	Larkspur, *o*	Salvia, Blue, *f* or *o*
Browallia, *f*	Daisy, in variety,	Lobelia, *f*	Scarlet, *f* or *o*
Calendula, *f*	*f* or *o*	Lupine, *o*	Scabiosa, *f* or *o*
Calliopsis, *f* or *o*	Everlasting, *f* or *o*	Mallow, *f*	Snapdragon, *f* or *o*
Candytuft, *o*	Feverfew, *f*	Marigold, *o*	Stock, Dwarf, *f*
Chinese Forget-	Forget-me-not, *f* or *o*	Nasturtium, *o*	Strawflower, *f* or *o*
me-not, *f*	Four-o'clock, *o*	Penstemon, *o*	Sweet Pea, Early, *o*
Cleome, *o*	Gayfeather, *o*	Petunia, *f* or *o*	Late, *o*
		Phlox, Drummond, *o*	Tobacco, Flowering,
			f or *o*

PLANTS which may now be placed in the open ground, weather permitting

Ageratum	Daisy, English	Lupine	Scabiosa
Alyssum, Sweet	Michaelmas	Pansy	Shrimp Plant
Arctotis	Shasta	Petunia	Shrubs
Bluebells	Delphinium	Phlox, Creeping	Snapdragon
Calendula	Forget-me-not	Drummond	Stock
Chinese Forget-	Four-o'clock	Louisiana	Sweet William
me-not	Gaillardia	Physostegia	Trees
Columbine	Gerbera	Pinks (Dianthus)	Verbena
Coreopsis	Hollyhock	Queen Anne's-lace	Viola
Cornflower	Honeysuckle	Roses	Violet
	Larkspur	Salvia, Blue	Wallflower

BULBS, TUBERS, RHIZOMES which may now be placed in the open ground

Agapanthus	Dahlia	Hemerocallis	Ornithogalum
Allium	Dietes	Hymenocallis	Oxalis
Alpinia (Ginger)	Gladiolus	Iris, Bearded	Ranunculus
Alstroemeria	Gloriosa (Climbing	Dwarf	Scilla
Amarcrinum	Lily)	Ismene	Sisyrinchium
Amaryllis	Habranthus	Kniphofia	Sprekelia
Blackberry Lily	Haemanthus	(Torch Lily)	Tigridia
Canna	Hedychium (Butterfly	Liriope	Tuberose
Chlidanthus	Lily)	Marica	Tulbaghia
Crinum		Milla	Zephyranthes
Cooperia		Montbretia	

VEGETABLES which may now be sown in flats *(f)* or open ground *(o)*

Artichoke tubers, *o*	Celtuce, *o*	Jerusalem	Pepper plants, *o*
Asparagus roots, *o*	Chard, Swiss, *o*	artichokes, *o*	Pepper, *f*
Beans, Snap, *o*	Chinese Cabbage, *o*	Kale, *o*	Potatoes, Irish, *o*
Pole, *o*	Chives, *o*	Kohlrabi, *o*	Sweet, *o*
Lima, *o*	Collards, *f*	Lettuce, *o*	Radish, *o*
Beets, *o*	Corn, sweet, *o*	Mirliton (Vegetable	Roquette, *o*
Broccoli, *o*	Cos, *o*	pear)	Rhubarb roots, *o*
Brussels sprouts, *f*	Cress, *o*	Mustard, *o*	Spinach, *o*
Cabbage, *f*	Cucumber, *f*	Onions, seeds, sets,	Squash, *f*
Carrots, *o*	Eggplant, *f*	plants, *o*	Tendergreens, *o*
Cantaloupe, *f*	Endive, *o*	Parsley, *o*	Tomatoes, *f*
Cauliflower, *f*	Horseradish roots, *o*	Parsnips, *o*	Turnips, *o*
Celery, *o*		Peas, English, *o*	

Azaleas: Plants may be moved. Keep watered. They must have good drainage (see "Azaleas").

Bulbs: Summer flowering bulbs may be planted now. Gladioli every two weeks from January through May and from July through October for succession of bloom. Divide daylilies if clumps are too large; side dress with fertilizer.

Camellias: Pick up and burn all old blooms. Reproduce plants by grafting.

Cuttings: Most favorable month to set cuttings of hardwood shrubs, trees and vines.

Fertilize: Lawns, trees, shrubs (except azaleas, camellias, pink magnolias) with complete fertilizer, watered in, keeping it away from trunk.

Maidenhair: While dormant and thin, work bone meal into the soil. May be divided and reset. Will spread quickly.

Perennials: Divide, separate, and transplant.

Pruning: Last chance for many shrubs to avoid losing summer bloom (see "Pruning").

Roses: Plant not later than February. Check new leaves and buds for aphids. Annual pruning now if not previously done. Spray rose beds with fungicide to prevent Black Spot. DO NOT fertilize newly planted rose bushes until after first blooming.

Spray: Peach and plum trees when 75% of flowers have fallen to control fruit or brown rot. Spray shrubs for scale.

Vegetables: Set out cool weather varieties. Sow seeds of summer varieties in flats (see "Vegetables.")

Winter Protection: February 10th is average date of last frost, but freezes can come later. Budding of pecan trees seems to be reliable sign danger is past.

PLANTS WHICH BLOOM IN FEBRUARY

t—Tree *s*—Shrub *v*—Vine *b*—Bulb, Tuber or Rhizome *e*—Evergreen
d—Deciduous *p*—Perennial *bn*—Biennial *a*—Annual

Alyssum, Sweet, *a*	Gerbera, *p*	Lantana, Weeping, *s d*	thunbergi
Azalea, *s e*	Heather, Mediter-	Moss Pink, *p*	Stock, *a* and *bn*
Bougainvilleas, *v e*	ranean, *s c*	Narcissus, *b*	Sweet Olive, *s e*
Calendula, *a*	Honeysuckle, *s d*	Oxalis, *b*	Sweet Pea, *a*
California Poppy, *a*	fragrantissima	Pansy, *a*	Verbena, *p*
Calla Lily, *b*	morrowi	Petunia, *a*	Viburnum, *s e*
Calycanthus Floridus, *s d*	tartarian	Phlox, Drummond, *a*	tinus
Camellia Japonica, *s e*	Hyacinth, Roman, *b*	Pinks, *a* and *bn*	suspensum
Candytuft, *a*	Ice Plant, *a*	Quince, Japanese	japonicum
Chinese Forget-met-not, *a*	Iris, *b*	Flowering, *s d*	Vinca, *v e*
Cornflower, *a*	Jasmine	Scilla, *b*	Viola, *a*
Daisy,	Carolina, *v e*	Snowdrop, *b*	Violet, *p*
African Golden, *a*	nudiflorum, *s d*	Snowflake, *b*	
English, *a*	primrose, *s e*	Spirea, *s d*	
Daphne, Winter, *s e*	pubescens, *v* or *s e*	prunifolia	

Ah, March! we know thou art
Kind-hearted, spite of ugly looks and threats,
And, out of sight, art nursing April's violets.

—Helen Hunt Jackson

SEEDS which may now be sown in flats *(f)* or open ground *(o)*

Ageratum, *f*	Cleome, *o*	Gayfeather, *o*	Portulaca, *o* after 15th
or *o* after 15th	Cockscomb, *f* or *o*	Globe Amaranth,	Salpiglossis, *f* or *o*
Alyssum, Sweet, *f* or *o*	Coleus	*f* or *o*	Salvia, Blue, *f* or *o*
Arctotis, *f* or *o*	Coral Vine, *f* or *o*	Hollyhock, *f* or *o*	Scarlet, *f* or *o*
Balsam, Garden, *f* or *o*	Cosmos, Early, *f* or *o*	Hyacinth Bean, *o*	Scabiosa, *f* or *o*
Sultan, *f* or *o*	Cypressvine, *o*	Immortelle, *o*	Sunflower, *o*
Bells-of-Ireland, *f* or *o*	Dahlia, Dwarf, *o*	Mallow, *f* or *o*	Sweet Pea, Perennial, *o*
Blanketflower, *f* or *o*	Daisy, African	Marigold, *o*	Tithonia, *o*
Browallia, *o*	Golden, *o*	Moonflower, *o*	Tobacco, Flowering,
Calliopsis, *f* or *o*	Dusty Miller, *o*	Morning-Glory, *o*	*f* or *o*
Candytuft, *o*	Feverfew, *f*	Nasturtium, *o*	Torenia, *f*
Castor Bean, *o*	Forget-me-not, *o*	Periwinkle, *f* or *o*	Verbena, *f* or *o*
Chinese Forget-	Four-o'clock, *o*	Petunia, *f* or *o*	Zinnia, *f*
me-not, *f* or *o*		Phlox, Drummond, *o*	

PLANTS which may now be placed in the open ground

Ageratum	Coreopsis	Hibiscus	Pansy
Alyssum, Sweet	Cornflower	Honeysuckle	Periwinkle
Arctotis	Cosmos, Klondyke	Hydrangea	Petunia
Azalea	Late	Jasmine, Day-	Physostegia
Balsam Sultan,	Dahlia, Dwarf	blooming	Phlox, Perennial
after 15th	Daisy, Michaelmas	Night-	Louisiana
Blanketflower	Shasta	blooming	Plumbago
Bluebell	Delphinium	Lantana	Salvia
Browallia	Dusty Miller	Larkspur	Scabiosa
Butterflyweed	Eranthemum	Lemon Verbena	Sedum
Calliopsis	Ferns	Lobelia	Shrimp Plant
Calendula	Feverfew	Lupine	Snapdragon
Camellia	Forget-me-not	Lythrum	Sweet Sultan
Chinese Forget-	Four-o'clock	Mallow	Verbena
me-not	Geranium, after 15th	Marigold, after 15th	Wallflower
Coleus	Gerbera	Mistflower	Zinnia
Coral Vine		Moonflower	

BULBS, TUBERS, RHIZOMES which may now be placed in the open ground

Achimenes	Calla	Haemanthus	Oxalis
Agapanthus	Canna	Hedychium	Sisyrinchium
Alstroemeria	Chlidanthus	(Butterfly Lily)	Sprekelia
Allium	Crinum	Hemerocallis	Strelitzia (pot)
Alpinia	Dahlia	Hymenocallis	Tigridia
Amarcrinum	Dietes	Iris, Louisiana	Tuberose
Amaryllis	Ginger Lily	Ismene	Tulbaghia
Billbergia	Gladiolus	Kniphofia	Water Hyacinth
Blackberry Lily	Gloriosa (Climbing	Liriope	Water Lily
Caladium	Lily)	Marica	Watsonia
	Habranthus	Montbretia	Zephyranthes

VEGETABLES which may now be sown in flats (f) or open ground (o)

Artichoke tubers, o	Chives, o	Lettuce, o	Pumpkin, o
Asparagus roots, o	Collard plants, o	Mirliton (Vegetable	Radish, o
Beans, Lima, o	Corn, o	Pear)	Rhubarb roots, o
Snap, o	Corn Salad, o	Muskmelon, o	Spinach, o
Beets, o	Cress, o	Mustard, o	Spinach,
Broccoli plants, o	Cucumber, o	Okra, o	New Zealand, o
Cabbage plants, o	Cushaw, o	Onion plants, o	Squash, o
Cantaloupe, o	Eggplant plants, o	Parsley, o	Tendergreens, o
Carrots, o	Endive, o	Peas, Blackeyed, o	Tampala, o
Cauliflower plants, o	Gourds, o	Crowder, o	Tomato plants, o
Celery, o	Herbs	English, o	Turnip, o
Celtuce, o	Horseradish roots, o	Pepper Plants, o	Watermelon, o
Chard, Swiss, o	Kohlrabi, o	Potatoes, Irish, o	
Chinese Cabbage, o	Leeks, o	Sweet, slips	

Azaleas: To avoid azalea petal blight, spray every week, as flowers open. Prune immediately after blooming and fertilize. May be sheared to thicken plants for screen or hedge.

Camellias: Spray for tea scale. Fertilize lightly.

Color: Plan and plant now for summer blooms.

Cultivation: Systematic surface cultivation of small bedding plants is essential to insure strong and rapid development. Mulch. Pinch chrysanthemums at main stem until fall. Divide and replant winter blooming iris. Sow most seeds now in Gulf Coast regions.

Fertilize: All roses, shrubs and plants with quick acting fertilizer to stimulate rapid spring growth. Do not allow dry fertilizer to touch stems or leaves of young plants. Read manufacturer's directions carefully BEFORE applying. Never use stronger dilution than recommended. It can burn plants, harm wildlife as well as people, and raise cost of gardening. Keep dry fertilizers away from stalks of plants and trunks of trees. ALWAYS KEEP ALL FERTILIZERS, PESTICIDES AND HERBICIDES OUT OF REACH OF CHILDREN. Feed flowering shrubs and trees following bloom. Fertilize early blooming bulbs (narcissus) with bone meal after bloom. Use high phosphorus fertilizer for more blooms on annuals and perennials. Exception: Nasturtiums, moonflowers and morning glories bloom best in poor, fairly dry soil.

Herbs: Most may be planted now from seeds, but germination is often slow; securing plants may be preferable. If seeds are planted, use flats of loose, well draining, slightly alkaline soil and protect from full sun until plants are at least 2″ tall; move gradually into part sun. Transplant. Check chart and chapter on Herbs.

Hydrangeas: Give shady locations—preferably north exposure—perfect drainage, and abundance of peat moss or leaf mold in soil. Mulch and water copiously after plants are in leaf. Prune only dead wood now.

Lawns: Rake or use a thatcher to remove dead growth. May apply a complete, controlled release or organic base fertilizer, manure or sludge type fertilizer. Raking, or thatching and aerating may be all lawn needs, especially if foundation soil contains quantity of humus and has good drainage. Application of gypsum can help drainage. Watch for new varieties of pest and disease-resistant grasses. Always water fertilizer in well after application (see "Lawns").

Maidenhair: A bed of this fern does well on north side of house, or in shade under trees. Pieces of well rotted bark or wood placed under the roots prove most helpful. Peat moss added to sandy loam is ideal, for spongy soil, perfectly drained. Keep beds pleasantly moist.

Pests: Watch for appearance of aphids on new growth; also, red spider and cut worm.

Pruning: Finish pruning roses and dormant shrubs. Any plants damaged by freeze should be cut back to green wood.

Roses: Begin monthly feeding program. Weekly fungicide spraying for Black Spot is recommended. Organic fertilizers excellent for seasonal balance. A handful of fertilizer high in phosphorus, such as 12-24-12, may be broadcast around each established bush. Water. Liquid fertilizers are faster, but do not feed the soil for long. Foliar feeding is helpful. A combination of methods, used at different times, is successful for many growers. DO NOT feed new bushes until after first blooming. Water by soaking. Try miniature roses.

Tuberose: Remove bulblets from old bulbs and plant separately for future bloom, or plant new bulbs now. Cover with two inches of soil.

Vegetables: Beds prepared at least two weeks earlier may be ready for planting. Weather permitting, transplant seedlings. If soil sticks to trowel, wait for dryer weather. Vegetables should grow quickly to be flavorful. Sun and well-drained, loose, rich soil are essential. If pecan trees have budded out, it should be safe to plant tender vegetables outdoors. Vegetables and herbs may be interplanted with annuals and perennials if their cultural needs can be met, and if they have enough space. Peppers, eggplants, asparagus roots, kale, chard, parsley, lettuce, radishes and others may be used successfully with flowers. Some say this diversity retards insect infestation. Set a plant of French marigold and sweet basil to every four tomato plants as an insect repellant (see Companion Planting). Weed, mulch and water. Hand pick insects early in morning. If pesticides or fungicides are needed, BE SURE BEFORE USING that they are intended for food crops, use exactly according to directions, and take note of the waiting date to harvest after spraying or dusting. Check calendar sections and the "Vegetables" chapter.

PLANTS WHICH BLOOM IN MARCH

t—Tree *s*—Shrub *b*—Bulb, Tuber or Rhizome *e*—Evergreen
d—Deciduous *p*—Perennial *bn*—Biennial *a*—Annual

Agarita, *s d*
Almond, Flowering, *s d*
Alyssum, Sweet, *a*
Amazon Lily, *b*
Anaqua, *t e*
Andromeda, *s e*
Anemone, *b*
Arctotis, *a*
Ardisia, *s e*
Azalea, *s d* and *e*
Bignonia, *v* and *p e*
Bluebonnet, *bn*
Calendula, *a*
Calla, *b*
Camellia, japonica, *s e*
Candytuft, *a*
Cerastium, *p*
Chinaberry, *t d*
Cherry Laurel, *t* or *s e*
Chionodoxa, *b*
Clivia, *b*
Cornflower, *a*
Crinum, *b*
Currant, Flowering, *s d*
Daffodil, *b*

Daisy, *p*
Daphne, *s e*
Delphinium, *a*
Dogwood, *t d*
Doxantha, *v d*
Flag, Native Iris, *b*
Fringetree, *t d*
Gerbera, *p*
Godetia, *a*
Grape-hyacinth, *b*
Guava, Pineapple, *s e*
Hawthorns, *t d*
Heather, Mediter-
    ranean, *s e*
Honeysuckle, *v d* and *s e*
Huisache, *t d*
Hyacinths, *b*
Iris, *b*
Ixia, *b*
Jasmines, *s e*
Jonquil, *b*
Kerria, *s d*
Laceflower, Blue, *a*
Lantana, *s d*
Larkspur, *a*

Laurel, Texas Mountain,
    s or *t e*
Magnolia, Star, *t d*
Mahonia, *s e*
Mexican Buckeye, *t d*
Milla, *b*
Moss Pink, *p*
Nandina, *s e*
Narcissus, *b*
Orchid Tree, *t d*
Oxalis, *b*
Pansy, *a*
Peach, *t d*
Pear, *t d*
Pearlbush, *s d*
Petunia, *a*
Phlox, *a* and *p*
Photinia, *s e*
Pinks, *a, bn* and *p*
Pittosporum, *s e*
Plums, *t d*
Poppies, *a*
Quince, Flowering, *s e*
Ranunculus, *b*
Redbud, *s* and *t d*

Roses, *s*
Scabiosa, *a, bn* and *p*
Silverbell Tree, *t d*
Snapdragon, *a*
Snowflake, *b*
Spireas, *s d*
Squill, *b*
Stock, *a* or *bn*
Styrax, native, *s d*
Sweet Olive, *s e*
Sweet Pea, *a s*
Trachelium, *a*
Tulip, *b*
Verbena, *p*
Viburnums, *s e*
Vinca, *v e*
Viola, *a*
Violet, *p*
Wallflower, *a*
Watsonia, *c*
Weigela, *s d*
Wisteria, *v* or *t d*

April

Oh, the lovely fickleness of an April day!
—W.H. Gibson

SEEDS which may now be sown in flats *(f)* or open ground *(o)*

Amaranthus, *o*
Ageratum, *f* or *o*
Alyssum, Sweet, *f* or *o*
Balsam, Garden, *f* or *o*
Blanketflower, *f* or *o*
Castorbean, *o*
Celosia, *o*
Cockscomb, *f* or *o*

Coleus, *o*
Coral Vine, *o*
Cosmos, *o*
Cleome, *o*
Cypressvine, *o*
Dahlia, Dwarf, *o*
Feverfew, *o*
Four-o'clock, *o*

Globe Amaranth, *o*
Gourd, *o*
Impatiens, *b*
Marigold, *o*
Moonflower, *o*
Morning-glory, *o*
Nasturtium, *o*
Periwinkle, *f* or *o*
Petunia, *f* or *o*

Portulaca, *o*
Queen Anne's-lace, *o*
Scabiosa, *o*
Sunflower, *o*
Sweet Pea, Perennial, *o*
Tithonia, *o*
Torenia, *f*
Zinnia, *o*

PLANTS which may now be placed in the open ground

Acalypha
Ageratum
Alternanthera
Amaranth
Aralia
Balsam, Garden
Banana
Begonia, Bedding
Blanketflower
Bluebells
Browallia
Butterflyweed
Calliopsis
Canterbury Bells

Chinese Forget-me-not
Chrysanthemum
Cockscomb
Coral Vine
Cosmos
Croton
Dahlia, Dwarf
Dusty-Miller
Eranthemum
Feverfew
Four-o'clock
Geranium
Gerbera
Hibiscus
Honeysuckle

Jasmine
Lantana
Lemon-grass
Lemon-verbena
Lythrum
Mallow
Marigold
Mistflower
Moonflower
Periwinkle
Petunia
Phlox, Louisiana
    Perennial
Physostegia

Plumbago
Potatovine
Queen Anne's-lace
Salpiglossis
Salvia
Sedum
Shrimp Plant
Sweet Sultan
Tobacco, Flowering
Torenia
Verbena
Violet
Wallflower
Zinnia

BULBS, TUBERS, RHIZOMES which may now be placed in the open ground

Achimenes	Chlidanthus	Haemanthus	Marica (Walking Iris)
Agapanthus	Crinum	Hedychium (Butterfly	Montbretia
Alpinia (Ginger)	Dahlia	Lily)	Oxalis
Amarcrinum	Dietes	Hemerocallis (Daylily)	Sprekelia
Amaryllis	Galtonia	Hymenocallis (Spider	Tigridia
Billbergia	Ginger Lily	Lily)	Tuberose
Caladium	Gladiolus	Lachenalia (Pot)	Tulbaghia
Calla	Gloriosa (Climbing	Liriope	Zephyranthes
Canna	Lily)	Lycoris	

VEGETABLES which may now be sown in open ground

Artichoke tubers	Chives	Leeks	Pumpkin
Asparagus roots	Celery	Mirliton (Chayote)	Radishes
Beans, Lima	Celtuce	Mustard	Shallots
Pinto	Collards	Parsley	Spinach
Snap	Corn	Parsnips	Spinach, New Zealand
Beets	Cress	Peanuts	Squash
Cabbage plants	Cucumber	Peas, Blackeye (Cow)	Tampala
Cantaloupe	Cushaw	Crowder	Tendergreens
Carrots	Eggplant plants	Potatoes, Irish	Tomato plants
Cauliflower	Herbs of all kinds	Sweet slips	Turnips
Chard, Swiss	Jerusalem artichokes	Pepper plants	

Azaleas: Prune now if not previously. Check soil acidity. Late April, spray for disease prevention and insect control; fertilize again only if necessary, 4 to 6 weeks after first feeding.

Bulbs: Fertilize with bone meal after blooming. Allow foliage of spring bloomers to die on plant to feed bulb. When cutting lilies, leave about ¼ of stem to mature bulb. Leave at least four leaves on lower part of stem when cutting gladioli. Separate waterlilies and renew earth in tubs.

Camellias: Check soil acidity. Spray with fungicide for dieback control. Prune.

Chrysanthemums: Divide last of April or early May. If divided earlier, plants are apt to grow woody and make poor flowers. New shoots make better plants than old central root. Pinch tips for bushier growth and more blooms.

Cutting of Blossoms: Cut flowers freely, especially stock, pinks, arctotis, coreopsis, snapdragon, and petunia to prolong blossoming period. Enjoy the blossoms of spring flowering shrubs, for cutting merely amounts to pruning, which should be done anyway as soon as the flowering season is over.

Fertilize: Hibiscus monthly with high phosphorus ratio fertilizer till September. Feed magnolias with azalea food (acid), placed in holes at drip line of branches. Water. Mulch with old manure.

Growth: Three main elements for healthy plant growth are: nitrogen for leaf and stem; phosphorus for fruit, bloom and root; and potash for vigor and winter protection.

Herbs: Set out plants of chamomile, coriander (cilantro), Italian parsley, basils, lemon balm, mints in variety, rosemary, sages, and thymes. Refer to "Companion Planting" for use of herbs as pest retardants.

Layering: Many trees and shrubs, including pink magnolia, japonica, viburnum, honeysuckle, and many vines, such as wisteria and jasmine, may be successfully layered this month. Slit bark on underside of a branch, bend and fasten securely to ground and cover with about two inches of earth. Treat verbenas in same manner, except cover with only a ½-inch of earth.

Mulch: All flowers, shrubs and trees at time of planting. Replace on established plants. A mulch keeps the soil from caking, promotes healthy growth of plants and deters weeds. Mixed mulch materials allow more aeration and better penetration of water. Keep mulches 2 to 4" thick.

Mildew: Dust—while the dew is on the plants—with sulphur; or spray with fungicide.

Prune: Flowering quince, bridalwreath, weigela, deutzia, and other flowering shrubs and trees after blooming. Prune and repot poinsettias.

Roses: Continue fungicide spray for Black Spot. For aphids use hard sprays of water or remove by hand, before resorting to pesticide such as rotenone or pyrethrum. Healthy plants are resistant to insects.

Vegetables: See **Mulch** above. Check in morning for insects, and hand pick when possible.

PLANTS WHICH BLOOM IN APRIL

t—Tree   *s*—Shrub   *v*—Vine   *b*—Bulb, Tuber or Rhizome   *e*—Evergreen
d—Deciduous   *p*—Perennial   *bn*—Biennial   *a*—Annual

Ageratum, *a* or *p*	Crinum, *b*	Laceflower, *a*	Roses, *s d*
Almond, Flowering, *t d*	Currant, Indian, *s d*	Lantana, *s d*	Salt Cedar, *s d*
Alyssum, Sweet, *a*	Dahlia, *b*	Larkspur, *a*	Salvia, blue, *p*
Amaryllis, *b*	Daisies, *a*	Ligustrum, Privet, *s e*	Gregg, *s d*
Anaqua, *t e*	Daphne, *s e*	Lilies, *b*	Scabiosa, *a, bn, p*
Anemone, *b*	Daylily, *tr*	Lobelia, *a*	Schizanthus, *a*
Aralia, *s d*	Delphinium, *a*	Locust, Black, *t d*	Sedum, *p*
Arctotis, *a*	Ebony, Texas, *t e*	Love-in-a-Mist, *a*	Shrimp Plant, *p*
Azalea, *s d* and *e*	Eucharis, *b*	Lupine, *a*	Silverbell Tree, *t d*
Babysbreath, *a*	False-Indigo, *s d*	Magnolia, *t e*	Snapdragon, *a*
Begonia, Bedding, *a*	Feverfew, *a* and *p*	Magnolia Fuscata, *s e*	Sparaxis, *b*
Bignonia, *v e p*	Forget-Me-Not, *a* and *p*	Milla, *b*	Spireas, *s d*
Bluebonnet, *bn*	Gazania, *p*	Mockorange, *s d*	Stock, *a* or *bn*
Bottlebrush, *s e*	Geranium, *p*	Narcissus, poeticus, *b*	Sweet Olive, *s e*
Bougainvillea, *v p e*	Gerbera, *p*	Nasturtium, *a*	Sweet Pea, *v a*
Calendula, *a*	Gladiolus, *b*	Oxalis, *b*	Sweet Rocket, *a* or *p*
Calla, *b*	Godetia, *a*	Pandorea, *v*	Sweetshrub, *s d*
Camellia, japonica, *s e*	Gorse, *s e*	Pansy, *a*	Tulip, *b*
Candytuft, *a*	Guava, Pineapple, *s e*	Parkinsonia, *t d*	Tulip Tree, *t d*
Canterbury Bell, *bn*	Strawberry	Pearlbush, *s d*	Verbena, *p*
Catalpa, *t d*	Hawthornes, *t d*	Penstemon, *p*	Viburnum, *s*
Chinaberry, *t d*	Honeysuckles, *s* and *v*	Petunia, *a*	Viola, *a*
Chinese Forget-Me-	Horse-Chestnut,	Phlox, Drummond, *a*	Violet, *p*
Not, *a*	Dwarf, *s d*	subulata, *p*	Wallflower, *a*
Chionodoxa, *b*	Huckleberry, *s* or *t d*	Louisiana, *p*	Watsonia, *c*
Citrus trees and	Hyacinths, *b*	Photinia, *s e*	Weigela, *s d*
shrubs, *e*	Indian Hawthorn, *s e*	Pinks, *a, bn, p*	Weaver's Broom, *s d*
Clethra, *s d*	Indian Paintbrush, *a*	Pittosporum, *s e*	Wild Olive, *t d*
Columbine, *p*	Iris, *b*	Pomegranate, *s d*	Winecup, *p*
Coralbean, *s d*	Jack-in-the-Pulpit, *b*	Poppies, *a*	Wisteria, *v p d*
Cornflower, *a*	Jasmines, *v* and *s e*	Pyracantha, *s e*	
Crabapples, *t d*	Kerria, *s d*	Queen Anne's Lace, *a*	

May

When Spring unlocks the flowers to paint the laughing soil.
—Bishop Heber

SEEDS which may now be sown in flats *(f)* or open ground *(o)*

Ageratum, *f*	Coral Vine, *o*	Gourd, *o*	Scabiosa, *o*
Alyssum, Sweet, *f* or *o*	Cosmos, *o*	Impatiens, *f* or *o*	Sunflower, *o*
Balsam, Garden, *f* or *o*	Cypressvine, *o*	Marigold, *o*	Sweet Pea, Perennial, *o*
Castor-bean, *o*	Dahlia, Dwarf, *o*	Moonflower, *o*	Tithonia, *o*
Cleome, *o*	Feverfew, *o*	Periwinkle, *o*	Torenia, *o*
Cockscomb, *f* or *o*	Four-o'clock, *o*	Petunia, *f* or *o*	Zinnia, *o*
Coleus, *f* or *o*	Globe Amaranth, *o*	Portulaca, *o*	

PLANTS which may now be placed in the open ground

Acalypha	Cleome	Hibiscus	Physostegia
Ageratum	Cockscomb	Impatiens	Plumbago
Alternanthera	Coleus	Jasmine	Potatovine
Amaranth	Coral Vine	Lantana	Salvia
Aralia	Cosmos	Lythrum	Sedum
Balsam, Garden	Croton	Mallow	Shrimp Plant
Banana	Dahlia, Dwarf	Marigold	Sweet Sultan
Begonia, Bedding	Eranthemum	Mistflower	Tithonia
Blanketflower	Foliage plants	Moonflower	Torenia
Browallia	Four-o'clock	Morning Glory	Verbena
Butterflyweed	Geranium	Periwinkle	Violet
Calliopsis	Gerbera	Petunia	Wallflower
Chrysanthemum	Godetia	Phlox, Louisiana	Zinnia

BULBS, TUBERS, RHIZOMES which may now be placed in the open ground

Achimenes	Dahlia	Hemerocallis	Marica (Walking Iris)
Alpinia (Ginger)	Dietes	Iris,	Montbretia
Alstroemeria	Gladiolus	Evansia	Sprekelia
Amaryllis	Gloriosa (Climbing	Kaempferi	Tulbaghia
Amarcrinum	Lily)	Louisiana	Tuberose
Billbergia	Habranthus	Lachenalia	Water Hyacinth
Caladium	Hedychium (Butterfly	Liriope	Water Lily
Canna	Lily)	Lycoris	Zephyranthes
Cooperia			

VEGETABLES which may now be sown in open ground

Asparagus roots	Chives	Mustard	Radishes
Beans, Lima	Corn	Okra	Shallots
Pinto	Cucumber	Onion sets	Spinach
Snap	Cushaw	Parsley	Spinach, New Zealand
Beets	Eggplant plants	Peanuts	Squash
Broccoli plants	Endive	Peas, Blackeyed (Cow)	Tampala
Carrots	Herbs	Crowder	Tendergreens
Cabbage plants	Jerusalem artichokes	Pepper plants	Tomato plants
Cantaloupe	Leeks	Popcorn	Turnips
Celtuce	Lettuce	Potatoes, Sweet, slips	Watermelon
Chard, Swiss	Mirliton	Pumpkin	

Azaleas: Last chance to prune. Keep mulch several inches thick at all times. Last month to fertilize.

Camellias: Fertilize lightly for second time. Spray for tea scale. Keep mulch several inches thick at all times.

Chrysanthemums: Best month to divide. (See April.)

Conifers: Water foliage, spray vigorously in late afternoon every two weeks from now on throughout the summer, on inner branches to prevent pests. Late afternoon spraying of conifers avoids scalding. Watch for red spider and bag or basket worm.

Fall Garden: Several varieties in the plant list above, will make garden rich in fall bloom.

Fertilize: Bearded Iris and Louisiana Iris after blooming.

Mulch: Maintain mulch at least two inches thick to keep roots cool, retain moisture in soil, add humus and deter weeds.

Peppers: Planted in sun or partial shade, they will ornament the August garden and supply peppers until frost for the kitchen and the mockingbirds.

Potted Plants: Leach soil of accumulated salts by filling and draining pot with water about ten times. Repot if needed, using just one pot size larger. May be moved outside to shady spot for a vacation, perhaps half burying pot in soil. Plants like the fresh air and additional light outside. Any plant of cascading habit is especially suitable for hanging baskets; also many succulents, herbs, vines or small bulbs. (See "Container Gardening.")

Pruning: Spring flowering shrubs may be safely pruned after blooming.

Transplanting: Retain sufficient earth around roots to prevent drying out and injury. Loosen soil in sides of planting hole for easier root penetration. Use transplanting solution, then water. Protect plant from sun, or transplant on cloudy day. Trees, roses and other shrubs should be partially defoliated. Keep moist for several days.

PLANTS WHICH BLOOM IN MAY

t—Tree *s*—Shrub *v*—Vine *b*—Bulb, Tuber or Rhizome *e*—Evergreen
d—Deciduous *p*—Perennial *bn*—Biennial *a*—Annual

Abelia, *s e*	Chaste Tree, *t d*	Impatiens, sultani, *a*	Petunia, *a*
Agapanthus, *b*	China Aster, *a*	India Hawthorn, *s e*	Phlox, Drummond, *a*
Ageratum, *a* or *p*	Chinese Forget-Me-	Iris, *b*	Pinks, *a, bn* and *p*
Alyssum, Sweet, *a*	Not, *a*	Jasmines, *v* and *s*	Plumbago, *p*
Amaryllis, *b*	Citrus shrubs and trees	Kerria, *s d*	Poinciana, *s d*
Anchusa, *a*	Clarkia, *a*	Laceflower, Blue, *a*	Pomegranates, *s d*
Arctotis, *a*	Columbine, *p*	Lantana, *s d*	Poppy, *a*
Azalea, *s e*	Coralbean, *s d*	Larkspur, *a*	Portulaca, *a*
Babysbreath, *a*	Coraltree, *t d*	Lavatera, *a*	Potatovine, *v p*
Balloon-flower, *p*	Coreopsis, *a*	Lily, Ace, *b*	Queen Anne's Lace, *a*
Balsam, *a*	Cornflower, *a*	Easter, *b*	Rose
Barbados Cherry, *s e*	Cosmos, Early, *a*	Estate, *b*	St. John's Wort, *s d*
Beargrass, *s e*	Crinum, *b*	Madonna, *b*	Salt Cedar, *s d*
Begonia, Bedding, *a*	Dahlia, *b*	Spider, Wild, *b*	Salvia, *s d*
Bignonia, *v p e*	Daisies	Regal, *b*	Scabiosa, *a, bn* and *p*
Blanket flower, *a*	Daylily, *t r*	Tiger, *b*	Schizanthus, *a*
Blue-eyed Grass, *b*	Delphinium, *a*	Liriope, *b*	Sedum, *p*
Bluebonnet, *bn*	Deutzia, *s d*	Lobelia, *a*	Shrimp Plant, *p*
Bottlebrush, *s e*	Duranta, *s d*	Lupine, *a*	Snapdragon, *a* and *bn*
Bougainvillea, *s e*	Elderberry, *s d*	Lythrum, *p*	Spirea, *s d*
or *v e*	Evening-primrose, *p*	Magnolia, *t e*	Stock, *a* and *bn*
Browallia, *a*	Feverfew, *a* and *p*	Mallow, *p*	Sunflower, *a* and *p*
Bushclover, *s d*	Forget-Me-Not, *p*	Mimosa, *t d*	Sweet Pea, Late, *a*
Butterflybush, *s d*	Four-o'clock, *p*	Mockorange, *s d*	Sweet Sultan, *a*
Butterflyweed, *p*	Geranium, *p*	Myrtle, Sweet, *s e*	Tobacco, Flowering, *a*
Calendula, *a*	Gerbera, *p*	Nasturtium, *a*	Torenia, *a*
Calla, *b*	Gladiolus, *b*	Nepeta, mussini, *p*	Trumpetvine, *v*
Calliopsis, *a*	Globe Amaranth, *a*	(catnip)	Verbena, *p*
Candytuft, *a*	Godetia, *a*	Oleander, *s e*	Veronica, *p*
Canna, *b*	Guava, Pineapple, *s e*	Oxalis, *b*	Viola, *a*
Canterbury Bell, *bn*	Hibiscus, *p*	Pansy, *a*	Water Hyacinth, *r*
Cape Jasmine, *s e*	Hollyhock, *a* or *bn*	Parkinsonia, *t d*	Waterlily, *b*
Catalpa, *t d*	Honeysuckle,	Penstemon, *a*	Waterpoppy, *p*
	Common, *v e*		Zephyr Lily, *b*
	Hydrangea, *s d*		Zinnia, *a*

𝒥une

It is the month of June, The month of leaves and roses,
When pleasant sights salute the eyes And pleasant scents the noses.
                                                          —N.P. Willis

SEEDS which may now be sown in flats (*f*) or open ground (*o*)

Ageratum, *f*	Castor-bean, *o*	Four-o'clock, *o*	Periwinkle, *f* or *o*
Alyssum, Sweet, *f* or *o*	Cockscomb, *f* or *o*	Impatiens, *o*	Portulaca, *o*
Balsam, Garden, *f* or *o*	Coleus, *f* or *o*	Marigold, *o*	Sunflower, *o*
Blanketflower, *o*	Cosmos, *o*	Moonflower, *o*	Tithonia, *o*
Blue Lace Flower, *o*	Dahlia, Dwarf, *o*	Moonvine, *o*	Torenia, *f* or *o*
Cleome, *o*	Feverfew, *o*	Morning Glory, *o*	Zinnia, *o*

PLANTS which may now be placed in the open ground

Acalypha	Chrysanthemum	Dahlia, Dwarf	Plumbago
Ageratum	Cleome	Feverfew	Salvia
Alternanthera	Cockscomb	Four-o'clock	Shrimp Plant
Aspidistra	Coleus	Hollyhock	Sweet Sultan
Balsam	Copperleaf	Impatiens	Tithonia
Blanketflower	Coreopsis	Marigold	Tobacco, Flowering
Bloodleaf	Cosmos, Klondyke	Michaelmas Daisy	Torenia
Browallia	Croton	Periwinkle	Wallflower
			Zinnia

BULBS, TUBERS, RHIZOMES which may now be placed in the open ground

Billbergia	Dietes	Iris, Evansia	Sisyrinchium
Caladium	Eucharis	Kaempferi	Sprekelia
Canna	Habranthus	Louisiana	Tulbaghia
Crinum	Haemanthus	Lycoris	Water Lily
Dahlia	Hemerocallis	Marica	Zephyranthes
		Oxalis	

VEGETABLES which may now be sown in open ground

Beans, Lima	Chard, Swiss	Mustard	Radishes
Pinto	Corn	Parsley	Shallot sets
Snap,	Corn Salad	Peanuts	Soy Beans
Beets	Cucumber	Peas, Blackeyed	Spinach, New Zealand
Broccoli	Cushaw	Crowder	Squash
Cabbage	Eggplant plants	Pepper plants	Tampala
Cantaloupe	Endive	Popcorn	Tomato plants
Carrots	Herb plants	Potato, Sweet, slips	Turnips
Cauliflower	Lettuce	Pumpkin	Watermelon
	Okra		

Azaleas and Camellias: Water by deep soaking once a week or as needed during hot weather.

Fertilize: Water annuals with solution of one tbsp. ammonium sulphate (21-0-0) dissolved in three gallons of water for a slow acting acidifying reaction. Manure, manure tea and phosphates encourage blooms. 13-13-13 in solution of one teaspoon to one gallon water is good general fertilizer.

Lawns: Brown spots indicate chinch bug or fungus damage.

Mulch: Keep beds well mulched. All iris except the bearded. Flowering quince likes a 3-4'' mulch of compost or pine needles; do not disturb shallow root system.

Perennials: To bloom well geraniums like good garden soil low in nitrogen, with pH 6.5-7.5, fairly dry soil, sun. In hottest months, full morning sun is enough. Dusty Miller *(Centaurea cineraria argentea)* has gray-white leaves which provide a fine color and texture contrast to bright geranium blossoms; same cultural needs.

Pests: Busy month for insects. Frequent spraying and dusting may be necessary. Take care, use weaker solutions. Do not use sulphur dust when temperature is over 85°.

Roses: After the blossom period of climbing roses, the old and new wood is easily distinguishable. Cut out oldest canes and all dead wood. Since bloom is produced on new wood, many of next year's blossoms will be lost if pruning is delayed. Feed roses lightly. They need 2'' of water per week. Groom bushes as flowers are cut, keeping center of bush open. Cut just above outside bud.

Staking: Many tall-growing plants will be less apt to overcrowd and will better attain their proper beauty and strength if not allowed to spread over the beds. Bamboo stakes are good. Tie firmly to the stake, but loosely about the stems of the plant.

Vegetables: Pick okra pods young to avoid sucking insects which cause curling and bumpy pods. Try cherry tomatoes, climbing (Malabar) spinach, Japanese eggplant and herbs in hanging baskets.

Watering: As in May. Bougainvillea, geraniums, moonflowers, morning glories are among plants that like dryish soil. Do not overwater. Potted plants outside may need watering once or more a day. Wilting in noon sun does not signify dryness, but wilting in early morning or late afternoon does. Plants benefit from spraying water on foliage, but not during heat of day. Always water before and after fertilizing.

PLANTS WHICH BLOOM IN JUNE

t—Tree   *s*—Shrub   *v*—Vine   *b*—Bulb, Tuber or Rhizome   *e*—Evergreen
d—Deciduous   *p*—Perennial   *bn*—Biennial   *a*—Annual

Abelia, *s e*
Achimenes, *b*
Agapanthus, *b*
Ageratum, *a* or *p*
Allamanda, *v p e*
Althea, *s d*
Alstroemeria, *b*
Alyssum, Sweet, *a*
Balloon-flower, *p*
Balsam, *a*
Barbados Cherry, *s e*
Bean, Scarlet
  Runner, *v a*
Begonia, Bedding, *a*
Blackberry Lily, *b*
Blanketflower, *a*
Bluebell, Texas, *bn*
Blue-Eyed Grass, *b*
Bougainvillea, *v e*
Browallia, *a*
Bushclover, *s d*
Butterflybush, *s d*
Butterflyweed, *p*
Buttonbush, *s d*
Caladium, *b*
Calliopsis, *a*
Canna, *b*
Cape Jasmine, *s e*
Cardinal Climber, *v a*
Catnip, *p*
Celosia, *a*
Chaste Tree, *s* or *t d*
China Aster, *a*
Chinese Forget-Me-
  Not, *a*
Clarkia, *a*

Clematis, *v pt*
Cleome, *a*
Clerodendron, *p*
Clitoria, *s a*
Cockscomb, *a*
Coneflower, *p*
Confederate Rose, *s d*
Coraltree, *t d*
Coral Vine, *v p*
Coreopsis, *p*
Cosmos, *a*
Crapemyrtle, *s* or *t d*
Crinum, *b*
Cypressvine, *v a*
Dahlia, *b*
Daisies, *a* or *p*
Datura, *a*
Daylily, *b*
Duranta, *s d*
Elderberry, *s d*
Everlastings, *a*
False-Dragonhead, *p*
Feverfew, *a* and *p*
Forget-Me-Not, *p*
Four o'clock, *p*
Geranium, *p*
Gerbera, *p*
Gladiolus, *b*
Globe Amaranth, *a*
Hibiscus, *p*
Hollyhock, *a* or *bn*
Honeysuckle, *v e*
  and *v p d*
Hydrangea, *s d*
Impatiens, sultani, *a*
Iris, *b*

Ismene, *b*
Jacobean Lily, *b*
Jacobinia, *s e*
Jasmines, *s*
Kerria, *s d*
Lantana, *s d*
Larkspur, *a*
Lemon Verbena, *s d*
Leucophyllum, *s e*
Lilies, *b*
Liriope, *b*
Lobelia, *a*
Lythrum, *p*
Madeira-vine, *v p*
Marica, *b*
Marigold, *a*
Magnolia, *t e*
Mallow, *p*
Mimosa, *t d*
Montbretia, *b*
Morning Glory, *v a*
Morning Glory Tree, *s d*
Moss Pink, *p*
Nasturtium, *a*
Oleander, *s e*
Parkinsonia, *t d*
Passionflower, *v p*
Periwinkle, *a*
Petunia, *a*
Phlox, Drummond, *a*
  perennial, *p*
Pinks, *a, bn* and *p*
Plumbago, *p*
Plumepoppy, *p*
Poinciana, *s d*
Pomegranate, *s d*

Portulaca, *a*
Potatovine, *v p*
Rainlily, *b*
Roses, *s d*
Rose Acacia, *s d*
Rosemallow, *p*
Sage, Desert, *s e*
St. John's-Wort, *s d*
Salpiglossis, *a*
Salt Cedar, *s d*
Salvias, *s d* and *a*
Scabiosa, *a, bn* and *p*
Sedum, *p*
Shrimp Plant, *p*
Silver-lace Vine, *v p*
Snapdragon, *a* and *bn*
Spirea, *s d*
Stokesia, *a*
Sunflower, *a*
Thunbergia, *v a*
Tithonia, *a*
Tobacco, Flowering, *a*
Torenia, *a*
Trumpetvine, *v p*
Tuberose, *b*
Turk's Cap, *s e*
Valeriana, *a*
Verbena, *p*
Veronica, *p*
Water-hyacinth, *b*
Waterlily, *b*
Waterpoppy, *p*
Willow, Flowering, *s d*
Yucca, *s e*
Zephyr Lily, *b*
Zinnia, *a*

July

The summer looks out from her brazen tower,
Through the flashing bars of July.
  —Francis Thompson

SEEDS which may now be sown in flats *(f)* or open ground *(o)*

Ageratum, *f*
Alyssum, Sweet, *f* or *o*
Balsam, Garden, *f* or *o*
Blanketflower, *o*
Bluebonnet, *o*

Castor-bean, *o*
Cockscomb, *f* or *o*
Cosmos, Late, *o*
Four-o'clock, *o*
Marigold, *o*

Moonflower, *o*
Moonvine, *o*
Morning-Glory, *o*
Pansy, *f*
Petunia, *f* or *o*

Portulaca, *o*
Sunflower, *o*
Tithonia, *o*
Vinca, *f* or *o*
Zinnia, *o*

PLANTS which may now be placed in the open ground

Acalypha	Calliopsis	Croton	Periwinkle
Ageratum	Chrysanthemum	Dahlia, Dwarf	Salvia
Alternanthera	Cockscomb	Foliage Plants	Tithonia
Aspidistra	Coleus	Four-o'clock	Tobacco, Flowering
Blanketflower	Copperleaf	Gerbera	Torenia
Bloodleaf	Cosmos, Klondyke	Marigold	Zinnia

BULBS, TUBERS, RHIZOMES which may now be placed in the open ground

Amaryllis	Hemerocallis	Liriope	Oxalis
Billbergia	Iris, Evansia	Lycoris	Tulbaghia
Cooperia	Kaempferi	Marica	Water Hyacinth
Dahlia	Roof		Water Lily
Gladiolus			

VEGETABLES which may now be sown in open ground

Beans, Lima	Cantaloupe	Okra	Shallot sets
Snap	Chard, Swiss	Parsley	Soy Beans
Beets	Collards	Peanuts	Spinach, New Zealand
Broccoli	Corn	Peas, Crowder	Squash
Brussels Sprouts	Cucumber	Pepper	Tampala
Cabbage	Cushaw	Potatoes, Sweet	Tendergreens
Carrots	Endive	Pumpkin	Turnips
Cauliflower	Mustard	Radishes	Watermelon

Annuals: Apply complete fertilizer such as 8-8-8. Water. To extend color into late summer sow seeds of quick-growing varieities.

Azaleas: If azaleas have failed to bloom well, look overhead in July and August to be certain that the plants are receiving sunlight during these two months when they are setting buds. A *high* canopy of trees usually allows enough sunlight, but low branches may not. Water regularly and well.

Beds: Clean up between seasons and alter design if desired. Make out lists of seeds, bulbs, and plants for next year's garden.

Bluebonnets: Sow now as nature does, with this year's seed. Scatter on ground, rake lightly and allow natural rainfall to germinate seed. May sow from now until January to have flowers next spring, but early sowing brings best results and longer flowering. Bluebonnets prefer gravelly, well drained, alkaline soil.

Fertilize: Guernsey lilies and lycoris with superphosphate worked into soil. Water.

Hollyhocks: Don't water too freely after bloom, as this often destroys the roots.

Lawns: Cut St. Augustine 2½″ high, Bermuda and Zoysia 1½″, and Tif Bermudas 1″ to conserve moisture and prevent burning.

Mulch: Maintain mulches. Allow grass clippings to compost, or dry out, before using thinly as mulch. Green plant matter used as mulch takes nitrogen from the soil, and might burn tender plants during the hot decomposition process.

Poinsettias: Keep pinched back until August to make bushy plants.

Vegetables: Plant proven varieties and those recommended by your Agricultural Extension Service. Keep mulched and watered. Prepare soil in new beds for planting late in August and September. Start seeds in flats.

Water: Soak as needed. Leaves appreciate water, too, but not when sun is on them. Do not overwater drought-resistant: lantana, pampas grass, yucca, vitex, and oleander. All plants in hanging baskets require more water.

Wisteria: Good time to prune.

PLANTS WHICH BLOOM IN JULY

t—Tree   *s*—Shrub   *v*—Vine   *b*—Bulb, Tuber and Rhizome   *e*—Evergreen
d—Deciduous   *p*—Perennial   *bn*—Biennial   *a*—Annual

Abelia, *s e*
Achimenes, *b*
Ageratum, *a* or *p*
Allamanda, *v p*
Althea, *s d*
Alyssum, Sweet, *a*
Balloon-flower, *p*
Balsam, *a*
Barbados Cherry, *s e*
Bean, Scarlet Runner, *v a*
Begonia, Bedding, *a*
Bignonia, *v p*
Blackberry Lily, *b*
Blanketflower, *a*
Bluebell, Texas, *bn*
Bougainvillea, *v e*
Browallia, *a*
Bushclover, *s d*
Butterflybush, *s d* or *e*
Butterflyweed, *p*
Buttonbush, *s d*
Caladium, *b*
Calliopsis, *a*
Canna, *b*
Cape Jasmine, *s e*
Cardinal Climber, *v a*
Catnip, *p*
Celosia, *a*
Chaste Tree, *s* or *t d*
Chinese Forget-Me-Not, *a*
Clematis, *v p*
Cleome, *a*
Clitoria, *s a*
Cockscomb, *a*

Coleus, *a*
Coneflower, *p*
Confederate Rose, *s d*
Coraltree, *t d*
Coral Vine, *v p*
Coreopsis, *p*
Cosmos, *a*
Crapemyrtle, *s* or *t d*
Crinum, *b*
Cypressvine, *v a*
Dahlia, *b*
Daisies, *p*
Datura, *a*
Daylily, *b*
Duranta, *s d*
Elderberry, *s d*
Everlastings, *a*
False-Dragonhead, *p*
Feverfew, *a* and *p*
Forget-Me-Not, *p*
Four o'clock, *p*
Gayfeather, *p*
Geranium, *p*
Gerbera, *p*
Gladiolus, *b*
Globe Amaranth, *a*
Habranthus, *b*
Hibiscus, *p*
Hollyhock, *a* or *bn*
Honeysuckle, *v e*
Ice Plant, *a*
Impatiens, sultani, *a*
Iris, *b*
Jackbean, *v a*
Jacobinia, *s e*
Jasmines, *s d* and *e*

Kerria, *s d*
Kniphofia, *b*
Lantana, *s d*
Lapeirousia, *c (b)*
Lemon Verbena, *s d*
Leucophyllum, *s e*
Lilies, *b*
Liriope, *b*
Lobelia, *a*
Lythrum, *p*
Madeira-vine, *v p*
Marigold, *a*
Mallow, *p*
Mexican Flame Vine, *a*
Mimosa, *t d*
Montbretia, *b*
Moonflower, *v a*
Morning Glory, *v a*
Morning Glory Tree, *s d*
Moss Pink, *p*
Nasturtium, Climbing, *a*
Oleander, *s e*
Oxalis, *b*
Parkinsonia, *t d*
Passionflower, *v p*
Periwinkle, *a*
Petunia, *a*
Phlox, Drummond, *a* perennial, *p*
Plumbago, *p*
Plumepoppy, *p*
Poinciana, *s d*
Pomegranate, *s d*

Portulaca, *a*
Potatovine, *v p*
Rainlily, *b*
Rangooncreeper, *v p e*
Roses, *s d*
St. John's-Wort, *s d*
Salt Cedar, *s d*
Salvias, *s d* and *a*
Sedum, *p*
Shrimp Plant, *p*
Silver-lace Vine, *v p*
Snapdragon, *a* and *bn*
Spirea, *s d*
Strawflower, *a*
Sunflower, *a*
Thunbergia, *v a*
Tigridia, *b*
Tithonia, *a*
Tobacco, Flowering, *a*
Torenia, *a*
Trumpetcreeper, *v p d*
Tuberose, *b*
Tulbaghia, *b*
Turk's Cap, *s e*
Valeriana, *a*
Verbena, *p*
Veronica, *p*
Water-hyacinth, *b*
Waterlily, *b*
Waterpoppy, *p*
Willow, Flowering, *s d*
Wisteria, Summer Flowering, *v e*
Yucca, *s e*
Zephyr Lily, *b*
Zinnia, *a*

August

O for a lodge in a garden of cucumbers!
O for an iceberg or two at control!
O for a vale that at midday the dew cumbers!
O for a pleasure trip up to the Pole!   —Rossiter Johnson

SEEDS which may now be sown in flats *(f)* or open ground *(o)*

Ageratum, *f*
Alyssum, Sweet, *f* or *o*
Amaranthus, *f*
Balsam, Garden, *f* or *o*
Bluebonnet, *o*

Calendula, *f* or *o*
Castor-bean, *o*
Cockscomb, *f* or *o*
Cornflower, *o*
Cosmos, Late, *o*

Four-o'clock, *o*
Gerbera, *f*
Hollyhock, *f*
Marigold, French, *o*
Pansy, *f*

Pinks, *f*
Snapdragon, *f*
Tobacco, Flowering, *f* or *o*
Tithonia, *o*

PLANTS which may now be placed in the open ground

Acalypha
Aspidistra
Azaleamum
Chrysanthemum
Cockscomb

Cosmos, Klondyke
Dahlia, Dwarf
Eranthemum
Four-o'clock
Gerbera

Marigold
Michaelmas Daisy
Periwinkle
Portulaca
Salvia

Shrimp Plant
Tithonia
Torenia
Verbena
Vinca

BULBS, TUBERS, RHIZOMES which may now be placed in the open ground

Amaryllis	Dahlia	Iris, Evansia	Water Hyacinth
Belladonna Lily	Dietes	Kaempferi	Water Lily
Canna	Habranthus	Lycoris	Watsonia
Chlidanthus	Haemanthus	Sparaxis	Zephyranthes
	Hemerocallis	Tulbaghia	

VEGETABLES which may now be sown in open ground

Beans, Lima	Chard, Swiss	Kohlrabi	Peppers, sweet
Snap	Chinese Cabbage	Lettuce	Potatoes, Irish, seed
Pole	Collards	Mustard	Radishes
Broccoli	Corn	Okra	Roquette
Brussels Sprouts	Corn Salad	Onion Seeds	Shallot sets
Cabbage	Cucumber	Parsley	Spinach New Zealand
Carrots	Eggplant	Peas, Blackeyed (Cow)	Squash
Cauliflower	Endive	Crowder	Tampala
Cantaloupe	Green Onions	English	Tomato plants
Celery	Kale	Parsnips	Turnips
			Watermelon

Azaleas: Water regularly and well. Plants are setting buds. (See **July.**)

Camellias: Continue watering. Check soil acidity.

Clean Up: Rose and flower beds of fallen foliage, yellowed leaves and dead wood. Cut off faded blossoms. Light green leaves may signify lack of iron (chlorosis). Correct with iron chelates, applied carefully as manufacturer directs, and water well. Cut leggy annuals back for new growth and bloom.

Cold Frames: Prepare now for fall planting when seedlings may need protection from rain.

Crapemyrtles: Prolong bloom by removing faded flowers and seed pods.

Dahlias: Cut back after first crop, leaving about half the growth.

Fall or Early Spring Garden: August is the traditional month to sow seed in flats for fall and early spring gardens. Almost all perennials should be sown early in order to bloom the following season.

Fruits: Prune blackberries after fruiting. Cut out old canes and fertilize with high-phosphate food. Keep watered. Water figs with slow soaking, 1' deep, but do not fertilize.

Iris: Cut off and burn old dead foliage, for it has already stored the rhizomes with nourishment and now only harbors disease. Dig in a little bone meal around the roots.

Maidenhair: This fern is partially dormant now and may look a little rusty. Do not permit it to dry out. Keep moist and well-drained. It will flourish again in the fall.

Pests: Scale insects, resembling small white round scabs often appear on foliage now. Use SUMMER oil spray in dilution suitable for hot weather. Sprays are apt to burn foliage in very hot weather, causing defoliation. Plants need as many leaves as possible now.

Pink Magnolia: Water thoroughly and maintain soil acidity.

Potted Plants: Overwatering is most frequent cause of failure with indoor plants. Use kitchen bulb baster to remove excess water easily from saucer under pot.

Shasta Daisies: Do not water too freely following bloom since this often destroys the plant.

Watering: Water to sustain life, saturating the soil thoroughly each time so the roots will not be drawn too near the surface. Water or mist in late afternoon to avoid danger of scalding.

Vegetables: Keep watered, weeded, and mulched. Plant seed potatoes whole in mid-August.

PLANTS WHICH BLOOM IN AUGUST

t—Tree *s*—Shrub *v*—Vine *b*—Bulb, Tuber or Rhizome *e*—Evergreen
d—Deciduous *p*—Perennial *bn*—Biennial *a*—Annual

Abelia, *s e*	Confederate Rose, *s d*	Kniphofia, *b*	Potatovine, *v p*
Achimenes, *b*	Coraltree, *t d*	Lantana, *s d*	Rainlily, *b*
Ageratum, *a* or *p*	Coral Vine, *v p*	Lemon Verbena, *s d*	Roses, *s d*
Allamanda, *v p*	Cosmos, *a*	Leucophyllum, *s e*	Rosemallow, *p*
Althea, *s d*	Crapemyrtle, *s* or *t d*	Lilies, *b*	Rudbeckia, *p*
Balloon-flower, *p*	Crinum, *b*	Liriope, *b*	St. John's-Wort, *s*
Balsam, *a*	Cypressvine, *v a*	Lobelia, cardinalis, *p*	Salvias, *s d* and *a*
Barbados Cherry, *s e*	Dahlia, *b*	Lycoris, *b*	Senna, Cassia, *s d*
Bean, Scarlet Runner,	Daisies, Shasta, *p*	Lythrum, *p*	Shrimp Plant, *p*
v a	Gloriosa	Madeira-vine, *v p*	Silver-lace Vine, *v p*
Begonia, Bedding, *a*	Datura, *a*	Marigold, *a*	Spirea, *s d*
Bignonia, *v p*	Daylily, *b*	Mallow, *p*	Strawflower, *a*
Blanketflower, *a*	Duranta, *s d*	Mexican Flame Vine, *a*	Sunflower, *a*
Bluebell, Texas, *bn*	Elderberry, *s d*	Mistflower, *p*	Thunbergia, *v a*
Bougainvillea, *v e*	Everlastings, *a*	Montbretia, *b*	Tigridia, *b*
Browallia, *a*	False-Dragonhead, *p*	Moonflower, *v a*	Tithonia, *a*
Bushclover, *s d*	Feverfew, *a* and *p*	Morning Glory, *v a*	Tobacco, Flowering, *a*
Butterflybush, *s d*	Flamevine, *p e*	Morning Glory Tree, *s*	Torenia, *a*
Butterfly Lily, *b*	Forget-Me-Not, *p*	*d*	Trumpetvine, *v p*
Butterflyweed, *p*	Four o'clock, *p*	Moss Pink, *p*	Tuberose, *b*
Buttonbush, *s d*	Gayfeather, *p*	Nepeta, mussini, *p*	Tulbaghia, *b*
Caladium, *b*	Geranium, *p*	Oleander, *s e*	Turk's Cap, *s e*
Calliopsis, *a*	Gerbera, *p*	Oxalis, *b*	Verbena, *p*
Canna, *b*	Gladiolus, *b*	Parkinsonia, *t d*	Veronica, *p*
Cape Jasmine, *s e*	Globe Amaranth, *a*	Passionflower, *v p*	Water-hyacinth, *b*
Cardinal Climber, *v a*	Globethistle, *a*	Periwinkle, *a*	Waterlily, *b*
Celosia, *a*	Goldenrod, *p*	Petunia, *a*	Waterpoppy, *p*
Chinese Forget-Me-	Hibiscus, *p*	Phlox, Drummond, *a*	Willow, Flowering, *s d*
Not, *a*	Honeysuckle, *v e*	perennial, *p*	Wisteria, Summer
Cistus, Rockrose, *s e*	Ice Plant, *a*	Plumbago, *p*	Blooming, *v e*
Clematis, *v p*	Impatiens, sultani, *a*	Plumepoppy, *p*	Yucca, *s e*
Cleome, *a*	Jacobinia, *s e*	Poinciana, *s d*	Zephyr Lily, *b*
Cockscomb, *a*	Jasmines, *s*	Pomegranate, *s d*	Zinnia, *a*
Coleus, *a*	Kerria, *s d*	Portulaca, *a*	

September

*When bounteous autumn rears her head,
he joys to pull the ripened pear.* —Dryden

SEEDS which may now be sown in flats *(f)* or open ground *(o)*

Alyssum, Sweet, *f* or *o*	Cleome, *o*	Four-o'clock, *o*	Pinks, *f* or *o*
Arctotis, *f* or *o*	Cockscomb, *o*	Gayfeather, *o*	Poppy, *o*
Babysbreath, *f* or *o*	Coreopsis, *f* or *o*	Gerbera, *f*	Salpiglossis, *f*
Balsam, Garden, *f* or *o*	Cornflower, *f* or *o*	Hollyhock, *f*	Salvia, Blue, *f* or *o*
Bluebell, Texas, *f* or *o*	Daisy, African	Laceflower, Blue, *f* or *o*	Scabiosa, *f* or *o*
Bluebonnet, *o*	Golden, *f* or *o*	Larkspur, *o*	Snapdragon, *f* or *o*
Calendula, *f*	English, *f* or *o*	Lupine, *f*	Stock, *f* or *o*
Candytuft, *o*	Shasta, *f* or *o*	Mallow, *f* or *o*	Stokesia, *f*
Chinese Forget-	Delphinium, *f*	Pansy, *f*	Sweet William, *f* or *o*
me-not, *f* or *o*	Everlasting, *f* or *o*	Petunia, *f* or *o*	Viola, *f*
		Phlox, Drummond, *o*	Wallflower, *f*

PLANTS which may now be placed in the open ground

Ageratum	False-dragonhead	Lupine	Portulaca
Aspidistra	Four-o'clock	Marigold	Violet
Cosmos, Klondyke	Gerbera	Petunia	Zinnia
Dahlia Dwarf	Lantana	Phlox, Louisiana	

BULBS, TUBERS, RHIZOMES which may now be placed in the open ground

Allium	Iris, Bearded	Lapeirousia	Liriope
Amaryllis	Bulbous	Leucojum	Marica
Anemone	Evansia	Lilies, Centifolium	Muscari
Banana	Kaempferi	Creole	Ornithogalum
Calla	Louisiana	Croft	Oxalis
Camassia	Siberian	Estate	Ranunculus
Chlidanthus	Spuria	Madonna	Scilla
Cooperia (Rain Lily)	Unguicularis	Philippine	Tritonia
Dietes	(Winter	Regal	Veltheimia (pots)
Gladiolus tristis	Blooming)	Speciosum	Watsonia
Hemerocallis	Ismene	Sunset	Zephyranthes
	Ixia	Tiger	

VEGETABLES which may now be sown in open ground

Beans, Lima	Chard, Swiss	Leeks	Potatoes, Irish
Dwarf snap	Chicory (French	Lettuce	Radishes
Pole	Endive)	Mustard	Roquette
Beets	Chinese cabbage	Onion, seeds, sets	Rutabaga
Broccoli	Collards	and plants	Salsify
Brussels sprouts	Corn salad	Parsley	Spinach
Cabbage plants	Cos (Romaine lettuce)	Parsnips	Squash
Carrots	Cress	Peas, Blackeyed	Tendergreens
Cauliflower	Endive	Crowder	Tomato plants
Celery	Kale	English	Turnips
Celtuce	Kohlrabi	Field	

Azaleas: Check soil acidity and mulch. Keep watered.

Camellias: Water by deep soaking. To disbud or gib see Camellias.

Chrysanthemums: Give liquid manure or commercial fertilizer every two or three weeks until flower buds appear; then weekly until buds show color. Water as necessary. For large flowers, leave center bud in each cluster and pinch off all lateral buds before they start stemming. This applies only to the large flowered and not to pompon, anemone-flowered, or singles. For garden display, pinch out center bud and leave others.

Compost: Arrange for compost pile in hidden area. (See Compost, in "Soil and Soil Improvement.")

Cultivation: After first cool spell, clean up beds, burning old stalks and leaves which may harbor insects. Add fertilizer if needed. Dust lightly with sulphur to combat fungus when temperature is under 90°. Prepare beds or boxes into which pansy and other seedlings must go when first pricked out. (See "Propagation.")

Fertilize: Gardenias regularly with acid food. Gerberas like rose food every four to six weeks; plant with crowns high in friable, humusy soil.

Herbs: Plant chives, coriander, dill, garlic, lovage, and winter savory.

Pests: Spray for scale, red spider on shrubs and plants. Grayish, stippled leaves mean red spider; try hard water spray first and improve air circulation.

Potted Plants: For indoors, select varieties suitable to your light and temperature conditions. Light intensity more than 6' from a window is usually not enough for most plants. (See "Container Gardening").

Roses: Keep mulched fed and watered. Collect infected leaves and burn. Cut out blind, dead and weak wood. As cool weather approaches water in the mornings, to discourage black spot and mildew. Black spot must be *prevented* from entering leaf tissues. May apply fungicide before disease appears. Continue regular dust and spray schedule. (see Roses). Fall roses are often finest of the year. Foliar feed only when temperature drops below 85° to avoid burning.

Soil: Unless soil has the texture to allow drainage, aeration, and penetration of food additives, neither seeds nor plants will prosper. (See "Soil and Soil Improvement.")

Vegetables: Need sun, excellent drainage and fairly loose, not too acid, soil and at least 6 hours sun, preferably morning. Prepare new beds now. 1 part soil, 1 part sand, and 1 part pinebark mulch or moistened peat moss 12 to 18″ deep is good soil mixture for beets, carrots, onions and turnips. Strawberries and parsley like mix of pine bark and manure. Cauliflower, brussel sprouts, Chinese cabbage, and broccoli need cool weather. (See "Vegetables" and "Soil and Soil Improvement.") Be aware of safe waiting periods if using pesticides on food crops. Do not use weed killers or herbicides on or near food crops because they last up to 18 months in the soil.

Violets: If not already divided, separate old clumps to single crowns with roots. Reset, fertilize, and reap a wealth of early bloom.

PLANTS WHICH BLOOM IN SEPTEMBER

t—Tree *s*—Shrub *v*—Vine *b*—Bulb, Tuber or Rhizome *e*—Evergreen
d—Deciduous *p*—Perennial *bn*—Biennial *a*—Annual

Abelia, *s e*	Confederate Rose, *s d*	Leonotis, *s e*	Portulaca, *a*
Achimenes, *b*	Coral Vine, *v p*	Leucophyllum, *s e*	Potatovine, *v p*
Ageratum, *a* or *p*	Cosmos, *a*	Lilies, *b*	Rainlily, *b*
Allamanda, *v p*	Crapemyrtle, *s* or *t d*	Liriope, *b*	Roses, *s d*
Althea, *s d*	Crinum, *b*	Lobelia, cardinalis, *p*	St. John's-Wort, *s d*
Balsam, *a*	Cypressvine, *v a*	Lycoris, *b*	Salvias, *s d* and *a*
Barbados Cherry, *s e*	Dahlia, *b*	Lythrum, *p*	Shrimp Plant, *p*
Begonia, Bedding, *a*	Datura, *a*	Madeira-vine, *v p*	Silver-lace Vine, *v p*
Bignonia, *v p*	Daylily, *b*	Marigold, *a*	Spirea, *s d*
Blanketflower, *a*	Duranta, *s d*	Mallow, *p*	Sunflower, *a*
Boltonia, *p*	Feverfew, *a* and *p*	Mexican Flame Vine,	Thunbergia, *v p*
Bougainvillea, *v e*	Forget-Me-Not, *p*	*a*	Tigridia, *b*
Browallia, *a*	Four o'clock, *p*	Mistflower, *p*	Tithonia, *a*
Butterflybush, *s d*	Geranium, *p*	Moonflower, *v a*	Tobacco, Flowering, *a*
Butterfly Lily, *b*	Gerbera, *p*	Morning Glory, *v a*	Torenia, *a*
Butterflyweed, *p*	Globe Amaranth, *a*	Morning Glory Tree, *s*	Trumpetvine, *v p*
Buttonbush, *s d*	Gloriosa Daisy, *p*	*d*	Tuberose, *b*
Canna, *b*	Goldenrod, *p*	Moss Pink, *p*	Turk's Cap, *s e*
Cardinal Climber, *v a*	Guernsey Lily, *b*	Oleander, *s e*	Verbena, *p*
Cassia, *s d*	Hibiscus, *p*	Passionflower, *v p*	Veronica, *p*
Celosia, *a*	Honeysuckle, *v e*	Periwinkle, *a*	Water-hyacinth, *b*
Chinese Forget-Me-	Impatiens, sultani, *a*	Petunia, *a*	Waterlily, *b*
Not, *a*	Jacobinia, *s e*	Phlox, perennial, *p*	Waterpoppy, *p*
Cistus, Rockrose, *s e*	Jasmines, *s d* and *e*	Plumbago, *p*	Wisteria, megasperma,
Clematis, *v p*	Kerria, *s d*	Plumepoppy, *p*	*v e*
Cleome, *a*	Kniphofia, *b*	Poinciana, *s d*	Zephyr Lily, *b*
Cockscomb, *a*	Lantana, *s d*	Pomegranate, Dwarf, *s*	Zinnia, *a*
Coleus, *a*	Lemon Verbena, *s d*	*d*	

October

Behold congenial Autumn comes, the Sabbath of the year!
—Logan

SEEDS which may now be sown in flats *(f)* or open ground *(o)*

Alyssum, Sweet, *f* or *o*	Daisy, African	Larkspur, *o*	Salpiglossis, *f*
Arctotis, *f* or *o*	Golden, *f* or *o*	Mallow, *f* or *o*	Salvia, Blue, *f* or *o*
Babysbreath, *f* or *o*	English, *f* or *o*	Pansy, *f*	Scabiosa, *f* or *o*
Blanketflower, *f* or *o*	Shasta, *f* or *o*	Petunia, *f* or *o*	Sedum, *f*
Bluebell, Texas, *f* or *o*	Delphinium, *f*	Phlox, Drummond, *o*	Snapdragon, *f* or *o*
Bluebonnet, *o*	Everlasting, *f* or *o*	Pinks, *f* or *o*	Stock, *f* or *o*
Calendula, *f*	Forget-me-not, *f* or *o*	Poppy, California, *o*	Stokesia, *f*
Chinese Forget-	Gerbera, *f*	Iceland, *o*	Sweet Pea, *o*
me-not, *f* or *o*	Godetia, *f*	Shirley, *o*	Sweet William, *f* or *o*
Coreopsis, *f* or *o*	Hollyhock, *f* or *o*	Queen Anne's-	Viola, *f*
Cornflower, *f* or *o*	Laceflower, Blue, *f* or *o*	lace, *f* or *o*	Wallflower, *f*

PLANTS which may now be placed in the open ground

Ageratum	Daisy, English	Petunia	Snapdragon
Alyssum, Sweet	Shasta	Phlox, Drummond	Stock
Aspidistra	Delphinium	Louisiana	Sweet William
Bluebonnet	Forget-me-not	Perennial	Verbena
Calendula	Four-o'clock	Physostegia	Viola
Candytuft	Gerbera	Pinks	Violet
Coreopsis	Hollyhock	Salvia, Blue	Wallflower
Cornflower	Pansy	Shrimp Plant	

BULBS, TUBERS, RHIZOMES which may now be placed in the open ground

Agapanthus	Crocus	Estate	Muscari
Allium	Dietes	Goldband	Narcissus
Alstroemeria	Freesia	Madonna	Ornithogalum
Amarcrinum	Ginger	Philippine	Oxalis
Amaryllis	Gladiolus	Regal	Ranunculus
Anemone	Hemerocallis	Speciosum	Scilla
Banana	Iris, all kinds	Sunset	Sparaxis
Calla	Ismene	Tiger	Spuria
Camassia	Ixia	Liriope	Strelitzia
Chlidanthus	Leucojum	Lycoris	Tulbaghia
Clivia (pots)	Lilies, Centifolium	Marica	Veltheimia (pots)
Cooperia	Creole	Milla	Watsonia
Crinum	Croft	Montbretia	Zephyranthes

VEGETABLES which may now be sown in open ground

Beans, Snap	Chard, Swiss	Kale	Potatoes, Irish
Pole	Chicory (French	Kohlrabi	Radishes
Lima	endive	Leeks	Roquette
Beets	Chinese cabbage	Lemon Balm	Rutabaga
Broccoli	Collard	Lettuce	Salsify
Brussels sprouts	Corn salad	Mustard	Shallots
Cabbage plants	Cos	Onion, seeds, sets	Spinach
Carrots	Cress	and plants	Strawberry plants
Cauliflower plants	Eggplant plants	Parsley	Tendergreens
Celery	Endive	Parsnips	Turnips
Celtuce	Horseradish roots	Peas, English	

Azaleas: Check soil pH. If above 5.5, dress with 1 part agricultural sulphur and 2 parts copperas, mixed and sprinkled dry around edges of bushes to maintain acidity. Do not disturb shallow root system. Carefully hand water at once to liquify chemicals. Check for signs of root rot. Groom bushes by pruning long unsightly branches down near base of bushes to maintain symmetry and promote bushiness. Azaleas bud out where cut.

Bulbs: Spring flowering bulbs may be planted now. Plant in rich loam with plenty of humus and good drainage. Mix 1 tbsp. bone meal in soil at bottom of hole. DO NOT PLANT TULIPS BEFORE LATE DECEMBER. Dig caladiums now and store in dry, ventilated place. Bearded and Dutch irises like bone meal; Louisiana irises like cotton seed meal and manure; spurias are gross feeders and want a fertilizer such as 8-8-8 mixed with half as much sheep manure. Feed other bulbs now with bone meal and superphosphate. Fertilize daylilies. They need six hours sun to bloom well.

Camellias: Before October 15th spray for tea scale if necessary.

Compost: Keep leaves, clippings and small branches in pile or containers to decompose. Compost helps the soil and saves money (See "Soil and Soil Improvement").

Container Gardening: Gradually accustom plants to less light for their winter quarters.

Cultivation: Clean up beds; plan changes. Correct drainage problems, perhaps by raising beds. Check and correct pH factor according to plant needs. Add humus, compost, and manure to beds and work in at least 8", but never work soil unless it is dry enough to crumble in hand.

Fertilize: Withhold nitrogen-high fertilizer to avoid stimulating growth which would be suceptible to freezing. Exception: winter vegetables. Feed spring-blooming shrubs lightly with 4 parts superphosphate mixed with 1 part sulphur of potash. Sprinkle lightly, away from trunk, and water in.

Forget-Me-Nots: Clumps may be moved to a partially shaded exposure with morning sun. Add quantities of old manure to the soil, for these plants are greedy feeders. They prefer a bed to themselves where they will form a dense mat with tiny blue flowers from spring to fall. Water freely during hot weather and protect from frost.

Frost: Be prepared to protect against frost even though average date of first frost is December 10th.

Fruits: Plant strawberries between October 15 and November 15 in beds with good drainage, slightly acid, rich, loose soil with ample humus. Set crown even with soil level. Mulch with straw, paper or plastic to keep fruit clean.

Herbs: Divide and replant: chives, garlic and multiplying onions.

Iris: Fertilize existing beds with well rotted manure or a balanced fertilizer. Plant all kinds.

Lawns: Determine whether lawn appears to need fungicide for brown patch, insecticide for chinch bugs, or fertilizer for nutrition. Read and heed directions on packages. Water (See "Lawns.")

Perennials: Cut tops after blooming; divide roots and transplant any time from now until March, but the sooner the early-blooming varieties are moved, the earlier and more satisfactory will be their blooms.

Pests: Beware of stinging caterpillars (asps) usually seen on limbs and twigs of oak trees, but may be on other trees or shrubs also; wear gloves as a safeguard. Their sting is vicious.

Roses: Soak beds. Groom to cut out dead wood but do not prune heavily until January or February. Feed lightly with 0-10-10 in solution to harden off for dormancy and improve bloom.

Trees and Evergreens: Feed and water, but do not prune now, except to remove dead wood.

Watering: Water in the morning to avert fungus disease. Avoid wetting bloom and foliage.

Wisteria: To encourage flowering the following spring, root-prune wisteria that has failed to bloom. Cut through the roots with a spade in a circle about 30 inches from the stem of the vine, and feed with bone meal through this cut.

PLANTS WHICH BLOOM IN OCTOBER

t—Tree   *s*—Shrub   *v*—Vine   *b*—Bulb, Tuber or Rhizome   *e*—Evergreen
d—Deciduous   *p*—Perennial   *bn*—Biennial   *a*—Annual

Ageratum, *a* or *p*	Cassia, *s d*	Ginger, Shell, *b*	Petunia, *a*
Alyssum, Sweet, *a*	Celosia, *a*	Gladiolus, *b*	Plumbago, *p*
Amaranthus, *a*	Chrysanthemum, *p*	Globe Amaranth, *a*	Plumepoppy, *p*
Anemone, Japanese, *b*	Clematis, *v p*	Hibiscus, *s e*	Pomegranate, *s d*
Angel's Trumpet, *s d*	Cleome, *a*	Honeysuckle, *s* or *v e*	Portulaca, *a*
Arbutus, *t e*	Clethra, *s d*	Impatiens, sultani, *p*	Potatovine, *v p*
Azaleas, *s e*	Coleus, *a*	Jasmines	Raintree, Golden, *t d*
Balsam, *a*	Confederate Rose, *s d*	Lantana, *s d*	Roses, *s d*
Barbados Cherry, *s e*	Coral Vine, *v p*	Lapeirousia, *b*	Salvia, *a* and *p*
Begonia, Bedding, *a*	Cosmos, *a*	Lobelia, cardinalis, *p*	Shrimp Plant, *p*
Bignonia, *v p*	Crinum, *b*	Lycoris, *b*	Silver Lace Vine, *v p*
Blanketflower, *a*	Cypressvine, *v a*	Mallow, Rose, *p*	Tea Plant, *s e*
Boltonia, *p*	Dahlia, *a* or *p*	Marigold, *a*	Thunbergia, *v a*
Bougainvillea, *v e*	Daylily, *b*	Michaelmas Daisy, *p*	Tithonia, *a*
Bouncing-Bet, *p*	Elaeagnus, *s e*	Mistflower, *p*	Tobacco, Flowering, *a*
Bouvardia, *s e*	Forget-Me-Not, *p*	Moonflower, *v a*	Turk's cap, *s e*
Butterflybush, *s d* or *e*	Four o'clock, *p*	Morning Glory, *v a*	Verbena, *p*
Butterflylily, *b*	Franklinia, *t d*	Narcissus, *b*	Violet, *p*
Canna, *b*	Garlic, *h*	Oxalis, *b*	Water Hyacinth, *b*
Cardinal Climber, *v a*	Geranium, *p*	Perennial Phlox, *p*	Waterlily, *b*
Caryopteris, *s d*	Gerbera, *p*	Periwinkle, *a*	Zinnia, *a*

November

Divinest Autumn! who may paint thee best,
Forever changeful o'er the changeful globe.

—R.H. Stoddard

SEEDS which may now be sown in flats *(f)* or open ground *(o)*

Alyssum, Sweet, *f* or *o*	Cornflower, *f* or *o*	Larkspur, *o*	Salpiglossis, *f*
Arctotis, *f* or *o*	Daisy, African	Lobelia, *f*	Salvia, Blue, *f* or *o*
Babysbreath, *f* or *o*	Golden, *f* or *o*	Mallow, *f* or *o*	Scabiosa, *f* or *o*
Blanketflower, *f* or *o*	English, *f* or *o*	Pansy, *f*	Snapdragon, *f* or *o*
Bluebell, Texas, *f* or *o*	Shasta, *f* or *o*	Petunia, *f* or *o*	Stock, *f* or *o*
Bluebonnet, *o*	Delphinium, *f*	Phlox, Drummond, *o*	Sweet Pea, *o*
Calendula, *f*	Everlasting, *f* or *o*	Pinks, *f* or *o*	Sweet William, *f* or *o*
Candytuft, *o*	Forget-me-not, *o*	Poppy, California, *o*	Verbena, *f* or *o*
Chinese Forget-me-	Four-o'clock, *o*	Iceland, *o*	Viola, *f*
not, *f* or *o*	Gerbera, *f*	Shirley, *o*	Wallflower, *f*
Cleome, *o*	Hollyhock, *f* or *o*	Queen Anne's-	
Coreopsis, *f* or *o*	Laceflower, Blue, *f* or *o*	lace, *f* or *o*	

PLANTS which may now be placed in the open ground

Alyssum, Sweet	Daisy, English	Lobelia	Queen Anne's-lace
Arctotis	Shasta	Lupine	Salvia, Blue
Aspidistra	Delphinium	Pansy	Shrimp Plant
Bluebonnet	Forget-me-not	Penstemon	Snapdragon
Calendula	Four o'clock	Petunia	Stock
Candytuft	Gerbera	Phlox, Drummond	Sweet William
Coreopsis	Hollyhock	Louisiana	Verbena
Cornflower	Honeysuckle	Perennial	Viola
	Larkspur	Pinks	Violet

BULBS, TUBERS, RHIZOMES which may now be placed in the open ground

Agapanthus	Crinum	Ismene	Narcissus
Allium	Crocus	Ixia	Ornithogalum
Alstroemeria	Dietes	Lachenalia	Oxalis
Amarcrinum	Freesia	Leucojum	Ranunculus
Amaryllis	Gladiolus tristis	Lilies, all kinds	Scilla
Anemone	Habranthus	Liriope	Sisyrinchium
Calla	Hemerocallis	Lycoris	(Blue-eyed Grass)
Camassia	Hyacinth, Roman	Marica	Sparaxis
Chlidanthus	Iris, Evansia	Milla	Tulbaghia
Clivia (pots)	Bearded	Montbretia	Watsonia
Cooperia	Louisiana	Muscari	Zephyranthes
	Unguicularis		

VEGETABLES which may now be sown in open ground

Beets	Chicory	Kohlrabi	Radishes
Broccoli plants	Chinese Cabbage	Leeks	Roquette
Brussels sprouts	Collards	Lettuce	Rutabaga
Cabbage plants	Corn salad	Mustard	Salsify
Carrots	Cos	Onion, seeds, sets	Shallots
Cauliflower plants	Cress	and plants	Spinach
Celery	Endive	Parsley	Strawberry plants
Celtuce	Horseradish roots	Parsnips	Tendergreens
Chard, Swiss	Kale	Peas, English	Turnips

Azaleas and Camellias: May be moved. Keep moist to lessen cold weather damage. Maintain mulch. (See **October**).

Bulbs: See **October**. Tulips should be put in refrigerator now to remain at least three weeks to induce a strong root system which, in turn, will produce better flowers.

Cultivation: See **October**. Cut back perennial tops. Thin out and transplant volunteer seedlings. Beds made now will profit by weathering before being planted. If soil is heavy, dig six inches deep, leave rough, cover with gypsum, leaves or strawy manure and allow to mellow.

Fruit Trees: Plant these and flowering shrubs, deciduous and evergreen, now.

Garden Sanitation: Remove dead foliage to help eradicate insects and disease organisms which can overwinter in debris. Add healthy prunings to compost.

Lilies-of-the-Valley: Force pips to bloom for Christmas by planting in sand or sphagnum moss in a shallow bowl. Keep moist in a dark room. Allow to grow 4 inches high, bring gradually to light. They should bloom about 25 days after planting.

Pansies: Place in the beds after weather has cooled. Use a little blood meal under each plant.

Perennials: As chrysanthemums and other perennials finish blooming, cut flowering stalks to ground to permit all the strength to be used in making root growth. Pinch off the tops of calendula, delphinium, snapdragon, stock and wallflower, to induce bushy growth and prevent flowers from forming so early that they may be destroyed by frost. Cultivate lightly.

Roses: Feed lightly, but avoid nitrogen fertilizers. DO NOT prune now. Keep up spraying program. Water deeply.

Vegetables: See **March.**

Violets: Manure heavily any time between now and March 15 for a full harvest of bloom.

Winter Protection: Be prepared from now until April for quick freezes. Plastic coverings should not touch plants. In the southern zones there can be as much damage to covered plants from heat following freeze as from the cold itself, so remove plastic covers as soon as temperature rises. Low plants may be covered with leaves; but remove when weather warms.

PLANTS WHICH BLOOM IN NOVEMBER

t—Tree *s*—Shrub *v*—Vine *b*—Bulb, Tuber or Rhizome *e*—Evergreen
d—Deciduous *p*—Perennial *bn*—Biennial *a*—Annual

Ageratum, *a* or *p*	Chrysanthemums, *p*	Jasmines, *s, d* and *e*	Potatovine, *v p*
Alyssum, Sweet, *a*	Clematis, *v p*	Lantana, *s d*	Roses, *s d*
Balsam, *a*	Confederate Rose, *s d*	Loquat, *s e*	Salvias, *p* and *a*
Bougainvillea, *v e p*	Crinum, *b*	Marigold, *a*	Scabiosa, *a, bn* and *p*
Calendula, *a*	Dahlborg Daisy, *a*	Michaelmas Daisy, *p*	Shrimp Plant, *p*
Camellia, japonica, *s e*	Dahlia, *b*	Pansy, *a*	Silver Lace Vine, *v p*
sasanqua, *s e*	Eranthemum, *s*	Periwinkle, *a*	Sweet Olive, *s e*
Canna, *b*	Geranium, *p*	Petunia, *a*	Turk's cap, *s e*
Cardinal Climber, *v a*	Gerbera, *p*	Pinks, *a, bn*	Verbena, *p*
Chinese Forget-Me-	Gladiolus, *b*	Plumbago, *p*	Violet, *p*
Not, *a*	Hibiscus, *p*	Poinsettia, *s d*	Waterlily, *b*
	Honeysuckle, *s v e*		Zinnia, *a*

December   *See, Winter comes to rule the varied year.*
—Thomson

SEEDS which may now be sown in flats *(f)* or open ground *(o)*

Alyssum, Sweet *f* or *o*	Cleome, *o*	Gerbera, *f*	Salvia, Blue, *f* or *o*
Arctotis, *f* or *o*	Coreopsis, *f* or *o*	Hollyhock, *f*	Salpiglossis, *f*
Babysbreath, *f* or *o*	Cornflower, *f* or *o*	Larkspur, *o*	Scabiosa, *f* or *o*
Blanketflower, *f* or *o*	Daisy, African	Lobelia, *f*	Snapdragon, *f* or *o*
Bluebell, Texas, *f* or *o*	Golden, *f* or *o*	Mallow, *f* or *o*	Stock, *f* or *o*
Bluebonnet, *o*	English, *f* or *o*	Petunia, *f* or *o*	Sweet Pea, *o*
Calendula, *f*	Shasta, *f* or *o*	Phlox, Drummond, *o*	Sweet William, *f* or *o*
Candytuft, *o*	Everlasting, *f* or *o*	Pinks, *f* or *o*	Verbena, *f* or *o*
Chinese Forget- me-	Forget-me-not, *o*	Poppy, California, *o*	Wallflower, *f*
not, *f* or *o*	Four-o'clock, *o*	Shirley, *o*	

PLANTS which may now be placed in the open ground

Alyssum, Sweet	Daisy, English	Lobelia	Queen Anne's-lace
Arctotis	Shasta	Pansy	Salvia, Blue
Aspidistra	Delphinium	Petunia	Snapdragon
Bluebonnet	Forget-me-not	Phlox, Drummond	Verbena
Calendula	Hollyhock	Louisiana	Viola
Candytuft	Honeysuckle	Perennial	Violet
Coreopsis	Larkspur	Physostegia	Wallflower
Cornflower		Pinks	

BULBS, TUBERS, RHIZOMES which may now be placed in the open ground

Agapanthus	Crinum	Jack-in-the-Pulpit	Lycoris
Allium	Crocus	Kniphofia	Narcissus
Alstroemeria	Dietes	Lachenalia	Ornithogalum
Amarcrinum	Freesia	Leucojum	Oxalis
Amaryllis	Gloriosa	Lily-of-the-Valley	Ranunculus
Anemone	Hemerocallis	(pots)	Scilla
Billbergia	Hyacinth	Liriope	Sisyrinchium
Blackberry Lily	Hymenocallis	Marica	Sprekelia
Calla	Iris, Bulbous	Milla	Tulbaghia
Camassia	Spuria	Montbretia	Tulip
Chlidanthus	Louisiana	Muscari	Water Hyacinth
Clivia (pots)	Ixia		Waterlily
Cooperia			Zephyranthes

VEGETABLES which may now be sown in open ground

Asparagus roots	Chicory	Kohlrabi	Roquette
Beets	Chinese cabbage	Lettuce	Rutabaga
Broccoli	Chives	Mustard	Salsify
Brussels sprouts	Collards	Onion, seeds, sets	Shallot plants
Cabbage	Corn salad	and plants	Spinach
Carrots	Cos	Parsley	Tendergreens
Cauliflower plants	Cress	Parsnips	Tomatoes
Celtuce	Endive	Peppers	Turnips
Chard, Swiss	Kale	Radishes	

Azaleas and Camellias: Plants may be moved. Keep moist to lessen cold weather damage. May acidify again. See **October.**

Bulbs: Last month to plant early blossoming spring bulbs, speciosum and other varieties of lilies. Mulch.

Cultivation: A season of heavy garden work begins this month. Clean up beds where fall flowers have bloomed. Prepare soil in new beds now, to allow time for settling before planting. Add leaves to compost heap but burn diseased or bug-infested refuse.

Fertilize: Established trees, spring-blooming shrubs, spurias, and sweet peas (after they are a foot tall) with fertilizer such as 13-13-13; Louisiana iris with cotton seed meal and manure.

Maidenhair: Even if frozen it will come back from roots in the spring. Allow fallen leaves to remain on bed as mulch.

Pansies: If long flowering period is desired, plants should be placed in their permanent beds not later than this month. Fertilize monthly with manure, superphosphate or a liquid high-phosphate product. Keep flowers picked for more bloom.

Shrubs and Trees: This month and the next two are considered best for planting.

Tulips: Take tulips out of cold storage and plant late this month.

Watering: Keep evergreens well watered to prevent damage from freezing.

Winter Protection: Be prepared to protect tender plants.

144

PLANTS WHICH BLOOM IN DECEMBER

t—Tree *s*—Shrub *v*—Vine *b*—Bulb, Tuber or Rhizome *e*—Evergreen
d—Deciduous *p*—Perennial *bn*—Biennial *a*—Annual

Alyssum, *a*
Calendula, *a*
Calla, *b*
Camellia, Japonica, *s e*
  Sasanqua, *s e*
Chinese Forget-Me-Not, *a*
Chrysanthemums, *p*
Daisy, African

Golden, *a*
Elaeagnus, *s e*
Eranthemum, *s*
Forget-Me-Not, *p*
Gerbera, *p*
Honeysuckle, *s d*
Iris, unguicularis, *b*
  stylosa, *b*
Jasmine, *v e*

floridum, *s e*
Loquat, *s e*
Michaelmas Daisy, *p*
Narcissus, *b*
Oxalis, *b*
Pansy, *a*
Pinks, *a, bn*
Plumbago, *s*
Poinsettia, *s d*

Quince, Japanese Flowering, *s d*
Roses
Salvia, *p a*
Sweet Olive, *s e*
Sweet Pea, Early, *a*
Turk's Cap, *s e*
Viola, *a*
Violet, *p*

BULBS, TUBERS, RHIZOMES, CORMS AND TUBEROUS ROOTS

B—Bulbs
T—Tubers
R—Rhizomes
C—Corms
TR—Tuberous Roots

To bloom well most bulbs need at least some sun, a fast draining soil of equal parts rich loam, sand and humus. The usual planting depth is twice the bulb's diameter. A pinch, each, of bone meal and superphosphate under the soil in the bottom of the hole helps. Careful selection from the different categories can bring the pleasure of monthly bloom. See BULBS chapter.

COMMON NAME *Botanical Name*	Color	When to Plant	Depth to Cover	Space Apart	COMMENTS
ACHIMENES, T *Achimines*	White, Pink, Blue, Lavender	Nov.-Dec.	1"	3"	Grown from tubers and divisions. Semi-shade. Fibrous loam; no fertilizer at planting. Shallow rooting. May be left in same pots for several years. Summer blooming. Thrives in sphagnum moss baskets. Naturalizes.
AGAPANTHUS, B (LILY-OF-THE-NILE) *Agapanthus Orientalis* *Agapanthus albus*	Blue White	Oct.-Feb.	2"	12"	Grown from bulbs and bulblets. Half loam and half peat. Sun or partial shade. Water freely. Excellent near edge of pool. Blooms in May and June. Very beautiful. Also grown from seeds. Dwarf forms. Plant high. Fertilize after blooming and again in the early spring.
ALLIUM, B *Allium Neopolitanum grandiflorum*	White	Sept.-Mar.	2"	6"	Grown from bulbs. Sun. Sandy loam. Excellent for cutting. Same culture as Grape-Hyacinths. New varieties come in shades of pink, yellow and blue. Blooms all summer. Other species. Naturalizes.
ALSTROEMERIA, T (PERUVIAN LILY) *Alstroemeria aurantiaca*	Orange, Yellow	Oct.-May	6"	8"	Grown from tubers and seeds. Half-hardy, semi-tropical. Light soil. Excellent for cutting. Requires winter mulch. Azalea-like blossoms in May and June.
AMARCRINUM, B *Amarcrinum Howardi*	Shell-Pink	Oct.-May	2"	18"	Culture same as Agapanthus. Blooms periodically during summer.
AMARYLLIS, B *Amaryllis*	White thru Red	Nov.-Feb.		12"	Grown from bulbs, bulblets and seeds. Any rich garden soil. Sun or semi-sun. Blooms April-May. Plant high, about one-fourth out of soil. Feed after blooming and again in the fall. Keep mulched. California and Dutch hybrids.
ANEMONE, B *Anemone St. Brigid*	Blue, Scarlet, White	Oct.-Dec.	4"	6"	Grown from bulbs. Light loam on sand base. Semi-shade or sun. Requires moisture. Blooms early spring. DeCaen and Tecolete strains.
ANTHURIUM, B (FLAMINGO FLOWER) *Anthurium Scherzerianum*	Coral	Oct.-Dec.	2"		Potting mixture should contain shredded sphagnum moss as humus. Semi-shade. Water from bottom of pot. Ample water needed while budding and flowering. Blooms March-June.
ASPIDISTRA *Aspidistra*	Green or variegated foliage	Any time	2"	8"	Grown from divisions and roots. Will withstand much heat and poor soil. Semi-shade or shade. Acid tolerant. Leaves last well when cut. Grown in old gardens as borders or used in urns.
BANANA, ROSE-FLOWERED *Musa rosacea*	Vivid Pink-Lavender	Nov.-Dec.	2"	2'	Rich, loamy soil, well drained. Propagated by suckers. Exotic flower stalk. Good patio plant. Protect from wind.
BEGONIA, FIBROUS ROOTED *Begonia semperflorens*	White, Pink, Red	Feb.-May	2"	12"	Grown from seeds or roots. Single and double varieties. Pot early indoors in well-drained rich soil. May be placed outdoors for summer bloom.
BLACKBERRY LILY, R *Pardanthus (Belamcanda)*	Yellow with Black spots	Aug.-Mar.	2"	12"	Grown from roots, seeds and divisions. Any soil. Sun. Naturalizes easily. Blooms June and July. Flowers followed by ornamental black seed clusters which may be used in arrangements.
BLUE-EYED GRASS, B *Sisyrinchium*	Blue	Any time	Just cover	3"	Grown from fibrous roots. Naturalizes. Sandy loam. Succession of bloom during spring and early summer.
BUTTERFLY LILY, R *Hdeychium coronarium*	White	Feb.-Mar.	2"	15"	Grown from divisions. Part shade. Give generous amount of fertilizer. Fragrant clusters of flowers resemble butterflies. Blooms late summer and fall.
CALADIUM, T *Caladium bicolor*	Variegated foliage Red, White. Pink, Green	Mar.-May	2"	12"	Semi-shade. Mildly acid soil. Popular as bedding plants. Lift and store in the fall in dry peat moss.

BULBS, TUBERS, RHIZOMES, CORMS AND TUBEROUS ROOTS

COMMON NAME *Botanical Name*	Color	When to Plant	Depth to Cover	Space Apart	COMMENTS
CALLA LILY, R *Zantedeschia aethiopica* Var. Elliottiana (Corm)	White Yellow, with spotted foliage	Sept.	2"	6-12"	Grown from roots or corms. Loose, rich soil, leaf mold. Partial shade. Water freely. Must be protected against cold. Blooms March-May. Dwarf species: *Z. Godefreyana*, white prolific bloomer; *Z. Rehmanni*, pink.
CAMASSIA, B *Camassia scilloides* (wild hyacinth)	Pale Blue, White	Sept.-Oct.	6"	6"	Grown from bulbs and seeds. Hardy. Naturalizes. Good for mass planting. Semi-shade or sun. Good garden loam. Blooms April and May.
CANNA, R *Canna*	Various	Feb.-April	3"	18-24"	Grown from divisions and seeds. Good garden soil. Sun or partial shade. Water freely. Good for color masses. Blooms May-November. Many lovely hybrids of low and medium height. Some varieties have mottled flowers.
CHLIDANTHUS, B *Chlidanthus fragrans*	Yellow	Aug.-April	3"	5"	Plant with neck above soil. Sun. Flowers resemble miniature amaryllis. Bulbs should be lifted and stored. Blooms spring. Tender.
CHIONODOXA, B (GLORY-OF-THE-SNOW)	Blue, White, Pink	Sept.	2-3"	3-4"	Grown from offsets or seeds. Sun or partial shade. Naturalizes. Star-shaped flowers. Most effective when planted in large clumps. Blooms March and April.
CLIVIA, B *Clivia*	Yellow, Apricot, Orange	Oct.-Dec.	4"	10"	Grown from divisions and seeds. Potting mixture of sand, humus and bone meal with charcoal for drainage. Occasional feedings of liquid manure. Outdoors in summer in shady location, then brought to cool but protected porch to bloom in Feb. and March.
CRINUM, B *Crinum*	Pink, White, Wine	Nov.-Mar.	6"	12-24"	Grown from bulbs and offsets. Any rich garden soil. Sun or partial shade. Water freely. Blooms March-December. Beautiful named varieties may now be secured. Plant bulb high on mound of sand. Feed after blooming and again in the fall with mixture of old manure and superphosphate.
CROCUS, C *Crocus*	White, Yellow, Blue	Sept.-Dec.	2"	3"	Winter sun. Best in clumps or drifts. 4" to 6" high. Light, sandy soil. Good drainage. 1 T. bonemeal, covered with soil, in planting hole. Early spring bloom.
DAFFODIL, B *Narcissus Pseudo-Narcissus*	White, Yellow	Oct.-Dec.	4"	6"	Grown from bulbs and bulblets. Any rich garden soil. sandy best. Sun or partial shade. Some varieties naturalize. Blooms February-March. See special article on Narcissus.
DAHLIA, T *Dahlia*	Various	Feb.-Mar.	2"	2-3'	Grown from seeds and divisions. Single varieties valuable for cutting. Blooms June-November. See special article on Dahlias. Miniature hybrid types excellent for bedding.
DAYLILY, TR *Hemerocallis*	Shades of Orange, Lemon, Red, Pink	Oct.-Mar.	1"	18"	Grown from roots and divisions. Also from proliferations (plantlets) which sometimes develop on the flower stem. Any soil. Sun or partial shade. Blooms April-Oct. Free bloomer. Hardy. See special article on Daylilies.
DIETES, R (SOUTH AFRICAN IRID) *Moraea iridioides*	White with orange or yellow throat	Sept.	1"	4"	Tender. Morning sun. Average garden soil. Blooms during summer. Reflowers on same bloom stalk. Other species also desirable.
EUCHARIS, B (AMAZON LILY) *Eucharis grandiflora*	White	Nov. to Jan.	4"	10"	Culture same as Clivia. Large clusters of exquisite star-shaped flowers. Blooms Jan.-May. Plant neck of bulb above soil. Excellent in pots.
FREESIA, C *Freesia*	Various	Sept.-Dec.	1"	4-6"	Sandy loam with peat moss. Sun. Fragrant.
GALTONIA, B (SUMMER HYACINTH) *Galtonia candicans*	White	Mar.	6"	7-8"	Grown from bulbs and seeds. Hardy. Fragrant. Culture same as gladiolus. Will produce a succession of blooms if flowers are kept cut as they fade. Blooms midsummer.
GINGER, HIDDEN, R *Curcuma petiolata*	Pink, Yellow	Mar.	2"	18"	Grown from tuberous roots. Feed in growing season. Keep moist year round. Partial shade.

COMMON NAME / *Botanical Name*	Color	When to Plant	Depth to Cover	Space Apart	COMMENTS
GINGER LILY, R (KAHILI GINGER) / *Hedychium gardnerianum*	Yellow, Scarlet Tipped	Feb.-Mar.	4-5"	18"	Grown from divisions. Larger than Butterfly lilies. Rich, loamy soil. Morning sun. Exotic flowers. Ample water while growing. Blooms summer and fall. Tender.
GINGER, SHELL, R / *Alpinia speciosa*	Pink	Feb.-May	2"	15"	Pink buds opening to white flowers with yellow lip, red striped. Fragrant. Grown from rhizomes and divisions. Large tropical plants. Rich loamy soil. Abundant water. Summer blooming.
GLADIOLUS, C / *Gladiolus*	Various	Feb.-Mar. July-Sept.	3-5"	6"	Grown from bulbs and bulblets. Any rich garden soil, sandy best. Sun or partial shade. Water freely. More lovely in groups than rows. Blooms April-June, October and November. Plant every two weeks.
BABY GLADIOLUS (Dwarf type)			1"	3"	See special article on Gladiolus. *G. tristis* fragrant. Dwarf species.
GLORIOSA, T (CLIMBING LILY) / *Gloriosa rothschildiana* / *Gloriosa superba*	Scarlet margined with yellow	Feb.-Mar.	2"	14"	Grown from tubers. Plant horizontally. Full sun. Rich, moist soil. Hardy along Gulf coast. Exotic blooms excellent for cutting. Tubers may be stored like dahlias. Summer blooming.
GLOXINIA, T / *Gloxinia*	Red, Purple, White	Feb.-Mar.	1"	10"	Grown from tubers, seeds and leaves. Peaty, sandy soil. Humid atmosphere. Shade. Ample water while growing. Recommended for greenhouse.
GRAPE-HYACINTH, B / *Muscari*	Blue, White	Oct.-Jan.	2"	6"	Grown from bulbs and bulblets. Good garden soil. Sun or partial shade. Blooms March. Naturalizes. Useful for edging and for ground cover.
GUERNSEY LILY, B / *Nerine sarniensis*	Coral, Red	Mar.	Just below surface	12"	Grown from bulbs. Any soil. Sun or shade. Very beautiful. Divide every 2 or 3 years. Naturalizes. Fertilize with superphosphate worked in and watered in. July or August. Blooms Sept.
HABRANTHUS, B / *Habranthus brachyandrus* / *Habranthus robustus*	Pink to Maroon Shell-Pink	Oct.	3-4"	6"	Good drainage. Sun or partial shade. Flowers resemble zephyranthes. Same culture as amaryllis. Plant in groups. Summer blooming. Rain lilies.
HAEMANTHUS, B (BLOOD LILY) / *Haemanthus katherinae* / *Haemanthus multiflora*	Red	Jan.-Mar.	4"	10"	Slightly acid soil containing leafmold. Partial shade. Plant bulb high, half out of soil. Culture same as Clivia. Blooms late summer and fall. Tops die down in winter. Bulbs need winter rest without water.
HYACINTHS, B / *Hyacinthus*	All colors	Nov.-Dec.	3-5"	5"	Grown from bulbs. Rich soil, preferably sandy. Water freely while developing. Withhold while blooming. Bulbs should be lifted after leaves turn brown. Blooms February-April. Several varieties. Roman hyacinths precede Dutch varieties. Plant in sandy loam with bone meal as fertilizer. For water culture, keep in cool, dark place until growth starts, then expose to light.
IRIS, ALGERIAN (WINTER), R / *Iris unguicularis (stylosa)*	White, Lavender thru Purple	March	1"	12"	Grown from divisions. Good garden soil. Sun or shade. Drainage. Blooms November-February.
IRIS, BEARDED, R	Wide color range	Aug.-Feb.	1"	12"	Grown from divisions. Alkaline soil. Sun. Good drainage. Blooms Jan.,-April.
IRIS, DUTCH, B	Blue, Yellow, White, Wine-Red	Sept.-Oct.-Nov.	3"	4-5"	Light well drained soil. Excellent for cutting. Blooms Feb. to May. Cut when color shows at tip, stand in water until open. See Iris.
IRIS, R / *Iris pseudacorus*	Yellow	Sept.-Nov.	1"	18"	Grown from division. Fertile moist soil. Sun or shade. 3' to 4' tall. Nearly evergreen. Erect growth. Grows well around pools. Blooms March-April.
IRIS, EVANSIA, R (CRESTED IRIS) / *Iris cristata*	Blue, White	May	Just cover	4"	Shade loving. Acid tolerant. Plant in Azalea soil mixture. Good for bordering azaleas. Resemble miniature spray orchids. Bloom Feb. and Mar.
Iris tectorum (ROOF IRIS) / *Iris japonica*	Lavender, Blue	Sept. Oct.		16"	Grown from seeds. Hardy. Dwarf. Linear crested. Blooms April. Good hybrid. Nada. Tender. Mulch deeply for freeze protection.
IRIS, JAPANESE, R / *Iris kaempferi*	White	Sept.-Oct.	1"	12"	From roots, seeds and divisions. Soil rich in humus. Sun or shade. Blooms May-June. See Iris.

BULBS, TUBERS, RHIZOMES, CORMS AND TUBEROUS ROOTS

COMMON NAME / Botanical Name	Color	When to Plant	Depth to Cover	Space Apart	COMMENTS
IRIS, LOUISIANA, R	White, Pink, Red, Purple, Yellow	Sept. to Nov.	1-2"	8"	Grown from divisions and seed. Soil requires leaf mold. Keep mulched. Water freely. Many lovely hybrids. Shade from afternoon sun. Blooms April-May.
IRIS, NATIVE, R (FLAG) / Iris hexagona	White, Purple	May-Nov.	1"	18"	Grown from divisions. Any moist soil. Sun or shade. Good in rock gardens and around pools. Blooms March, April.
IRIS, RETICULATA, B / Iris reticulata	Violet, Purple	Oct. to Jan.	4"	4"	Grown from seeds and bulbs. Dwarf variety about 8 inches high. Sun, good drainage. Naturalizes. Fragrant. Good companion planting for narcissus. Blooms February.
IRIS, SIBERIAN, R / Iris sibirica	Blue, Purple, White	Sept.-Nov.	1"	12"	Grown from seeds and divisions. Friable moist soil. Water freely. Sun. Blooms early spring. Leave in clumps undisturbed.
IRIS, SPURIA, R / Iris spuria	White, Yellow, Blue, Lavender, Bronze, Purple and Bicolors	Oct.-Nov.	1-2"	2"	Sun, good drainage. Moist, friable, neutral soil with abundance of food. Excellent for cutting. Blooms April to June.
ISMENE (PERUVIAN DAFFODIL), B / Hymenocallis calathina	White	Feb.-Mar.	4"	18"	Grown from bulbs. Any soil. Sun or partial shade. Water freely. Very fragrant. Blooms May and June.
IXIA, B	Various	Oct.-Dec.	1"	4"	Grown from bulbs. Sandy soil. Sun. Rare. Worth trying. Blooms early spring.
JACK-IN-THE-PULPIT, B / Arisaema triphyllum	Mottled, Brown, Green	Oct.-Dec.	2"	6"	Grown from bulbs. Soil rich in humus. Water freely. Shade. Blooms early spring.
JACOBEAN LILY, B / Sprekelia formosissima	Scarlet	Nov.	2"	5"	Same culture as Amaryllis. Flowers resemble butterflies. Plant shallow. Fertilize with bonemeal and superphosphate. Blooms June. May also be grown in pots.
JONQUIL, B / Narcissus jonquilla	Yellow	Oct.-Dec.	3"	5"	Grown from bulbs. Light, sandy soil. Sun or partial shade. Naturalizes easily. Blooms March. Also N. odorus.
KNIPHOFIA (root) / (Red Hot Poker Plant)	Red, Yellow	Jan. to Mar.	Just cover	6"	Grown from divisions and seed. Formerly called Tritoma. Full sun. Light garden soil. Plant in clumps. Blooms summer.
LACHENALIA, B / (CAPE COWSLIP)	White, Red, Yellow	Oct.	½"	2"	Grown from bulbs and seeds. Same culture as Clivias. Need moisture while growing, but keep on dry side during summer months. Will grow in same pots for years. Use liquid manure. Blooms Dec. and Jan.
LAPEIROUSIA, C	Rose, White	Jan.-Mar.	2"	6"	Dwarf plants, flowers resemble freesias. Naturalizers. Sheltered position. Mulch in winter. Light porous soil. Blooms summer and fall.
LIRIOPE (root) (LILY TURF) / Liriope muscari / Liriope spicata	Purple / Pale lilac	Oct.-Dec.	1½"	4"	Grown from divisions. Acid tolerant. Sun or shade. Flowers resemble Grape-Hyacinths. Ideal as border plant or ground cover. Excellent for cutting. Blooms summer and fall. Monroe White, giant Majestic, and variegated forms.
LILY, CENTIFOLIUM, B / Lilium centifolium	White	Sept.	6"	10"	Semi-shade. Plant in clumps of 3 or 5. Hybrid of Regal Lily. Same culture as Creole Lily. Blooms May. Olympic hybrids most popular.
LILY, GOLDBAND, B / Lilium auratum	White with Gold band	Oct.-Feb.	6"	12"	Grown from bulbs. Well drained soil, rich in humus. Semi-sun. Water freely. Blooms May-June. Stem rooting.
LILY, LONGIFLORUM, B / var. ACE / var. EASTER / var. CREOLE / var. CROFT / var. ESTATE	White / White / White / White / White	Oct. / Oct.-Feb. / Sept. / Sept. / Sept.	6" / 6" / 4-6" / 4-6" / 4-6"	10-12"	Grown from bulbs. Well drained, light soil, rich in humus. Use sand and bonemeal under bulbs when planting. Sunny location. When growth begins, water freely. Bulbs multiply readily. Bulblets may be removed from mother bulb, resetting immediately. Blooms April, May.
LILY, MADONNA, B / Lilium candidum	White	Oct.	6"	12"	Grown from bulbs. Loose, rich, well drained soil. Plenty of moisture. Partial shade. Blooms April. Basal rooting. Slight alkalinity good.

COMMON NAME / *Botanical Name*	Color	When to Plant	Depth to Cover	Space Apart	COMMENTS
LILY, PHILIPPINE, B / *Lilium philippinense formosanum*	White with rose tints	Sept.-Oct.	8"	12"	Grown from bulbs or seeds. Plant in sun with ground cover, away from other lilies. Mulch during summer. Wilson hybrid strain most satisfactory. Blooms late summer.
LILY, REGAL, B / *Lilium regale*	Ivory-White shaded Pink White with Yellow throat	Oct.	6"	10"	Best from bulbs. Good, well drained soil rich in humus. Blooms April-May. Very beautiful. Gaining in popularity. Stem rooting.
LILY, SPECIOSUM, B / *Lilium speciosum* Var. RUBRUM Var. ALBUM	Pale Pink with crimson spots White	Oct.	6"	12"	From bulbs. Soil rich in humus, well drained. Water freely. Sun or partial shade. Blooms June-July. Stem rooting.
LILY, TIGER, B / *Lilium tigrinum*	Orange-Brown spotted	Oct.	6"	8"	Grown from bulbs and bulblets. Any good garden soil. Sun or partial shade. Water sparingly. Showy. Blooms May-June. Stem-rooting.
LILY, TURK'S-CAP, B / *Lilium superbum*	Yellow to Scarlet spotted	Oct.	9"	10"	Soil rich in humus. Summer blooming. Basal rooting.
LILY, UMBELLATUM, B (GOLDEN CHALICE) / *Lilium umbellatum*	Yellow, Red, Deep Copper	Oct.	6"	10"	Sun. Stem-rooting. Free flowering. Early blooming.
LILY-OF-THE-VALLEY, R / *Convallaria*	White	Nov.-Dec.	2"	1"	Pips may be forced in water or damp moss for early indoor bloom. Fragrant.
LYCORIS, B / *Lycoris aurea* *Lycoris radiata*	Yellow Red	Apr.-Aug.	Tips showing	6-8"	Sun and shade. Bulbs multiply if not disturbed. Any soil fortified with bonemeal. Blooms appear without foliage in the fall. Feed during winter growth.
MARICA (WALKING IRIS) / *Neomarica gracilis*	White with Purple markings	Any Time	1"	8"	Shade-loving. Acid tolerant. Naturalizes. Blooms June. Grown from divisions.
MILLA, B (TRITELEIA) / *Milla uniflora*	White, edged with Blue	Oct.-Dec.	1"	6"	Sun. Light sandy soil. Fragrant. Star-shaped flowers on six inch stems. Blooms early spring.
MONTBRETIA, B / *Tritonia*	Orange-Red	Oct.-Feb.	1"	6"	Grown from bulbs and bulblets. Any good garden soil. Sun or shade. Blooms June-August. Fine for cutting. Feed.
NARCISSUS, B / *Narcissus*	White, Yellow	Oct.-Jan.	3"	6"	Grown from bulbs and bulblets. Any rich garden soil, sandy best. Sun or partial shade. Water freely. Blooms about 70 days after planting. See special article on Narcissus.
OXALIS, B / *Oxalis*	Pink, White, Yellow	Any Month	1"	8"	Any soil. Sun or shade. Naturalizes. Suitable for borders and rock gardens. Watch for Red Spider. Blooms often.
RAIN LILY, B / *Cooperia*	White	Nov.-Feb.	2"	6"	Grown from bulbs and bulblets. Any soil. Sun or shade. Water freely. Naturalizes easily. Blooms July-September after rains.
RANUNCULUS, B / *Ranunculus asiaticus*	Various	Sept. to Dec.	1½"	4-5"	Well-drained soil. Bulbs may be soaked overnight in water. Plant prongs down. Excellent for cutting. Plant for succession of bloom. Winter and spring blooming.
SANSEVIERIA (root) (SNAKE PLANT) / *Sansevieria zeylanica*	Variegated Foliage Small white flower	Any time	1"	8"	Grown from leaf cuttings and divisions. Requires little sun. Does best in heavy soil with bonemeal. Must be pot-bound to bloom.
SNOWDROPS, B / *Galanthus nivalis*	White	Oct.	2"	6"	Well drained garden loam. Partial shade. Winter bloom.
SNOWFLAKE, B / *Leucojum aestivum*	White with Green dot	Oct.-Dec.	2"	6"	Grown from bulbs. Sandy garden loam. Partial shade. Free bloomer. Naturalizes easily. Blooms February-March.

150

BULBS, TUBERS, RHIZOMES, CORMS AND TUBEROUS ROOTS

COMMON NAME / Botanical Name	Color	When to Plant	Depth to Cover	Space Apart	COMMENTS
SPARAXIS (corm) (HARLEQUIN FLOWER)	Yellow to Flame	Nov.	2"	3-4"	Well-drained, sandy loam. Sun. Same culture as Ixias. Excellent for cutting. Spring blooming.
SPATHIPHYLLUM, R / Spathiphyllum clevelandi	White	Feb.	2"		Grown from root divisions in pots. Very decorative. Commonly called White Anthurium. Dwarf form also.
SPIDER LILY, B / Hymenocallis	White	Oct.-Mar.	5"	18"	Grown from bulbs and bulblets. Any well drained soil. Sun or shade. Water freely. The wild lily of this region. Blooms June-August.
SQUILL, B / Scilla	Blue, Pink, White	Nov.	2"	6"	Grown from bulbs. Sandy loam. Partial shade. Plant in masses. Blooms March.
STAR OF BETHLEHEM, B / Ornithogalum umbellatum	White	Sept.-Oct.	2-3"	3-4"	Average, well-drained soil. Sun. O. arabicum has dark center.
STRELITZIA, (BIRD-OF-PARADISE) / Strelitzia reginae	Blue and Orange	Sept.-Oct.	4"	12"	Grown from seeds, suckers and root-stalks. Potting mixture same as Clivia. Sunny garden location in summer, protection during winter. Feed occasionally in summer with liquid manure. Winter blooming.
TIGRIDIA, B (SHELL FLOWER) / Tigridia	Variegated Scarlet, Yellow, Orange	Feb.-Mar.	3"	6"	Grown from seeds, divisions and bulbs. Hot sunny location. Same culture as Gladiolus. Beautiful Iris-like flowers. Ample water at blooming time. Blooms July to frost.
TUBEROSE (SINGLE AND DOUBLE), T / Polianthes tuberosa	White	Mar.	2"	8"	Grown from tubers. Any soil. Full sun. Water freely. Very fragrant. Blooms June-September.
TULBAGHIA, B / Tulbaghia violacea (dwarf) / Tulbaghia fragrans	Orchid Lavender	Nov.-Mar.	Just cover	6"	Sun or shade. Almost continuous bloomer. Plant in groups in rich, well-drained soil. Excellent for cutting. Summer blooming. T. violacea.
TULIP, B / Tulipa	Various	Dec. 26-Jan.	6"	6"	Grown from bulbs. Sandy soil, plenty of humus. Pinch of bonemeal, super-phosphate under bulb when planting. Sun or partial shade. Blooms March-April. Darwin and Breeder types do best in this area. Should be refrigerated from 3 to 6 weeks before planting.
WATER-HYACINTH, R / Eichhornia	Lavender	Any time			Fine for pools. Blooms May-Oct. Multiplies rapidly. Beautiful.
WATERLILY, T / Nymphaea	Blue, Pink, White, Yellow, Red	Any time			Plant 6-18 inches under water, 2-3 feet apart. Blooms May-November. Fragrant. Day and night-blooming varieties.
WATERPOPPY (root) / Hydrocleis nymphoides	Yellow	Any time			For ponds, pools and aquariums. Grown from divisions. Blooms May-August. Resembles California poppies.
WATSONIA, C / Watsonia	Various	Sept. to Nov.	3"	5"	Culture same as Gladiolus. Fertilize with bonemeal. Naturalizes. Excellent for cutting. Spring blooming.
YUCCA (SPANISH DAGGER), R / Yucca dioifolia	White	Any month	6"	3-4'	Evergreen. Showy spikes of bell-shaped flowers. Plant in small groups for effect
YUCCA, RED FLOWERED / Hesperaloe parviflora	Coral Red	Any month		2'	Not a true yucca. May be grown from seed. Sun. Native. May be used in hot dry locations. Summer bloom.
ZEPHYR LILY, B (FAIRY or RAIN LILY) / Zephyranthes ajax / Zephyranthes candida / Zephyranthes citrina / Zephyranthes grandiflora	Yellow White Gold Pink	Nov.-Feb.	2"	4-6"	Grown from bulbs and bulblets. Any soil. Sun or shade. Water freely. Naturalizes. Blooms May-September. Especially beautiful. Effective for massed planting.

FLOWERING SHRUBS AND TREES

S—Shrubs
T—Trees
D—Deciduous
E—Evergreens

In the Houston and Gulf Coast areas of heavy annual rainfall and often flat terrain it is of paramount importance to assure satisfactory drainage first; then prepare the soil to make it fertile and friable, preferably allowing some weeks before planting to allow the soil to settle. Attention to these two necessities will save time, effort and expense later, as well as give greater assurance of success. Refer to Soil and Drainage in the index.

COMMON NAME / Botanical Name	Color	Approx. Height	Space Apart	To Plant	TIME Of Blooming	COMMENTS
ABELIA, S E / Abelia grandiflora	Pinkish white	4-6'	3-4'	Nov.-Mar.	May-Sept.	Good in groups. Valuable for hedge, planted one foot apart. Sun. Fragrant glossy foliage, bronzy in fall.
AGARITA, S E / Mahonia trifoliata	Yellow	3-4'	3-6'	Nov.-Mar.	March	Handsome. Native. Likes dry soil. Lovely in Spanish garden. Fruit makes good jelly.
ALMOND, FLOWERING, S D / Prunus glandulosa (Amygdalus)	White, Pink	3-5'	3'	Nov.-Mar.	Mar.-April	Best in full sun. Good in groups. Sandy well-drained soil.
ALTHAEA, S D / Hibiscus syriacus	Lavender, Rose, White	8'	4'	Nov.-Mar.	June-Sept.	Good as specimen plant, in group or hedge. Free blooming. Any garden soil. Sun.
ANAQUA, T E / Ehretia anacua	White	30'	30'	Nov.	Mar.-Apr.	Flowers small and profuse followed by orange fruit. Hardy tree which should be used more. Rich soil. Attracts birds.
ANDROMEDA, S E (LILY-OF-THE-VALLEY TREE) / Andromeda japonica / Pieris japonica	White	3-15'	6'	Oct.-Nov.	Feb.-Mar.	Semi-shade. Acid soil. Good drainage. Dainty flowers, beautiful foliage. Keep mulched.
ANGEL'S TRUMPET, S D / Datura arborea	White	6-12'	5'	Nov.-Mar.	June-Oct.	Full sun. Tender. If frozen back will come out from roots. Easily grown from divisions. Best used as a specimen tree. Drought resistant. Attractive double variety.
APPLE, T D / Malus sylvestris	Pink	10-12'	12'	Nov.-Mar.	March	Southern varieties advised. Flowers exquisite. Garden soil.
ARBUTUS UNEDO, T E (STRAWBERRY TREE)	White, Red fruit	8-15'		Feb.	Sept.-Dec.	Propagated by cuttings or seed. Average soil. Use as specimen tree or in shrubbery border. Sun or partial shade.
ARDISIA, S E / Ardisia crenulata	White, Red Berries	2-3'		Nov.-Mar.		Shade. Acid soil. Often planted in tubs. Useful for foundation planting.
AUCUBA, S E and D / Aucuba japonica / var. variegata (Gold Dust Plant)	Red Berries	4-5' / 3-5'		Nov.-Mar.		Semi-shade. Acid soil. Ample water. Good specimen shrub. Var. variegata has yellow spotted foliage.
AZALEA, S D and E / Azalea	Yellow, Lavender, Pink, White, Red, Purple	1-8'	1-3'	Any month	Oct.-May	Best in semi-shade. Exceedingly beautiful. Requires moisture, leafmold and mulch. Acid soil. See Azaleas. Many varieties.
BARBADOS CHERRY, S E / Malpighia glabra	Pink	2-3'	3'	Nov.-Mar.	May-Oct.	Beautiful red berries while blooming. Effective in groups or foundation planting. Sun. Any soil.
BEARGRASS / Sotol Texana	White	1-2'	2'	Nov.-Mar.	May	Perennial. Likes dry, sandy, alkaline soil. Graceful foliage.
BEAUTYBERRY, S D / Callicarpa americana	Pink, Lilac, Red, White	3-5'	3'	Nov.-Mar.	May	Beautiful purple berries in late summer. Attracts 10 species birds. Garden soil. Semi-sun.
BOTTLEBRUSH, S E / Callistemon	Red	4'	4'	Feb.-Mar.	April-May	Beautiful. Water sparingly. Excellent as specimen plant. Difficult to transplant. Full sun. Any soil. Dwarf forms fine.
BOUVARDIA, S E / Bouvardia	White	2-3'	2'	March	Sept.-Jan.	Shade. Loamy soil. Tender. Often grown in pots. Fragrant. Waxy flowers. Winter blooming.
BRUNFELSIA, S E (LADY-OF-THE-NIGHT) (YESTERDAY-TODAY-AND TOMORROW) / Brunfelsia americana	White	4-5'	4'	Mar.	Summer	Good soil. Partial shade. Uniform moisture. Tender. Fragrant.
Brunfelsia calycina	Dark purple fading to white			Mar.-June	Mar.-Apr.	Fragrant. Tender. Feed while growing.

FLOWERING SHRUBS AND TREES

COMMON NAME / *Botanical Name*	Color	Approx. Height	Space Apart	TIME—To Plant	TIME—Of Blooming	COMMENTS
BUSHCLOVER, S D / *Lespedeza formosa*	Purple	3-4'	3-4'	Oct.-Mar.	May-Aug.	Delicate foliage and sprays of blossom. Contrasts well with other shrubs. Open, sandy soil.
BUTTERFLYBUSH, S D / *Buddleia alternifolia*	Lavender	6'	3-4'	Nov.-Mar.	May-Oct.	Graceful, spreading. Lilac-like, sweet-scented bloom. Attracts butterflies. Sun. Rich, well drained soil.
BUTTERFLYBUSH, S E / *Buddleia davidi*	Lavender	5-6'	6'	Nov.-Mar.	May-Oct.	Very showy. Good as specimen or in groups. Suitable for cutting. Blue-green leaves four inches long. Sun. Rich soil. Drainage.
BUTTONBUSH, COMMON, S D / *Cephalanthus occidentalis*	White	6-18'	4'	Oct.-Mar.	June-Sept.	Handsome foliage and flowers. Likes extremely moist, good soil.
CAMELLIA, S E / *Camellia japonica* / *Camellia sasanqua*	White thru Red	6-10' / 6-10'	4' / 3'	Nov.-Mar. / Nov.-Mar.	Feb.-Mar. / Dec.-Jan.	Very beautiful. Best in semi-shade. Both varieties do best in acid soil. Japonica varieties good as specimen plants. See Camellias.
CARYOPTERIS, S D (BLUE SPIREA) / *Caryopteris incana*	Pale Blue	2-5'	2'	Nov.-Mar.	July to frost	Attracts bees and butterflies. Full sun. Tender. Powder blue fringed flowers, grown in clusters. Humusy loam.
CASSIA, S D / *Cassia alata* (Candle Tree) / *Cassia beareana* / *Cassia corymbosa* (Flowery Senna)	Yellow / Yellow / Yellow	3-8' / 6-10' / 6-8'	6' / 6' / 4'	Nov.-Apr. / Nov.-Apr. / Nov.-Apr.	Aug.-Oct. / Oct.-Dec. / Aug.-Oct.	Light sandy loam. Sun and water. If killed by freeze, worth replanting. Fast growing. Free flowering.
CATALPA, T D / *Catalpa speciosa*	White	30'	20'	Nov.-Mar.	April-May	Symmetrical. Handsome foliage and flowers. Any good soil.
CHASTE TREE, S D / *Vitex agnus-castus* / *Vitex negundo incisa*	Lavender / Lavender	10' / 6'	6' / 6'	Nov.-Mar. / Nov.-Mar.	May-July / May-July	Lovely. Aromatic foliage. Foliage very beautiful. Free bloomer. Both varieties combine effectively with Crapemyrtle. Drainage. Any good soil.
CHENILLE PLANT, S E / *Acalypha hispida*	Red-Purple	6-15'	10'	Feb.	July-Sept.	Tender. Cylindrical flowers. Large heart-shaped leaves. Garden soil.
CHINABERRY, T D / *Melia azedarach* / *Melia azedarach umbraculiformis*	Lavender / Lavender	25' / 25'	20' / 20'	Nov.-Mar. / Nov.-Mar.	Mar.-April / Mar.-April	Ornamental foliage. Any soil. Sun. The Umbrella China. Good for quick shade.
CHINESE HAT PLANT, S E / *Holmskioldia sanguinea*	Rust-Red	8'	6-9'	Any time	Continuous	Sun. Rich soil. Long clusters of flowers. Good for tropical effect. Plant in tub. Protect in winter.
CIGARETTE PLANT, S E / *Cuphea micropetala*	Red and Yellow	5-6'	3'	Nov.-Mar.	Summer and Fall	Sun. Average soil. Prune after blooming to insure almost continuous blooms.
CLETHRA, S D / *Clethra alnifolia*	White, Pink	3-6'	3'	Nov.-Mar.	Aug.-Oct.	Neat growing. Fragrant. Appropriate for Colonial garden. Acid soil. Part shade.
CONFEDERATE ROSE, S D / *Hibiscus mutabilis*	White thru Crimson	8'	6'	Nov.-Mar.	June-Oct.	Striking feature—flowers white at morning, pink at noon, crimson at night, then fall. New flowers each day. Acid. fertile soil.
CORALBEAN, S D / *Erythrina herbacea*	Scarlet	2'	2'	Nov.-Mar.	April	Effective. Long handsome sprays of slender flowers. Showy red seeds in dark brown pods. Native. Sun. Any soil.
CORALTREE, T D / *Erythrina crista-galli*	Coral	6'	5'	Nov.-Mar.	May-Aug.	Semi-hardy. Sunny location. Showy clusters of large pea-shaped flowers. Any soil.
COTONEASTER, S E / *Cotoneaster*	White, Pink	2-6'	3-4'	Nov.-Mar.	Mar.-April	Good in groups, foundation planting and rockeries. Shade. Well drained soil. Red berries. Alkaline soil.
CRABAPPLE (SOUTHERN), T D / *Malus angustifolia*	Pink	10-20'	10'	Dec.-Mar.	April	Handsome. Delightfully fragrant. Rich, draining soil. Dormant spray for scale.
CRABAPPLE, FLOWERING, S D / *Malus ioensis* (Pyrus Texana)	Pink	10-20'	10'	Dec.-Mar.	April	Lovely clusters. Fragrant. Well-drained, deep clay soil with manure.

COMMON NAME / *Botanical Name*	Color	Approx. Height	Space Apart	TIME To Plant	TIME Of Blooming	COMMENTS
CRAPEMYRTLE, S or T D / *Lagerstroemia indica*	White thru Red, Lavender-Purple	6-15'	4-6'	Nov.-Mar.	June-Sept.	Hardy. Prune annually for heavy growth. Clipping of old flower-heads encourages repeated blooming. Hybrids especially desirable. Near East is pale pink. Rich soil. Manure. Sun.
CUPHEA, S E / *Cuphea hyssopifolia*	Lavender	1'	1'	Feb.-April	Constant bloomer	Dainty. Good for borders. Part shade. Average soil. Frequent watering.
CURRANT, INDIAN (CORALBERRY), S D / *Symphoricarpos orbiculatus*	White	5-7'	3'	Nov.-April	April	Red berries. Excellent for border. Native plant. Sun or shade. Any soil.
DAPHNE, ROSE, S E / *Daphne cneorum*	Pink	1'	2'	Dec.-Jan.	Mar.-April	Fragrant. Exquisite coloring. Part shade. Mulch with peat moss and sand, mixed. 'Ruby Glow' good.
DAPHNE, WINTER, S E / *Daphne odora*	Rose-Purple	3-5'	2'	Dec.-Jan.	Feb.-Mar.	Fragrant. Partial shade. Fast drainage. Good soil. Feed once after bloom.
DEUTZIA, S D / *Deutzia gracilis* *Deutzia rosea*	White, Pink	2-5'	3-4'	Nov.-Mar.	May	Upright growth. Requires sun. Good for spring bloom. Water freely. Garden soil. Prune after bloom.
DOGWOOD, T D / *Cornus florida*	White	8-15'	6-8'	Dec.-Mar.	March	Native. Very striking in bloom. Best in semi-shade. Grows in any good soil, slightly acid, with manure. Fast drainage. Mulch.
DURANTA, S E (GOLDEN DEWDROP) / *Durania repens*	Blue, Yellow Berries	6-15'	3-5'	Nov. to Feb.	May	Average soil. Full sun. Berries follow flowers. Tender but recovers quickly. May be trimmed as a small tree or used as a hedge. Grown from seeds and cuttings.
EBONY, TEXAS, T E / *Pithecellobium flexicaule*	Green-White	20'	30'	Oct.	Mar.-Apr.	Small, dense, black-green foliage. Very thorny. Fragrant. Flowers frequently.
ELDERBERRY, S D / *Sambucus canadensis*	White	6-10'	4-5'	Nov.-Mar.	May-Aug.	Fragrant flowers followed by conspicuous dark purplish berries. Likes plenty of room, and moist rich soil. Attracts birds.
ELAEAGNUS, S E / *Elaeagnus pungens*	Silver-White, Orange-Red fruit	8-10'	6'	Nov.	Fall	Sun or shade. Hardy. Foliage silver underneath. Fast growing. Loose spreading habit. Several varieties. Fragrant. Dry soil.
ERANTHEMUM, S / *Daedalacanthus nervosus*	Blue	3'	2-3'	Mar.-April	Nov.-Dec.	Very tender. Coarse foliage but flowers beautiful. Shade. Garden soil. Water. Good in pots.
EUCALYPTUS, T E / *Eucalyptus undulata* *Eucalyptus pulverulenta* (Silver Dollar)	White, White	40', 16'	20'	Feb.-Mar.	April, March	Tender until established. Rapid growing. Plant closely for very high screen. Beautiful gray-green round leaves effective in arrangements. Any soil.
FALSE-INDIGO, S D / *Amorpha paniculata*	Purple	6'	4'	Nov.-Mar.	April	Likes moist soil.
FRANKLINIA, T D / *Gordonia alatamaha*	White	15-25'	15'	Feb.	Aug.-Nov.	Well drained acid soil, well supplied with humus. Hardy. Magnolia-like flowers.
FRINGETREE, T D (GRANNY-GRAYBEARD) / *Chionanthus virginica*	White	6-8'	4'	Nov.-Mar.	March	One of the most beautiful of our native trees. Dark green foliage and fragile panicles of fragrant flowers. Sun. Moist sandy loam.
GORSE (WHIN), S E / *Ulex europaeus*	Yellow	3-4'	3-4'	Nov.-Mar.	April	Very showy. Thorny. Sandy. slightly acid soil. Difficult to transplant. Sun.
GRAPEFRUIT, T E / *Citrus paradisi*	White, Yellow fruit	6-10'	10'	Dec.-Jan.	April	Good sandy loam. Protect in freezing weather. Sun. Drainage.
GUAVA, PINEAPPLE, S E / *Feijoa sellowiana*	White, Red stamens	6-15'	8'	Nov.-Mar.	Mar.-April	Showy. Gray-green foliage. Excellent for jelly. Several varieties. Sandy loam rich in humus. Sun.
GUAVA, STRAWBERRY, S E / *Psidium cattleianum*	White, Purple fruit	4-6'	8'	Nov.-Feb.	April	Any soil with good drainage. Tender. An attractive ornamental bearing edible fruits.
HAW, MAY, T D / *Crataegus monogyna opaca*	White, Red fruit	20'		Nov.-Mar.	Feb.-Mar.	Native. Fruit makes delicious jelly. Some varieties have pink double flowers. Sandy, limey soil. Sun or part shade.
HAW, RED (HAWTHORN), T D / *Crataegus mollis*	White	20'	6-8'	Nov.-Mar.	Mar.-April	Native. Beautifully shaped. Highly colored foliage and berries in fall. Rich soil. Sun or part shade. Parsley Haw, *C. marshallii*, beautiful foliage, white flowers, red fruit, recommended.

FLOWERING SHRUBS AND TREES

COMMON NAME. *Botanical Name*	Color	Approx. Height	Space Apart	TIME To Plant	TIME Of Blooming	COMMENTS
HAW, RUSTY BLACK, T D *Viburnum rufidulum*	White Black fruit	8-15'	6-10'	Nov.-Mar.	Mar.-Apr.	Native. Handsome. Glossy foliage. Brilliant autumn coloring. Favorite of birds.
HEATHER, MEDITERRANEAN, S E *Erica mediterranea*	Lavender	2'	2'	Nov.-Mar.	March	Likes peat or leaf mold. Shady place.
HIBISCUS, S D *Hibiscus rosa-sinensis* *Hibiscus grandiflorus*	White thru Red Yellow, Orange White, Pink	2-6'	3-4'	Mar.-May.	May-Dec.	Sandy slightly acid loam with manure. Drainage. Sun with afternoon shade. Water freely. Feed in summer months with 8-8-8. Good in tubs. Fine on coast. Tender.
HOLLY, T E *Ilex opaca* *Ilex decidua*, T D	White Greenish	15-40' 15'	15' 6-10'	Dec.-Feb. Dec.-Mar.	Feb.	Acid, sandy, draining soil. Sun, part shade. Male and female plant needed for berry production. *I. cassine, I. crenata* and Hume varieties good in this area. Dormant oil spray for scale.
HOLLY, CHINESE, T E *Ilex cornuta burfordi*	Red Berries	10-15'	4'	Dec.-Mar.		Sun or shade. Acid soil. Large berries. May be adapted to many landscape purposes. May be sheared. Rank growing. Subject to white fly. Dwarf forms.
HONEYSUCKLE, BUSH, S D *Lonicera fragrantissima*	Cream	8-10'	4-6'	Nov.-April	Dec.-Feb.	Very fragrant. Excellent as specimen, hedge or screen. Any good soil. Sun.
HONEYSUCKLE, MORROW, S D *Lonicera morrowi*	White turning Yellow	6-8'	4'	Nov.-April	March	Handsome red berries in summer. Fertile soil. Sun.
HONEYSUCKLE, TATARIAN, S D *Lonicera tatarica*	White thru rosy pink	4-6'	4'	Nov.-April	March	Very showy. Commonest of bush honeysuckles. Rank grower.
HORSECHESTNUT, DWARF, S D (BUCKEYE) *Aesculus pavia*	Red, White	4-6'	4'	Nov.-Mar.	April	Handsome foliage. Long spikes of showy flowers. Garden soil.
HUCKLEBERRY, S or T E *Vaccinium arboreum*	White	6-12'	4-6'	Dec.-Mar.	April	Handsome. Native. Clusters of flowers like Lilies-of-the-valley. Acid soil. Part shade.
HUISACHE, T D *Acacia farnesiana*	Yellow	8-15'	15'	Dec.-Mar.	March	Any soil. Hardy. Fragrant. Especially appropriate in Spanish garden. Loves sun.
HYDRANGEA, S D *Hydrangea macrophylla* *Hortensia*	Blue, Pink, White	2-4'	3'	Oct.-April	May-June	Several types. Good for foundation and border planting. Soil half humus and half loam. Acidity changes pink flowers to blue. Aluminum sulfate to blue. Water freely. Best in partial shade, preferably north exposure. Prune after bloom.
INDIA-HAWTHORN, S E *Raphiolepis indica*	Pink, White	2-3'	3'	Nov.-Mar.	Feb.-May	Sun. Fertile soil. Blue berries in summer. Many varieties including dwarf forms. Good drainage. Mass well.
JACARANDA, S or T D *Jacaranda mimosifolia*	Blue	20-30'	15'	Mar.-May	May-June	Mimosa-type foliage. A sheltered south location may reward with fragrant blue blossoms. Tender. Sun. Sandy loam.
JACOBINIA, SCARLET, S E *Jacobinia coccinea*	Scarlet	2-3'	2'	Feb.-April	June-Sept.	Evergreen. Desirable in an old-fashioned garden. Semi-shade. Tender.
JASMINE, S E *Jasminum floridum*	Yellow	3-5'	3-4'	Nov.-April	Mar.-Nov.	Flowers freely. Trailing foliage. Rank grower. Regular garden soil. Sun or part shade. No scent.
JASMINE, CAPE, S E *Gardenia jasminoides fortuniana Veitch* JASMINE, DWARF CAPE, S E *Gardenia radicans and G. strict-nana*	White White	4-6' 2'	4' 2'	Nov.-April Nov.-April	May-June May-July	Sun or filtered sun. Well-drained moist acid rich soil of manure, pine bark and loam. Also other fine varieties. *G. thunbergia* coarser but resistant to nematodes. Dark glossy foliage. Fragrant. Good in tubs.
JASMINE, DAYBLOOMING, S D *Cestrum diurnum*	Cream	3-5'	3'	Mar.-May	July-Oct.	Easy to grow. Tender. Excellent as specimen. Beautiful berries in fall, shades lavender to purple.
JASMINE, GRAND DUKE, S E *Jasminum sambac*	White	4'	2'	Mar.-May	June-Sept.	Very double-flowered. Intensely fragrant. Foliage dark green and shining. Also 'Maid of Orleans'

COMMON NAME *Botanical Name*	Color	Approx. Height	Space Apart	To Plant	TIME Of Blooming	COMMENTS
JASMINE, ITALIAN, S E *Jasminum humile*	Yellow	6-8'	4'	Nov.-April	May-Aug.	Dark green foliage. Free bloomer. Fragrant. One of the finest of bush jasmines.
JASMINE, NIGHTBLOOMING, S D *Cestrum nocturnum*	Greenish White	3-4'	3'	Mar.-May	July-Oct.	Flowers inconspicuous but delightfully fragrant at night. White berries in the fall. Sun. Well-drained loam.
JASMINE, PRIMROSE, S E *Jasminum primulinum*	Yellow	4-8'	4'	Nov.-April	Jan.-Feb.	Drooping, attractive foliage. Beautiful, golden yellow flowers. Sun. Moist soil. Prune after bloom.
JUJUBE (CHINESE DATE), T D *Zizyphus jujuba*	Greenish-Yellow	20'	10'	Nov.-Mar.	April	Valuable for fruit and foliage. Grows in poor, sandy soil. Alkali and heat tolerant.
KERRIA, S D *Kerria japonica*	Yellow	3'	3'	Nov.-April	Mar.-Sept.	Small, golden globes in great profusion. Border or individual specimens. Likes shade. Drained humusy soil.
KUMQUAT, S E *Fortunella japonica*	White Orange fruit	3-6'	6'	Dec.-Jan.	May	Good, sandy loam soil. Prune for compact growth and increased fruit. Sun. Drainage. High nitrogen fertilizer.
LANTANA, S D *Lantana*	Various	2-8'	2'	Mar.-May	April-Nov.	Easily grown. Likes sunny exposure. Rank grower, profuse bloomer, flowers in small clusters. Any soil. Dwarf forms.
LAUREL, TEXAS MOUNTAIN, S or T E *Sophora secundiflora*	Blue, Lavender	4-8'	6'	Dec.-Mar.	March	Fragrant and ornamental. One of the loveliest blues in the garden. Bright red seeds. Likes alkaline soil, sun, drainage.
LAVENDER COTTON, S E *Santolina incana*	Yellow	1½-2'		Dec.-Mar.	June	Sun or partial shade. Aromatic silver-grey foliage. Cut back after blooming.
LEONOTIS, S E (LION'S TAIL) *Leonotis leonurus*	Orange-Red	4-6'	4'	Feb.	Sept.	Well drained soil. Grown from seeds and cuttings. Useful in shrubbery border when combined with Pyracantha. Sun.
LIGUSTRUM, AMUR RIVER PRIVET, S E *Ligustrum amurense*	White	4-10'	4'	Oct.-April	April	Hardy hedge plant, useful for tall screen, subject to white fly.
LIGUSTRUM, JAPANESE, S E *Ligustrum japonicum*	White	8-15'	4-6'	Oct.-May	May	Good as screen, hedge or individual specimen. Black berries in fall.
LIGUSTRUM, WAXLEAF, S E *Ligustrum lucidum*	White	6-12'	4-6'	Oct.-May	May	One of the handsomest of broad-leaved evergreens. Dark green glossy leaves. Dense clusters flowers. Excellent as hedge or screen. Any garden soil.
LOCUST, BLACK, T D *Robinia pseudo-acacia*	White	10-30'	20'	Nov.-Mar.	April	Flowers very fragrant, resembling white wisteria. Robust. Good street tree.
LOQUAT, T E *Eriobotrya japonica*	Cream Yellow fruit	8-15'	6-10'	Nov.-Mar.	Nov.	Edible fruit. Beautiful large olive green foliage. Fragrant winter bloom. Fast grower. Garden soil, sun, drainage.
MAGNOLIA, (SOUTHERN), T E *Magnolia grandiflora*	White	10-40'	10'	Dec.-Mar.	April-June	Likes humus. Native. Magnificent, large, fragrant flowers. Glossy ornamental foliage. Good drainage.
MAGNOLIA FUSCATA (BANANA SHRUB), S E *Michelia fuscata*	Cream	4-6'	4'	Nov.-Mar.	April-May	Sandy soil with humus. Fragrant. Profuse bloomer. Miniature blossoms. Part shade. Drainage.
MAGNOLIA, PINK S or T D *Magnolia soulangeana*	Pink	6-12'	6-10'	Dec.-Feb.	Jan.-Feb.	Very beautiful. Blooms before leaves appear. Hardy. Rich soil with humus. Other varieties white, purple and red also lovely. Drainage.
MAGNOLIA (STAR), D *Magnolia stellata*	White	6-10'	6'	Nov.-Dec.	Mar.-Apr.	White small, star-shaped blossoms. Light green foliage. Flowers appear before leaves. Rich, draining soil. Part sun. Tender.
MAHONIA (OREGON GRAPE), S E *Mahonia aquifolium*	Yellow	3'	3'	Nov.-Mar.	Feb.-Mar.	Holly-leaved Barberry. Lovely winter foliage. Ornamental berries. Shade or part sun. Soil with bonemeal, manure.
MESQUITE, T D *Prosopis iuliflora glandulosa*	Pale green	20'	20'	Dec.	Apr.-May	Will stand severe heat and drouth.

FLOWERING SHRUBS AND TREES

COMMON NAME / *Botanical Name*	Color	Approx. Height	Space Apart	TIME To Plant	TIME Of Blooming	COMMENTS
MEXICAN BUCKEYE, T D / *Ungnadia speciosa*	Pink	12'	6'	Nov.-Feb.	March	Prefers sandy soil. Water sparingly. Fragrant, spectacular flowers.
MIMOSA, T D / *Albizzia julibrissin*	Pink	12-15'	10'	Nov.-Mar.	May-June	Feathery foliage. Clusters of fragrant ball-shaped blossoms. Graceful, horizontal growth habit. 'Rosea' var. also.
MOCKORANGE, S D / *Philadelphus in species*	White	3-6'	4'	Nov.-April	April-May	Very decorative. Long sprays of white blossoms. Some varieties fragrant. Part shade. Garden soil.
MORNING-GLORY TREE, S D / *Ipomoea fistulosa*	Lavender	4-6'	4'	Mar.-April	June-Sept.	Coarse foliage but very effective with its clusters of large trumpet-shaped flowers. Easily grown from seed.
MYRTLE, TRUE, S E / *Myrtus communis*	White	6'	4'	Nov.-Mar.	May-June	Aromatic. Small dark green, glossy leaves. Blue berries all winter. Sun or part shade. Any well-drained soil.
NANDINA, S E (CHINESE "HEAVENLY" BAMBOO) / *Nandina domestica*		4-5'	4'	Nov.-Mar.		Valued for beautiful red berries and foliage during winter months. Effective in groups. Rich soil. Sun. Ample water. 'Alba' has white berries. Dwarf forms.
OLEANDER, S E / *Nerium*	White thru Red Yellow thru Orange	8-12'	5-6'	Nov.-April	Apr.-Sept.	Sun. Dwarf forms. All parts are poisonous if eaten. Don't use limbs for fuel or skewers.
ORANGE, HARDY, T D / *Citrus trifoliata*	White	6-10'	4'	Nov.-Mar.	April	Most defensive of all ornamental hedges. Beautiful as specimen. Do not plant near walk account of thorns.
ORANGE (LOUISIANA SWEET), T E / *Citrus*	White	10-12'	8-10'	Nov.-Mar.	April	One of the best varieties here. Should be protected in freezing weather.
ORANGE, SATSUMA T E / *Citrus nobilis unshiu*	White	8-10'	6'	Nov.-Mar.	April	Most reliable and productive of citrus fruits in this region. Sweet and delicious. Very ornamental.
ORCHID TREE, D / *Bauhinia forficata*	White	25'	15'	Any month	Mar.-April	Tender. Semi-shade or sun. Ornamental specimen tree. Lovely orchid-shaped flowers. Loam. Water freely.
PARKINSONIA (RATAMA), T D / *Parkinsonia aculeata*	Yellow	12-15'	12'	Nov.-Mar.	April-Aug.	Drooping feathery foliage. With care small trees may be transplanted throughout the year.
PEACH, T D / *Amygdalus persica*	Pink, Red, White	6-10'	8-10'	Nov.-Mar.	March	Well drained soil. Showy double flowers. Fine for cutting.
PEACH, WILD (CHERRY LAUREL), T E / *Laurocerasus caroliniana*	White	10-20'	6-10'	Nov.-April	March	One of our most beautiful native trees. Part shade. Rich soil. Excellent for screens and hedges, also as specimen.
PEAR, T D / *Pyrus*	White	10-15'	12'	Nov.-Mar.	Jan.-Feb.	Douglas, Pineapple, Garber, Kieffer recommended for fruit, flowers and early foliage. Kawakami evergreen, good espaliered dwarf variety good in tubs.
PEARLBUSH, S D / *Exochorda racemosa*	White	4-6'	4'	Nov.-April	Mar.-April	One of the showiest of the early spring flowering shrubs. Sun. Fertile soil. Prune after bloom.
PENTAS, S E	Various	3'	18"	Aug.-Sept.	Year round	Sun or partial shade. Rich, deep soil. Excellent cut flowers.
PEPPERTREE, CALIFORNIA, T E / *Schinus molle*	Cream	10-15'	10'	Feb.-April		Tender. Lacy, pungent foliage. Plant in protected spot.
PERSIMMON, T D / *Diospyrus Kaki*	Yellowish	30'	15'	Nov.-Mar.	June	Sun. Any soil. Hardy. Showy large orange fruit. *D. virginia*, smaller. Fine food for birds.
PHOTINIA, S E / *Photinia*	White	6-10'	4-6'	Nov.-Mar.	April	Valued for its beautiful foliage, colors changing throughout the year. Several species. Sun. Draining loam.

COMMON NAME / *Botanical Name*	Color	Approx. Height	Space Apart	TIME To Plant	TIME Of Blooming	COMMENTS
PITTOSPORUM, S E / *Pittosporum Tobira*	Cream	4–8'	4–6'	Oct.–April	Mar.–April	Sun, part shade. Rich, draining soil. Water. Feed. Dwarf and variegated forms. Excellent, spreading, fragrant.
PLUM, FRUITING, T D / *Prunus*	White	8–12'	10'	Nov.–Mar.	March	Best on plum roots. Excelsior, Bruce and Methley are good varieties.
PLUM, PURPLELEAF, T D / *Prunus cerasifera (pissardi)*	Pink	8–12'	6'	Nov.–April	March	Planted for ornamental reddish-purple foliage. Striking in groups.
PLUM, THUNDERBIRD, T D / *Prunus cerasifera*	Pink	25'		Nov.–Mar.	March	Hardy. Leaves rich red, gradually turning darker red.
PLUM, WILD, T D / *Prunus mexicana*	White	10–15'	10'	Nov.–Mar.	March	Most ornamental—like a Japanese etching in the garden with its black stems and exquisitely fragrant blossoms.
PLUMBAGO, S / *Plumbago Alba* / *Plumbago capensis*	White / Blue	2–3'	2'	Feb.–Apr.	Mar.–Dec.	Semi-shade. Sun or semi-shade. Long sprays. May be supported on trellis. Prolific bloomer. All summer. Poor soil. Good drainage.
PLUMBAGO, CREEPING / *Ceratostigma plumbagonoides*	Blue	1'	12"	Nov.–April	Mar.–Dec.	Evergreen ground-cover. Deep blue flowers. Loose, rich draining soil. Part shade. Winter prune.
PLUMBAGO, S D / *Plumbago rosea*	Rose	1½–2'	2'	Feb.–April	May–June	Blooms freely. Desirable for cutting. Not common here, but easily grown. Lovely shade of rose.
POINCIANA, (BIRD OF PARADISE), S D / *Caesalpinia gilliesi*	Yellow	6–8'	4–6'	Nov.–April	May–Sept.	Clusters of yellow flowers with long crimson stamens. Likes dry sandy soil. Graceful, spreading. Hot sun. Good drainage.
POINSETTIA, S D / *Euphorbia pulcherrima*	Red, Pink, White	4–8'	3'	Feb.–Aug.	Nov.–Dec.	Sun. Slightly acid soil. Summer feed. Pinch back till October. Tender. Double and dwarf forms. Prune hard in March. Root cuttings.
POMEGRANATE, DWARF, S D / *Punica granatum nana*	Orange-Scarlet	2–4'	3'	Nov.–April	April–Oct.	Very ornamental. Suitable for borders. Effective in pots, inside or outdoors. Sun. Well drained loam.
POMEGRANATE, FRUITING, S D / *Punica granatum*	Orange-Scarlet	8–12'	6'	Nov.–April	April–Sept.	Attractive flowers. Large showy fruit, edible. Fast growing. Deep heavy loam. Sun. Drainage. Many varieties.
PYRACANTHA (FIRETHORN), S E / *Pyracantha coccinea*	White / Yellow to red berries	10–20'	4–6'	Nov.–Mar.	April	Needs sun to flower. Well drained soil. Showy berries. Thorny. Prune after berrying to control rapid growth. Dwarf forms also.
QUINCE, JAPANESE FLOWERING, S D / *Chaenomeles lagenaria*	Crimson, Pink, White	4–6'	4'	Nov.–April	Dec.–Mar.	Likes sun. Beautiful winter-blooming shrub. Fine for cutting. Good in groups. Excellent as specimen.
RAINTREE, GOLDEN, T D / *Koelreuteria paniculata*	Yellow	20–30'		Feb.–Mar.	Sept.–Oct.	Hardy. Exotic seed pods excellent for dried arrangements. Sun. Well drained soil.
REDBUD, T D / *Cercis canadensis* / *Cercis canadensis alba*	Purple, Pink / White	12–15'	6–10'	Nov.–April	March	One of the most beautiful flowering native trees. Hardy. Also double-flowered form. Complements Formosa azaleas. Open sandy soil. Sun or part shade.
REDBUD, (DWARF), S D / *Cercis chinensis*	Rosy-Purple	4–8'	4'	Nov.–April	March	Extremely ornamental. Prolific bloomer. Flowers large and more abundant than those of native variety.
ROCKROSE, S E / *Cistus*	White, Rose	2–6'	3'	Feb.	Aug.–Sept.	Sun. Dry light soil. Will tolerate lime. Grown from seeds, cuttings and layers.
ROSE-ACACIA, S D / *Robinia hispida*	Rose	6–8'	6'	Nov.–Mar.	May to June	When planting seeds soak overnight. Hardy. Any soil. Clusters of wisteria-like flowers. A handsome locust.
RICE-PAPER PLANT, S E / *Tetrapanax papyriferus*	Greenish-white	8–18'	5'	Nov.	Dec.–Jan.	Sun or partial shade. Hardy. Flowers excellent for cutting. Dark green foliage resembles Castor bean.
SAGE, DESERT (SENISA), S E / *Leucophyllum texanum*	Orchid	4–6'	4'	Nov.–Mar.	June–Sept.	Likes well drained soil. Tolerates prolonged drought. Blossoms profusely after rain. Can be induced to bloom by sprinkling. Beautiful grey-green foliage. 'Compacta' is smaller.

FLOWERING SHRUBS AND TREES

COMMON NAME *Botanical Name*	Color	Approx. Height	Space Apart	TIME To Plant	TIME Of Blooming	COMMENTS
SALT CEDAR, S D *Tamarix gallica*	Pink, White	8–15'	4–8'	Nov.–April	April–June	Does well near seashore. Grey-green feathery foliage. Cuttings root easily in moist sand.
SILK OAK *Grevillea robusta*	Orange	50'	25'	July–Aug.		Sun. Well drained fairly poor soil. Tolerates heat and drought. Lacy foliage. Does well in pots.
SILVER-BELL TREE, T D *Halesia carolina*	White	15–20'	4'	Nov.	March–April	Sun or semi-shade. Acid or neutral soil. Good drainage. Flowers hang in small clusters. Native.
SPIREA, ANTHONY WATERER, S D *Spiraea Bumalda, Anthony Waterer*	Crimson	2'	2'	Nov.–April	April–Sept.	Good for shrub border, mass planting and cutting. Profuse bloomer. Does best in partial shade, any soil.
SPIREA (BRIDALWREATH), S D *Spiraea prunifolia plena*	White	4–5'	3–4'	Nov.–April	Feb.–Mar.	An old garden favorite. Double flowers.
SPIREA, REEVES, S D (BRIDALWREATH) *Spiraea reevesiana*	White	3–5'	4'	Nov.–April	Mar.–April	Most satisfactory and free blooming of the Bridalwreaths. Both double and single. Excellent for cutting. Better than S. *vanhouttei*.
SPIREA, THUNBERG, S D *Spiraea thunbergi*	White	2–3'	3'	Nov.–April	Jan.–Feb.	Its graceful drooping sprays with delicate blossoms are an exquisite addition to the early shrub border.
ST. JOHN'S-WORT, S D *Hypericum*	Yellow	2–3'	2–3'	Nov.–April	May–Aug.	Neat shrub for border or foundation planting. Likes partial shade. Several varieties.
SUMAC, S D *Rhus copallina*	Greenish	6–10'	4'	Nov.–Mar.		Brilliant autumn foliage and berries. Non-poisonous variety. Will grow in sandy or rocky soil.
SWEET OLIVE, S E *Osmanthus fragrans*	White	6–20'	5'	Nov.–Mar.	Jan.–April	Sun or shade. Any soil. Good drainage. Fragrant.
SWEETSHRUB, S D *Calycanthus floridus*	Reddish Brown	3–6'	3'	Nov.–Mar.	April	Very fragrant. Rich well-drained soil. Ample moisture.
TEA PLANT, S E (CAMELLIA THEA) *Thea sinensis*	Cream	4–5'	3'	Nov. to Feb.	Oct.–Nov.	Hardy. Same culture as Camellias. Fragrant flower.
THRYALLIS, S E *Thryallis glauca*	Yellow	3–5'	3'	Nov.–Mar.	Almost continuous	Good for mass or foundation planting. Stands pruning well. Yellow Plumbago. Bluish green foliage.
TULIP TREE (TULIP POPLAR), T D *Liriodendron tulipifera*	Greenish Yellow	30–40'	25'	Mar.	April	Rapid growing. Magnificent lawn tree. Plant only small trees, balled and burlapped. Rich, moist soil.
TUNG OIL TREE, T E *Aleurites fordi*	White, Pink	25'	20'	Nov.–Feb.	March	Makes a good specimen tree. Hardy. Fast growing. Loam with pH 5 to 6. Good drainage. Fertilize.
TURK'S CAP, S E *Malaviscus grandiflorus*	Red, Pink	4–10'	3'	Sept. to March	Sept.–Dec.	Grown from cuttings. Any soil. Flowers suggest Turkish fezzes. Rapid grower. Tender. If frozen will come back from roots.
VIBURNUM, S E and D *Viburnum*	White	6–8'	4–6'	Nov.–Mar.	Feb.–Mar.	Most beautiful. Dark green leaves. Flowers in clusters—fragrant. Sun or part shade. Garden soil. Attracts birds. See Shrubs.
WEAVERS-BROOM, S D *Spartium junceum*	Yellow	6'	3–4'	Nov.–Mar.	April	A glorious sight in bloom. Light, fast draining soil. Sun.
WEIGELA, S D *Weigela*	Pink, Red, White	4'	3'	Nov.–Mar.	Mar.–April	Lovely spring flowering shrub. Likes east exposure. Clusters of exquisite blossoms. Some varieties bloom all summer.
WILD OLIVE (ANACAHUITA) *Cordia boissieri*	White	25'	30'	Nov.	April	Showy trumpet shaped flowers from April to October. Growing in popularity and importance. Sun. Drainage.
WILLOW FLOWERING, (DESERT), T D *Chilopsis linearis*	Lavender White	8–20'	8–15'	Nov.–Mar.	June–Aug.	One of the few hot weather flowering trees. Graceful drooping foliage. Orchid-like blossoms.
WILLOW, PUSSY, S D *Salix discolor*	Grey-Green	6–8'	4–6'	Nov.–Mar.	February	Grows from cuttings. Beautiful. Fine for cutting. Catkins easily forced in water indoors. Any soil. Water. Needs cold winters.
YAUPON, S or T E *Ilex vomitoria*	White	6–12'	4–6'	Dec.–Jan.	March	Brilliant red berries during winter months. Native. Useful as hedge or screen. Sun. Rich drained soil. Attracts birds.

FLOWERING PLANTS GROWN FROM SEEDS

Since this region allows year-round planting it is enjoyable to keep lively color in our gardens. The basic necessities are: the soil must be loose and fine enough for the seedlings to break through and fertile enough to nourish them; watering should be by fine sprinkling so as not to uproot the young plants; the soil must be kept moist enough to avoid soil crusting; most seeds need sunlight to germinate; good drainage. With these needs met the miracle of the seed is accomplished.

A—Annuals
B—Biennials
P—Perennials

COMMON NAME *Botanical Name*	Color	Height	Space Apart	To Plant	TIME To Germinate	Of Blooming	COMMENTS
AGERATUM, A or P *Ageratum houstonianum*	Blue, White Pink	6-18"	8-12"	Mar.-Aug.	5-8 days	Apr.-Nov.	Grown also from divisions and cuttings. Tender. Good for bedding and cut flowers. Dwarf variety for edging.
ALYSSUM, SWEET, A *Lobularia maritimum*	White, Lavender, Rose	2-6"	6"	Oct.-Mar.	4-5 days	All year	Sun, light shade. Any soil, not too wet. Many varieties.
AMARANTHUS, A *Amaranthus tricolor*	Crimson Foliage	2-3'	20"	Mar.-Apr.	15-20 days	June-Oct.	Sun. Half-hardy. Good border plant. Gives tropical effect. Dwarf forms 12" high.
ANCHUSA, A or P *Anchusa azurea (A.italica)* *Anchusa capensis* (CAPE FORGET-ME-NOT)	Blue Blue	2-4' 18"	2'	Sept.-Nov.	20 days	Mar.-May	Grown also from cuttings. Full sun. Water sparingly. Good for cutting. Dropmore good tall variety.
ARCTOTIS, A *Arctotis grandis*	White and Lavender	24"	12"	Sept.-Mar.	10-12 days	Nov.-May	Best in sun. Flowers close late afternoon. Excellent for cutting.
BABYSBREATH, P *Gypsophila paniculata*	White	18"-2'	1'	Nov.-Mar.	20 days	Apr.-May	Grown also from roots. Sandy, well drained soil. Sun or partial shade. Good in perennial border. Excellent for cutting and drying.
BABYSBREATH, A *Gypsophila elegans*	White Rose	24"	6"	Sept.-Feb.	10-15 days	Jan.-May	Best in full sun. Excellent for cutting. Muralis variety, pink, good for border. Beautiful.
BALLOON-FLOWER, P *Platycodon*	Blue, White	24"	12"	Feb.-Mar.	14 days	May-July	Sun or partial shade. Good in perennial border. Fine for cutting.
BALSAM, GARDEN, A *Impatiens balsamina*	Various	12-18"	6-8"	Mar.-Sept.	3-8 days	May-Nov.	Good in border. Sun or partial shade. Camellia-flowered best variety.
BALSAM. SULTAN, A *Impatiens sultani*	Rose, Salmon White	18"	12"	Mar.-May	3-8 days	May-Oct.	Profuse bloomer. Best in border in partial shade. Rich moist soil. Dwarf and midget forms.
BEGONIA, WAX, A or P *B. semperflorens*	Various	8-18"	1'	Apr.-Sept.	15 days	May-frost	Need cool shade to germinate, then light sun or shade in moist humusy soil. Many varieties.
BELLS-OF-IRELAND *Molucella laevis*	Green bracts	24"	12"	Early spring		Spring Summer	Best grown from plants. Prized for arrangements. Well drained soil. Full sun.
BLANKETFLOWER, A *Gaillardia*	Yellow thru Red	12-18"	12"	Oct.-Apr.	10-14 days	May-Oct.	Best in full sun. Excellent for cutting. Good for rural planting. Native.
BLUEBONNET, A *Lupinus subcarnosus (texensis)*	Blue	12"	8-12"	July-Jan.	5-10 days	Apr.-May	Light, well drained soil. Full sun. Good for cutting. Naturalizes. Mass rural planting suggested.
BOLTONIA, P *Boltonia asteroides*	White, pink	2-3'	30"	Mar.-Sept.		Aug.-Sept.	Grown also from divisions. Good border plant. Dwarf forms better. Aster-like flowers. Profuse bloomer.
BOUNCING-BET, P *Saponaria officinalis*	Pink, White	2'	1'	Sept.-Mar.	20 days	May-Oct.	Grown also from root divisions. *S. ocymoides* excellent for rock garden.
BROWALLIA, A (AMETHYST) *Browalia Americana*	Blue, White	18"	6"	Mar.-Apr.	20 days	May-Aug.	Good for bedding and borders. Excellent for cutting and pot plants. Sun. Reseeds. Pinch plants back for more compact growth. Native.
BUTTERFLYFLOWER, A *Schizanthus*	All colors	12-18"	6"	Sept.-Mar.	20 days	Apr.-May	Likes sandy soil. Partial shade. Exquisite. Fine for cutting.
BUTTERFLYWEED, P *Asclepias tuberosa*	Yellow and Orange	1-4'	1-2'	Sept.-Nov.	10 days	May-Sept.	Coarse growth. Native milkweed. Good for rural planting. Dry, sandy soil.

FLOWERING PLANTS GROWN FROM SEEDS

COMMON NAME / Botanical Name	Color	Height	Space Apart	To Plant	TIME To Germinate	Of Blooming	COMMENTS
CALENDULA, A / Calendula officinalis	Lemon thru orange	8-15"	12"	Sept.-Feb.	4-10 days	Nov.-May	Heavy loam. Full sun. Good for border, bedding and cutting.
CALLIOPSIS, A / Coreopsis tinctoria	Yellow, Orange, Maroon	2-4'	6-15"	Feb.-Mar.	5-15 days	May-July	Sun or partial shade. Feathery foliage. Good for rural planting.
CANDYTUFT, A or P / Iberis	White thru Red. Lavender	10-18"	6"	Sept.-Mar.	5-8 days	Nov.-May	Full sun. Useful for border and cutting. I. sempervirens good for ground cover. Many varieties. Free bloomer.
CANTERBURY BELLS, A or B / Campanula medium	Bluish Purple White	18"	12"	Mar.-May	15 days	Apr.-May following yr.	Well drained soil. Sun or partial shade. Excellent for cutting. Ashes and copper sulphate prevent root and crown rot.
CASTOR-BEAN, A / Ricinus communis	Bronze Foliage	5-10'	60"	Apr.	15 days		Grown also from cuttings. Sun, moisture. Seeds poisonous. Warn children.
CERASTIUM (SNOW-IN-SUMMER), P / Cerastium tomentosum	White	3-8"	12-18"	Sept.-Nov.	15 days	Mar.-May	Sun. Grown from divisions and cuttings. Dry location. Good rock garden plant. Useful for edging or carpeting. Silvery foliage. Drainage.
CHINA ASTER, A / Callistephus chinensis	Various	6-18"	8"	Feb.-Mar.	12 days	May-June	Sun or partial shade. Fine for cutting. Good for bedding. Rich soil. Little water.
CHINESE FORGET-ME-NOT, A / Cynoglossum amabile	Blue, White, Pink	18"	8"	Sept.-Nov.	10 days	Apr.-Aug.	Sun or shade. Border plant. Beautiful. Firmament, dark blue dwarf variety. Water regularly.
CHINESE LANTERN PLANT. P / Physalis francheti	Whitish	12-18"	12"	Sept.-Mar.	10 days	June-Sept.	Light, well drained soil. Partial shade. Grown for ornamental orange seed pods, which may be dried.
CHRYSANTHEMUM, P / Chrysanthemum	White, Pink, Lavender, Maroon, Yellow, Bronze	2-4'	12"	Feb.-Mar.	15 days	Oct.-Dec.	Full sun. Best grown from cuttings and divisions. Numerous varieties and forms. Rich soil. Fertilize.
CLARKIA, A / Clarkia	White thru Red	12"	6"	Mar.-Apr.	7 days	May-June	Full sun. Good for mass planting. Native.
COCKSCOMB, A / Celosia argentea cristata / Celosia argentea plumosa	Red, Yellow	1-3'	8-12"	Mar.-Sept.	5-8 days	June-Dec.	Full sun. Best combined with evergreens. Do not plant with dainty flowers. May be dried. Dwarf forms.
COLEUS, A / Coleus	Variegated Foliage	12-24"	12"	Feb.-May	20-25 days	Continuous	Easily propagated by cuttings and divisions. Tender. Sun or partial shade. Rich soil.
COLUMBINE, P / Aquilegia	Various	18"	8-12"	Sept.-Mar.	15 days	Apr.-May of second year	Well drained, moist soil. Partial shade. Buy two-year-old plants for first season bloom.
COREOPSIS, P / Coreopsis grandiflora	Yellow	2'	12-18"	Sept.-Feb.	10-12 days	May-July	Sun or partial shade. Also grown from divisions.
CORNFLOWER, A (BACHELOR'S BUTTON) / Centaurea cyanus	Pink, Blue, Purple, White	3'	8-12"	Sept.-Feb.	10 days	Feb.-May	Full sun. Best combined with perennials. Excellent for cutting. Dwarf forms.
COSMOS, EARLY, A / Cosmos bipinnatus	Crimson, Pink, Lavender, White	4-5'	12"	Feb.-Mar.	5-8 days	Apr.-July	Light soil. Full sun. Good in background planting. Combines well with shrubbery.
COSMOS, KLONDYKE, A / Cosmos sulphureus	Orange, Red, Yellow	4-6'	2'	Apr.-June	5-8 days	July-Nov.	Good for cutting and as screen. Should be staked. Dwarf and double-flowered varieties.
DAHLBORG, DAISY, A / Thymophylla	Golden yellow	8"	6"	Oct. or Feb.	15 days	Mar.-Nov.	Sun. Well drained, light sandy loam. Aromatic foliage.

COMMON NAME / *Botanical Name*	Color	Height	Space Apart	To Plant	TIME To Germinate	Of Blooming	COMMENTS
DAHLIA, A or P / *Dahlia*	All colors except Blue	4-6'	18"	Jan.-Feb.	10 days	June-Nov.	Sandy soil. Also grown from cuttings and divisions. Sun. Water freely. Should be staked. Disbud for specimens. Dwarf varieties recommended.
DAISY, AFRICAN GOLDEN, P / *Dimorphotheca*	Cream to Orange	12-18"	12"	Sept.-Mar.	10-12 days	Nov.-June	Best in sun. Beautiful for display and cutting.
DAISY, ENGLISH, A / *Bellis perennis*	White, Pink, Red	4-6"	6-8"	Sept.-Dec.	4-5 days	Jan.-Apr.	Sun or partial shade. Used for border and bedding.
DAISY, GLORIOSA, P / *Rudbeckia hybrida*	Yellow, Gold, Mahogany	2-3'	14"	Apr.-Aug.	20 days	May-Aug.	Sun, light shade. Cut to encourage bloom.
DAISY, MICHAELMAS, P / *Aster novi-belsi*	Lavender, White	3-5'	12-18"	Jan.-Mar.	15 days	Sept.-Dec.	Best from divisions. Fine for cutting. Many new hybrids.
DAISY, PAINTED, A / *Chrysanthemum coccineum*	Various	12"	12"	Sept.-Mar.	8 days	Apr.-June	Sun or partial shade. Excellent for cutting. Plant in the bed or border.
DAISY, SHASTA, P / *Chrysanthemum maximum*	White	1-2'	12-18"	Aug.-Sept.	10-15 days	May-Aug.	Well drained soil. Sun or partial shade. Also grown from divisions. Good for cutting and display.
DAISY, SWAN-RIVER, A / *Brachycome iberidifolia*	Blue, White, Pink	12"	6"	Sept.-Mar.	8 days	Apr.-June	Blue variety very beautiful. Full sun. Rich soil.
DATURA, A / *Datura Metel*	Lavender, White, Yellow	3-4'	24"	Feb.-Apr.	15 days	June-Sept.	Full sun. Grown also from cuttings. Decorative. Long trumpet-shaped flowers. Double varieties. (See Angel's Trumpet.)
DELPHINIUM, A or P / *Delphinium*	Light to deep Blue Pink, White	1-2'	12"	Sept.-Nov.	10-15 days	Mar.-May	Best in sandy loam or leaf mold. Shade or sun. Excellent for cutting. Beautiful blue. Giant hybrids available in many colors.
FALSE-DRAGONHEAD, P (PHYSOSTEGIA) / *Dracocephalum virginianum*	Lavender, Pink, White	3-4'	12"	Sept.-Dec.	15 days	June-Aug.	Best in sandy soil. Sun or partial shade. Water freely. Also grown from divisions. Good for border planting and cutting.
FEVERFEW, A / *Chrysanthemum Parthenium*	White, Yellow	18"	12"	Feb.-Apr.	15-20 days	Apr.-Sept.	Sun or partial shade. Good for bedding, borders and cutting. Naturalizes.
FORGET-ME-NOT, A or P / *Myosotis palustris semperflorens*	Blue	6-8"	10"	Oct.-Nov.	12-15 days	Apr.-Dec.	Partial shade. Rich loose soil. Water freely. Also grown from divisions. Excellent for edging, mass planting and rock gardens. Blooms all summer.
FOUR-O'CLOCK, P / *Mirabilis jalapa*	White, Yellow Red	3'	18-24"	Jan.-Dec.	5-10 days	May-Oct.	Grown also from roots. Fast spreading. Free blooming. Fragrant. Dwarf variety good for bedding.
GAYFEATHER, P / *Liatris*	Lavender	2-3'	12"	Sept.-Mar.	20 days	July-Aug.	Dry for winter bouquets. Native wild flower.
GAZANIA, P / *Gazania*	White, Yellow, Orange	1'	12"	Oct.-Nov.	8 days	May-July	Sun. Propagated by divisions and cuttings. Daisy-like flowers close at night.
GERANIUM, P / *Pelargonium, in variety*	White thru Red and Purple	1-2'	12"	Feb.-Mar.	15 days	Apr.-Oct. year following.	Sun or partial shade. Water sparingly. Best from cuttings, or plants. Capitatum is rose-scented. Also trailing and variegated types.
GERBERA, P (TRANSVAAL DAISY) / *Gerbera jamesoni hybrida*	Various	1½'	12-15"	Feb.-Mar.	30 days	All year	Divisions easier. Sun. Deep rich humusy soil, excellent drainage. Plant with crown above soil level. Feed 5-10-5 often. Protect from freeze. Exquisite.
GLOBE AMARANTH, A / *Gomphrena globosa*	White thru deep Red	24"	12"	Feb.-May	10-12 days	May-Oct.	Best in sun. May be treated as Strawflower. Good for bedding and border.
GODETIA, A / *Godetia*	Red, Pink, White	12"	6"	Sept.-Nov.	15 days	Mar.-May	Light, sandy soil. Partial shade. Excellent for cutting. Blooms best in crowded plantings.

FLOWERING PLANTS GROWN FROM SEEDS

COMMON NAME *Botanical Name*	Color	Height	Space Apart	To Plant	TIME To Germinate	Of Blooming	COMMENTS
GOLDENROD, P *Solidago*	Yellow	2–4'	15–18"	Sept.–Mar.	20 days	July–Sept.	Best in sun. Also grown from divisions. Good for rural plantings. Hybrids advisable.
GOLDENTUFT, P *Alyssum saxatile*	Yellow	6"	6"	Sept.–Mar.	8 days	May–June	Variety Compactum good for crevices in terraces and pavements.
HOLLYHOCK, A or B *Althaea rosea*	Yellow, White thru Red	4–6'	1–2'	Sept.–Dec.	15 days	May–July	Sun or partial shade. Well drained soil. Lovely against wall, fence or in a border.
HONESTY, A (DOLLAR PLANT) *Lunaria annua*	Purple, White	18–30"	12"	July	21 days	April	Start seed in damp peat moss in shade. Transplant to rich soil in full sun. Shelter from north wind. Grown for silvery-white partitions of seed pods.
ICE PLANT, A *Cryophytum crystallinum*	Pink, White	8"	12"	May–June	15 days	All summer	Sun. Good drainage. Little water. Succulent foliage glistens. Interesting pot plant.
IMMORTELLE, A *Xeranthemum annuum*	Various	3'	1'	March	5–15 days	May–July	Sandy soil. Sun. Flowers may be dried.
LACEFLOWER, BLUE, A *Didiscus or Trachymene caerulea*	Blue, White	18"	12"	Sept.–Nov.	10 days	Mar.–May	Full sun. Good in border. Fine for cutting.
LARKSPUR, A *Delphinium ajacis*	White, shades of Blue, Purple and Pink	2–3'	6"	Sept.–Jan.	15 days	Mar.–June	Full sun. Good for bedding, border and cutting. Rich, loose soil. Feed often.
LAVENDER, SWEET, P *Lavandula officinalis*	Lavender	1–2'	2'	Sept.–Mar.	20 days	May–July	Well drained soil. Sun or partial shade. Grown also from cuttings and divisions. Fragrant when dried.
LOBELIA, P (CARDINAL FLOWER) *Lobelia cardinalis*	Red	2–3'	12"	Feb.–Mar.–Sept.	20 days	Aug.–Sept.–Oct.	May be grown from seeds or root divisions. Grows best in moist, semi-shade.
LOBELIA, A *Lobelia Erinus*	Blue	4"	6"	Nov.–Feb.	10 days	Apr.–July	Sandy loam. Full sun. Good for bedding, edging.
LOVE-IN-A-MIST, A *Nigella damascena*	Blue, White	12"	6"	Mar.–Apr.	8 days	Apr.–May	Sun. Garden soil. Lacelike flower and foliage. Good for cutting. Pods dry well.
LYCHNIS (MALTESE CROSS), P *Lychnis chalcedonica*	Scarlet	24"	12"	Feb.	10–20 days	May–Sept.	Grown also from divisions. Sun. Hardy. Good border plant. Pink family.
LYTHRUM, P *Lythrum Salicaria, roseum superbum*	Rose	3–4'	24"	June–July	15 days	June–July	Good rich soil. Moist. Propagated by division. Worth trying.
MALLOW, ROSE, P *Hibiscus Moscheutos*	White thru Red	4–6'	24"	Sept.–Mar.	15 days	June–Oct.	Moist soil. Sun or partial shade. Requires ample space. Good for shore planting. Very beautiful
MARIGOLD, AFRICAN, A *Tagetes erecta*	Lemon, Orange	3–4'	12"	Mar.–July	8 days	June–Nov.	Full sun. Good for the border and cutting.
MARIGOLD, FRENCH, A *Tagetes patula*	Yellow and Mahogany	12–18"	12"	Mar.–Aug.	8 days	June–Nov.	Full sun. Best for bedding. Colorful. Said to discourage nematodes. Dwarf forms also.
MISTFLOWER, P *Eupatorium*	Blue, White	24"	12"	Sept.–May	10 days	Aug.–Oct.	Moist soil. Also from divisions. Sun or partial shade.
MOSS PINK, P *Phlox subulata*	Purple, Pink, White	6"	24"	Feb.–Mar.	Side shoots	June–Oct.	Sun. Fertile soil. Moisture. Feed Often. Blooming ground cover. Divide every 3 or 4 years.
NASTURTIUM, A *Tropaeolum majus* *Tropaeolum minus*	Yellow to Mahogany	2–3' 6–12"	10" 6"	Feb.–Apr.	8 days	Apr.–June	Full sun. Flowers well in poor soil. Trailing variety left on ground produces long stems and more flowers. Dwarf and double varieties available.
PANSY, A *Viola tricolor*	Various	6"	6–8"	Aug.–Nov.	10–12 days	Nov.–May.	Rich, sandy loam and humus. Sun. Set plants out Nov. Feed often. *V. tricolor* is Johnny Jump Up.
PENSTEMON, A or P *Penstemon*	Various	2'	1'	Oct.–Dec.	10 days	Apr.–May	Light, sandy soil. Sun or partial shade. Some varieties native.

COMMON NAME *Botanical Name*	Color	Height	Space Apart	To Plant	TIME To Germinate	Of Blooming	COMMENTS
PERIWINKLE, A *Vinca rosea*	Pink, Lavender, White	15"	8–12"	Mar.–June	15 days	June–Nov.	Full sun. Excellent for mass planting and borders. Showy. Good for cutting.
PETUNIA, A *Petunia hybrida*	Various	12–18"	12"	Sept.–Mar.	6–8 days	Feb.–Nov.	Rich, drained soil. Sun or part shade. Many varieties. Fragrant. Feed monthly. Fine for massing and cutting.
PHLOX, DRUMMOND, A *Phlox drummondi*	Various	12"	4–6"	Sept.–Jan.	15 days	Jan.–June	Full sun best. Hardy. One of the best bedding plants. Colorful and fragrant. Good for cutting
PHLOX, LOUISIANA, P *Phlox divaricata*	Blue to mauve	8"	6"	Sept.–Oct.	Divisions	Feb.–Mar.	Sun or semi-shade. Will tolerate acid soil. When planting, cover entire plant with soil, only leaving tip exposed, in order to make joints take root.
PHLOX, PERENNIAL, P *Phlox paniculata*	Various	18–24"	12–15"	Sept.–Feb.	10 days	May–Oct.	Well drained soil. Sun or partial shade. Best from divisions or roots. Good in groups in the border, foundation planting and for cutting.
PINKS (DIANTHUS), B *Dianthus*	Various	8–12"	12"	Sept.–Feb.	12 days	Nov.–June	Full sun best. Good for bedding and edging. Fine for cutting. Fragrant. Many species.
POPPY, CALIFORNIA, A or P *Eschscholtzia californica*	Orange, Yellow, Pink thru Red	12"	6"	Oct.–Dec.	10–12 days	Feb.–May	Well drained sandy loam. Best in full sun. Glorious display in border or beds. Very difficult to transplant.
POPPY, ICELAND, A *Papaver nudicaule*	Yellow, Red, White	8–12"	6"	Oct.–Nov.	10–20 days	Apr.–May	Well drained sandy loam. Sun or partial shade. Best in border. Fernlike foliage. Exquisitely dainty blossoms.
POPPY, ORIENTAL, P *Papaver orientale*	Orange, Red, Flame	3'	2'	Sept.–Oct.	10 days	Apr.–May–June	Rich loam. Sun. Foliage dies to ground after blooming. Needs drainage.
POPPY, SHIRLEY (CORN). A *Papaver rhoeas*	White thru Blood Red, Lavender	2–3'	6"	Oct.–Dec.	15 days	Mar.–May	Well drained sandy loam. Sun or partial shade. Best in border. Excellent for cutting. Showy in mass planting. Carnation, Peony and other varieties good.
PORTULACA, A *Portulaca*	All colors except Blue	4–6"	4–6"	Mar.–July	12–15 days	May–Oct.	Best in sandy soil. Full sun. Brilliant in borders and beds. Flowers close in afternoon.
QUEEN ANNE'S-LACE, A *Daucus Carota*	White	3–4'	12"	Sept.–Nov.	20 days	Apr.–May	Excellent for cutting. Recommended for rural gardens.
ROCKET, SWEET, A or P *Hesperis matronalis*	Lilac, Purple, White	1–2'	6"	Sept.–Mar.	10 days	Apr.–June	Light sandy soil. Sun or partial shade. Fragrant. Double form called gilly flower.
SALPIGLOSSIS, A *Salpiglossis*	Cream, Yellow, Blue, Purple, Brown	18"	6"	Sept.–Mar.	5 days	May–June	Light, sandy soil. Partial shade. Fine for cutting. Rich velvety texture.
SALVIA (BLUE SAGE), P *Salvia farinacea*	Blue	2–3'	1'	Sept.–Mar.	15 days	April–Dec.	Grown also from cuttings and divisions. Freebloomer. Good in border and for cutting.
SALVIA (SCARLET SAGE), A *Salvia splendens*	Red	2–3'	1'	Feb.–Mar.	10 days	May–Dec.	Prefers partial shade. Grown also from cuttings. Best alone or with shrubbery. Good for cutting.
SALVIA, P *Salvia greggi*	Crimson	2–3'	2'	Nov.–April	15 days	Apr.–Oct.	Likes well-drained soil. Open sunny location. Frequent watering. Dwarf variety Salmon Pygmy.
SCABIOSA, A *Scabiosa*	Various to brown-black	2–3'	1'	Sept.–Mar.	20 days	Mar.–June	Protect from afternoon sun. Good in border. Excellent for cutting.
SHRIMP PLANT, P *Beloperone guttata*	Red–Brown bracts	2–3'	24"	From divisions and cuttings		Apr.–Nov.	Part shade. Rich, humusy soil, moist but drained. Pinch to shape. Good for cutting and in pots.
SNAPDRAGON, A *Antirrhinum*	Various	1–3'	6"	Sept.–Feb.	15 days	Mar.–June	Well drained soil. Sun or partial shade. Border and mass planting. Excellent for cutting.

264

FLOWERING PLANTS GROWN FROM SEEDS

COMMON NAME / Botanical Name	Color	Height	Space Apart	To Plant	TIME To Germinate	Of Blooming	COMMENTS
SPIDERFLOWER, A / Cleome spinosa	White, Pink with Crimson stamens	3'	1'	March	10 days	June-Oct.	Plant in the border or with shrubbery. Also pure white variety.
STATICE, A or P / Limonium latifolium	Pink, Blue, White	1½-2'	20"	Apr.	Plants	June-Aug.	Sun. Well drained soil. To dry cut when fully open. Hang upside down in shady, airy place.
STOCK, A or P / Matthiola incana	Various	1-2'	1'	Sept.-Jan.	5-8 days	Feb.-May.	Well drained rich soil. Sun or partial shade. Bedding and border plant. Night-scented good variety. Fine for cutting.
STOKESIA, A or P / Stokesia laevis / Stokesia caerulea rosea	Blue / Pink	1'	1'	Sept.-Oct.	10 days	May-June	Light, sandy soil. Sun or partial shade. Grown also from divisions. Good for cutting. Drainage.
STRAWFLOWER, A / Helichrysum bracteatum	Yellow white thru deep red	2-3'	1'	Jan.-Mar.	5-8 days	June-Aug.	Well drained soil. Flowers excellent for drying. Full sun.
SUMMER CYPRESS, A (BURNING BUSH) / Kochia scaparia var. trichophila	Red, Green, Yellow foliage	1-2'	24"	Mar.-Apr.	15-18 days		Soak seeds over night before sowing. Fine, dense foliage turns bronze in fall. Ornamental pyramidal plant used for borders and hedges.
SUNFLOWER, A or P / Helianthus	Yellow	6-8'	2'	Mar.-May	10 days	May-Sept.	Full sun. Attracts birds. Background or screen planting in rural areas.
SWEET-SULTAN, A / Centaurea moschata	Lavender, Purple, Rose, White	3'	1'	Sept.-Feb.	8 days	May-July	Sun. Plant in the border. Excellent for cutting.
SWEET-SULTAN, A or P / Centaurea imperialis hybrid	Lavender, Rose, White	2-3'	8"	Sept.-Mar.	8 days	Apr.-July	Light, sandy soil. Sun. Good as border background and for cutting. Fragrant.
SWEET WILLIAM, B / Dianthus barbatus	Various	8"	6"	Sept.-Dec.	10 days	Apr.-May following year	Well drained soil. Plant in protected border. Grown also from divisions. Splendid for cutting.
TITHONIA, A (MEXICAN SUNFLOWER) / Tithonia speciosa	Orange	4-6'	3'	Feb.-Apr.	21 days	July-Oct.	Sun. Robust grower. Excellent for cutting. Flowers resemble single dahlias.
TOBACCO, FLOWERING, A or P / Nicotiana alata grandiflora / Nicotiana sanderae / Nicotiana sylvestris	White and Violet / Red / White	5' / 3' / 5'	12-18"	Sept.-Mar.	10 days	May-Oct.	Sandy loam. Sun or partial shade. Water freely. Plant in perennial border. Fertilize for continuous bloom. Very fragrant.
TORENIA, A / Torenia fournieri	Blue, White	12"	8"	Mar.-June	10 days	May-Nov.	Sun or partial shade. Excellent for bedding and edging.
VERBENA, P / Verbena erinoides hybrids	Various	8-12"	12"	Nov.-Mar.	10 days	Jan.-Dec.	Sun. Fertile soil. Grown also from divisions and cuttings. Excellent for bedding, edging, window boxes. Naturalizes. Profuse bloomer.
VIOLA, A / Viola cornuta	Blue, White, Yellow, Purple	6"	6"	Sept.-Nov.	20 days	Jan.May	Light, rich soil. Full sun. Excellent for bedding, cutting and edging.
VIOLET, P / Viola odorata	Purple, White	6"	8"	Any time		Oct.-May	Grown usually from divisions. Rich loamy soil. Sun or semi-shade. Fertilize with bone meal.
WALLFLOWER, A / Cheiranthus cheiri	Yellow, Orange	8-12"	6"	Sept.-Dec.	5 days	Feb.-Apr.	Light, rich soil. Sun or partial shade. Plant in the border. Fragrant. Fine for cutting.
ZINNIA, A / Zinnia	Various	1-3'	1'	May-Aug.	5 days	May-Dec.	Any good, rich soil. Sun or partial shade. Most successful summer bloomer. Many forms.

VINES EASILY GROWN

VINES EASILY GROWN

A—Annual D—Deciduous
P—Perennial E—Evergreen

COMMON NAME / Botanical Name	Color	Best From	To Plant	Time To Germinate	Of Blooming	COMMENTS
ALLAMANDA (GOLDEN TRUMPET) P E / Allamanda hendersoni	Yellow	Plant	Mar.-April		Spring Summer	Tender. Fragrant. Long season of bloom. Large flowers. Sun. Humusy rich loam.
BEAN, SCARLET RUNNER, A / Phaseolus coccineus	Scarlet	Seed	Mar.-April	8 days	June-Aug.	Likes sun. Rapid growing. Flowers ornamental. Pods are edible. Loose fertile soil. P. caracalla (Snail Vine) odd and pretty.
BIGNONIA (CROSSVINE), P E / Bignonia capreolata	Yellowish-Red	Seed Cuttings	Mar.-May	15 days	Summer	Old favorite. Native. Large flowers. Acid soil. Prolific bloomer. Sun.
BIGNONIA, P E / Bignonia chamberlayni	Yellow	Seed Cuttings	Anytime	15 days	Aug.-Sept.	Sun. Rich soil. Tender. Stout climber. Showy funnel-shaped flowers.
BOUGAINVILLEA, P E / Bougainvillea	Magenta, Crimson, White, Orange	Plant Cuttings	Mar.-Aug.		April-Nov.	Tender. Sun. If frozen, cut back to live wood. Garden soil. Feed May, July. Prune and pinch for bloom. Don't overwater.
CARDINAL CLIMBER, A / Quamoclit sloteri	Red with white throat	Seed	Mar.-May	8 days	June-Nov.	Sun. Vigorous. Showy blossoms. Little water.
CLEMATIS (VIRGIN'S-BOWER), P E / Clematis paniculata, hybrids	White	Plant	Nov.-April		July-Aug.	Likes deep planting with roots shaded, tops in sun. Rich, fast draining slightly alkaline soil. Mulch. 2 yr. old plant best.
CLITORIA (BUTTERFLY-PEA), A / Clitoria mariana	Blue	Seed Cuttings	Mar.-May	15 days	June	Hardy. Attractive twiner. Sandy soil. Sun. C. ternatea, blue, is showier.
CLYTOSTOMA, E / Clytostoma callistegioides	Lavender	Plant	Nov.-Mar.		May	Sometimes known as Bignonia speciosa. Sun or partial shade, also from layers. Subject to freeze. Rich soil.
CORAL VINE, P D / Antigonon leptopus	Pink, White	Root	Mar.-May		June-Oct.	Easily grown. Sun. Cover with two inches of soil. Hardy and luxuriant. Garden soil, little water.
CYPRESSVINE, A / Quamoclit pennata	Red, White	Seed	Mar.-May	5 days	May-Oct.	Best in sun. Rapid growing. Dense, fernlike foliage. Any soil.
DOXANTHA / Doxantha unguis-cati	Yellow	Plant	Nov.-Mar.		Mar.	Sometimes offered as Bignonia tweediana. Grown also from layers. Sun or partial shade. Tender.
DUTCHMAN'S PIPE, P D / Aristolochia durior	Yellowish Brown	Seed	Mar.-May		June	Hardy. Thrives best when lime is added to soil. Semi-shade Exotic flowers. Heart-shaped foliage. Twiner.
FIG VINE P E / Ficus pumila (repens)		Plant	Any time			Grown also from divisions and layers. Best for wall cover. Glossy, dark green leaves. Roots are invasive. Keep pruned.
FLAMEVINE OF BRAZIL, P E / Pyrostegia ignea	Orange-Red	Cuttings	Any time		Midwinter Summer	Tender. Well-drained soil. Quick-growing. Tendrils cling to stone or wood. Hot sun.
GOURD, A / Cucurbia ovifera	Cream, Yellow	Seed	April-May	12 days	June-Sept.	Full sun. Very rapid, coarse growth. Fruits unique in shape. Other ornamental gourds in variety.
HONEYSUCKLE, BELGIAN, P E / Lonicera periclymenum (belgica)	Buff and Pink	Plant	Nov.-April		April-Nov.	Also grown from cuttings and layers. Likes sun. Very fragrant. Can be grown as bush or vine. Commonly called woodbine.
HONEYSUCKLE, COMMON (HALL'S), P E / Lonicera halliana japonica	White	Plant	Nov.-April		April-Nov.	Rapid growing. Very difficult to control. Becomes a pest except for ground cover with unlimited space. Caution.
HONEYSUCKLE, CORAL, P E / Lonicera sempervirens	Red	Plant	Nov.-April		Feb.-Mar. Oct.-Nov.	Grown also from cuttings and layers. Sun or partial shade. Colorful. Any soil.
HYACINTH BEAN (JACK BEAN), A / Dolichos lablab	White and Purple	Seed	Mar.-April	8 days	May-Aug.	Likes sun. Rapid growing. Both flower and fruit clusters ornamental.

VINES EASILY GROWN

COMMON NAME *Botanical Name*	Color	Best From	To Plant	TIME To Germinate	Of Blooming	COMMENTS
HYDRANGEA, CLIMBING, P D *Hydrangea petiolaris*	White	Seed	Nov.		May-June	Hardy. Fragrant flowers. Aerial roots enable it to climb stone and stucco walls.
IVY, BOSTON, P D *Parthenocissus (tricuspidata)*		Plant	Nov.-April			Grown also from cuttings and layers. Quick growing wall cover. Handsome autumn foliage. Virginia Creeper is *P. quinquefolia.*
IVY, ENGLISH, P E *Hedera helix*		Plant	Any time			Grown also from cuttings and layers. Excellent ground and wall cover. Slow growing. Shade. *H. canariensis* similar.
JASMINE, P E *Jasminum mesnyi*	Yellow	Plant	Nov.-April		February	Grown also from cuttings and layers. Sun or shade. Semi-climber. Easy to transplant. Good in window boxes.
JASMINE, CONFEDERATE, P E *Trachelospermum jasminoides*	White	Plant	Nov.-April		April-May	Grown also from layers. Likes sun. Beautiful. Small clusters fragrant flowers. Garden soil.
JASMINE, CAROLINA, P E *Gelsemium sempervirens*	Yellow	Plant	Nov.-Mar.		February	Grown from layers also. Sun or partial shade. Beautiful native vine. Fragrant. All parts are poisonous. Any soil.
LANTANA, WEEPING, P D *Lantana sellowiana*	Lavender	Plant	Mar.-May		All year	Grown also from cuttings. Fine for rock gardens, window boxes and ground covers. Prolific bloomer. Also 'Velutina White.'
MADEIRA-VINE, P D *Boussingaultia baselloides*	White	Tuber	Mar.-May		June-Sept.	Sun. Multiplies rapidly. Old garden favorite. Fragrant. Called mignonette vine.
MEXICAN FLAME VINE, A *Senecio confusus*	Orange	Seed	Nov.		June to Sept.	Sun. Average soil. Rapid grower. Daisy-like flowers bloom all summer. Excellent colorful vine.
MOONFLOWER, A *Calonyction aculeatum*	White	Seed	Mar.-May	10 days	July-Sept.	Likes sun. Rapid, coarse growth. Night-blooming. Fragrant. Soak before planting.
MORNING-GLORY, P D *Ipomoea leari*	Blue	Plant	Mar.-April		May-Oct.	Grown also from cuttings. Sun or partial shade. One of the prettiest of the Morning-Glories.
MORNING-GLORY, A *Ipomoea in variety*	Various	Seed	Mar.-April	8 days	May-Sept.	Sun or partial shade. Soak seed before planting. Rapid growing. Hot, dry spot. Fertile soil low in nitrogen.
MORNING-GLORY, P *Ipomoea horsfalliae*	Magenta	Tubers	Spring		Summer	Beautiful. Hawaiian variety. Rampant grower.
NASTURTIUM, CLIMBING, A *Tropaeolum majus*	Yellow, Orange	Seed	Spring	8 days	Summer	Blooms best in poor soil. Sun.
PANDOREA *Pandorea ricasoliana*	Pink	Seed Cutting	Nov.-Mar.		April	Sun. Rich soil. Tender. Slow to establish growth. Good for trellises and arbors.
PASSIONFLOWER, P D *Passiflora*	Lavender	Root	Mar.-April		June-Aug.	Grown also from divisions. Free bloomer. Interesting for curious flower formation. Many varieties. Sun. Garden soil.
POTATO VINE, P D *Solanum jasminoides*	Lavender, White	Plant	Mar.-May		May-Oct.	Grown also from cuttings and layers. Sun or partial shade. Half hardy. Free bloomer. Rapid growth. Beautiful.
RANGOON CREEPER, P E *Quisqualis indica*	Pink to Red	Seed Cuttings	Mar.-May		Summer	Tender. Fragrant. Vigorous grower. Twiner. Should be pruned after blooming to induce new growth.
ROSE, CLIMBER *Rosa,* in variety	Various	Plant	Feb.		Mar.-Aug.	Numerous types and sizes. Some everblooming. Support. Sun. Well-drained, rich soil. Prune after blooming. See ROSES.
SILVER LACE VINE, P E *Polygonum auberti*	White	Seed	Mar.-May		Midsummer	Sun. Hardy. Fragrant. Rapid grower. Excellent for screening. Twiner.
SWEET PEA, A *Lathyrus odoratus*	Various	Seed	Oct.		Mar.-May	Sow seeds 2" deep in 6" trench of rich manured well drained soil. Sun. As plants grow add soil. Train on support. Fragrant.

COMMON NAME / Botanical Name	Color	Best From	To Plant	TIME To Germinate	Of Blooming	COMMENTS
THUNBERGIA (SKY FLOWER), P / *Thunbergia grandiflora*	Blue	Seed	Feb. to June	2 weeks	July to Oct.	Sun. Rapid grower. Rich humusy soil. Tender. Black-eyed Susan vine, *T. alata*, yellow. *T. gibsoni*, dbl. orange.
TRUMPETCREEPER, P D / *Campsis radicans*	Orange-Red	Plant	Nov.-Mar.		April-Sept.	Grown also from root cuttings. Rampant grower. Very beautiful. Native. *C. tagliabuana*, var. Mme Galen, very fine. Hot sun.
VIRGINIA CREEPER, P D / *Parthenocissus quinquefolia*		Plant	Nov.-April			Grown also from cuttings and layers. Handsome autumn foliage. Excellent wall cover. Rapid growing.
WISTERIA, P D / *Wisteria floribunda* / *Wisteria sinensis, alba*	Violet-Blue / Blue, White	Plant / Plant	Nov.-Mar. / Nov.-Mar.		May / April-May	Sun. Good drainage. Rich deep soil. Fragrant. Prune severely after blooming to control. Needs very firm support.
WISTERIA, P E / *Wisteria megasperma*	Purple	Plant / Layers	Nov.		July, Aug., Sept.	Evergreen foliage, grows very tall. Rich, loamy soil, humus. Drought resistant, disease free.

FERNS FOR INDOORS AND OUTDOORS

General Culture: Loose, fibrous, sandy soil. Good drainage but moist. Shade or filtered sun. Feed often with organic fertilizer; blood meal or fish emulsion. Mist for humidity.

COMMON NAME / Botanical Name	Color	Description	Height	Propagation	COMMENTS
BIRD'S NEST FERN / *Asplenium nidus*		Formal rosette of fresh green, spatula-shaped leaves	2-3'	Sporelings	Excellent indoor fern. Requires moist, well-drained fibrous soil, filtered sunlight.
BOSTON FERN / *Nephrolepis exalata bostoniensis*		Clusters of clear, medium green pinnate fronds	2-3'	Runners from base of leaves	Foliage freezes. Recovers quickly from roots. Requires shade, peat moss and sandy soil. Dwarf: *compacta*.
FISHTAIL FERN / *Nephrolepis biserrata furcans*		Medium green fronds 6 to 10 inches wide. Segments rather distant, thick and forked.	2-4'	Runners from base of leaves	Good in pots or hanging baskets.
FLUFFY RUFFLES / *Nephrolepis exalata, var. fluffy ruffles*		Light green fronds of multiple curly pinnates	2-4'	Runners from base of leaves	Very beautiful for hanging baskets. Dwarf: Mini Ruffle.
HOLLY FERN / *Polystichum falcatum (Cyrtomium falcatum)*		Shiny evergreen leaves, sharply toothed.	3-5'	Sporelings, or division of rootstock	Very hardy. Semi-shade. See The Tropical Garden.
LEATHER-LEAF FERN / *Polystichum adiantiforme*		Dark evergreen fronds, segments heavy textured.	2-3'	Division of rootstock	Very hardy. Stands cold weather. Requires filtered light or morning sun.
MAIDENHAIR / *Adiantum*		Light green, delicate fronds with wedge-shaped segments.	12-15"	Division of rootstock	Multiplies rapidly. Foliage freezes. See Circle of the Year. Feb., Mar., Aug.
POLYSTICHUM SETOSUM / *Polystichum setosum*		Feathery fronds from single crown.	12-15"	Division of rootstock	Very hardy. Stands cold well. Requires rich moist loam. See The Tropical Garden.
SPRENGERI / *Asparagus sprengeri*		Apple green, multiple fronds with short, needle-like leaves.	1-2'	Division of rootstock	Hardy. Multiplies rapidly. Good fern for pots, cascading 3 or 4 feet.
STAGHORN FERN / *Platycerium alcicorne*		Exotic fronds, winged from base spreading into fan-shaped blades.	2-3'	Suckers from roots	Requires lots of peat moss or leafmold, indirect light and occasional syringing. Good basket fern.
TREE FERN, HAWAIIAN / *Cibotium chamissoi*		Lacy fronds develop pinnately from golden-haired trunks.	4-6'	Sporelings or by rooting top of tree trunks in water or moist, porous soil.	Excellent in modern buildings or offices. Pot in porous soil or in shallow water with pebbles. Requires humid atmosphere.
WHITTMANI / *Nephrolepis exalata, var. whitmani*		Light green, lacy fronds, thickly pinnated	2-3'	Runners from base of roots.	Beautiful in hanging baskets.
WOOD FERN / *Dryopteris*		Erect handsome fronds developing from a dense crown.	2-4'	Sporelings, or division of rootstock.	Excellent for garden. Requires shade, much water, well-drained fibrous soil.

A FEW POPULAR HERBS

COMMON NAME *Botanical Name*	Description	Height	Space Apart	Time to Plant	COMMENTS
BASIL, SWEET, A *Ocimum Basilicum*	Shiny green leaves. Tiny white flowers.	1–2′	18″	March	Sun. Pinch out tips for a bushy plant. Fairly rich soil. Water regularly. O. 'Dark Opal' purplish foliage.
BORAGE, A *Borago officinalis*	Stiff hairy foliage. Sky-blue flowers.	2″	1′	March	Hardy, Sun. Faint cucumber flavor.
CHERVIL, A *Anthriscus Cerefolium*	Fern-like leaf. White flower.	2′	6″	Monthly	Some shade. Do not transplant. Discourage flowers. Average moist soil. Faint licorice flavor.
CHIVES, P *Allium Schoenoprasum*	Grass-like leaves. Lavender flowers.	1′	6″	October	Sun. Propagate from seeds or divisions. Moist fairly rich soil.
DILL, A *Anethum graveolens*	Fine leaves. Small yellow flowers.	2½′	18″	March	Sun. Allow to develop flower tops. Use leaves and seeds. Average well-drained soil.
FENNEL, A *Foeniculum vulgare*	Feathery leaves. Small yellow flowers.	3–5′	2′	March	Sun. Light well-drained soil. Dried seeds are spices.
GARLIC, P *Allium sativum*	Onion-like leaves. Lavender flowers.	6–12″	8″	October	Sun. Hardy. Lift bulb when leaves turn yellow; dry in sun and hang in dry place. Increase is by division of cloves. Rich, well-drained soil.
LEMON BALM, P *Mellissa officinalis*	Lemon scent and flavor. Light green, veined leaves.	2′	16″	October	Hardy. Sun or part shade. Rich, moist soil. Shear to restrain.
MARJORAM, SWEET, P *Majorana Hortensis*	Tiny gray-green leaves. White or lavender flowers.	2′	1′	March	Sun. Tender. Propagate from seeds, cuttings, or roots. Moist, alkaline soil.
MINT, P *Mentha in variety*	Dark green leaves. Spikes of lilac flowers. Numerous flavors.	18–24″	1′	March	Some shade. Rich moist soil. Keep flowers cut. Propagate by runners. Fragrant leaves best used fresh.
OREGANO, P *Origanum vulgare*	Oval green leaves. Purple-pink blooms.	18–30″	2′	March	Sun. Hardy. Medium-rich soil, good drainage. Prevent flowering. Replant every three years.
PARSLEY, B *Petroselinum crispum*	Dark green, tightly curled leaves.	2–10″	3″	April-July	Part shade. Good moist soil. Soak seeds before sowing. Keep flowers cut.
ROSEMARY, PROSTRATE, P *Rosemarinus officinalis prostratus*	Dark needlelike leaves. Light blue flowers.	15″	1′	Sept.	Propagate from cuttings. Likes lean well-drained soil, and full sun. Good low hedge plant.
SAGE, P *Salvia officinalis*	Gray-green leaves. Spikes of violet-blue flowers.	18–24″	10″	March	Sun. Drought resistant. Drainage. Other species.
SAVORY, SUMMER, A *Satureja hortensia*	Lance-shaped leaves. Pink, white or lilac flowers.	18″	6″	March	Sun. Pinch out tips for bushier plants. Winter savory may also be propagated by cuttings or divisions of rootstocks in Sept. Light, well-drained soil.
SAVORY, WINTER, P *Satureja montana*		15″	12″	Sept.	
TARRAGON, P *Artemisia dracunculus*	Narrow dark-green leaves.	18″	12″	March	Sun or shade. Poor sandy soil results in best flavor. Propagated by division of roots or cuttings in fall or early spring. Do not fertilize.
THYME, P *Thymus in species*	Small green leaves. Tiny lavender flowers. Varying flavors.	6–8″	6″	March	Sun. Light sandy, moderately dry soil. Prune after flowering. Propagate from seed or cuttings.

METRIC CONVERSION CHART

Handy approximate conversions to metric measurements.

Linear

1 inch = 2.54 centimeters
1 foot = 30.48 centimeters or .31 meter
1 square foot = 929 square centimeters
1 square yard = .84 square meter

Liquid

1 teaspoon = 5 milliliters
3 teaspoons = 1 tablespoon = 15 milliliters
16 tablespoons = 8 ounces = 1 cup = 240 milliliters
2 cups = 1 pint = 16 ounces = 480 milliliters or about one-half liter
1 quart = .9463 liter
4 quarts = 1 gallon = 3.79 liters

Dry

1 pint = .55 liters (a bit over one-half liter)
1 quart = 1.1 liters
8 quarts = 1 peck = 8.81 liters
4 pecks = 1 bushel = 35.24 liters

Weights

1000 grams = 1 kilogram (kilo) = 2.2 pounds
1 avoirdupois ounce = 28.35 grams
1 avoirdupois pound = .45 kilograms

GARDENING HINTS

Plan before you plant. Know the plant before you buy.
How large does it grow? Height and width?
What are its soil, light and water requirements?
Do you have the space, the place and the time to grow it well?
Work with your plants, not against them.
Plants need more knowledgeable gardeners.

Index

Note: *Abbreviations in subentries denote genus name given in main entry; genus names that are also used as common names have not been set in italics.*